Beyond the Foster Care System

Beyond
the Foster Care System

The Future for Teens

Betsy Krebs
Paul Pitcoff

Rutgers University Press
New Brunswick, New Jersey, and London

Library of Congress Cataloging-in-Publication Data

Krebs, Betsy

Beyond the foster care system : the future for teens / Betsy Krebs and Paul Pitcoff.

    p.   cm.

Includes bibliographical references (p.   ) and index.

ISBN-13: 978-0-8135-3828-0 (hardcover : alk. paper)

   1. Foster home care—United States.   2. Social work with teenagers—United States.
I. Pitcoff, Paul.   II. Title.

HV881.K74 2006

362.73'30830973—dc22

2005024941

A British Cataloging-in-Publication record for this book is available from the British Library

Manufactured in the United States of America

Contents

Acknowledgments

Many of the ideas, analysis, and recommendations in this book derive from our work and relationships with youth in foster care. Their passion to become successful contributing citizens and to improve the foster care system was our motivation for writing *Beyond the Foster Care System*. If we have made any contribution to helping youth in foster care, it has been eclipsed by what they have taught us about resilience, independent thinking, loyalty, and optimism. These youth are the coauthors of this book.

Countless individuals, foundations, and organizations have encouraged us. Their support not only acknowledges our work but also recognizes the capacity and strengths of youth in foster care. Dr. Francine Cournos, professor of Clinical Psychiatry and deputy director of the New York State Psychiatric Institute, provided us with delightfully challenging and encouraging support throughout the process of developing this book. Sean Bolser and Deborah Hayes were with us when we began the Youth Advocacy Center in 1992 and have remained strong collaborators to this day.

The following people were instrumental in converting *Beyond the Foster Care System* from an idea into a book: Dr. Leon Botstein, president of Bard College; Philip Coltoff, chief executive officer, Children's Aid Society; Tracy Conn; Lauren Bank Deen; Rebecca Iwerks; Jeremy Kohomban, chief executive officer, Children's Village; Commissioner John Mattingly of the New York City Administration for Children's Services; Deirdre Mullane, the Spieler Agency; Gara LaMarche, vice president and director of U.S. Programs, the Open Society

Institute; Kristi Long, Rutgers University Press; Johanna Osburn; Xavier Reyes; Sashine Rivera; Earl Shorris, founder, the Clemente Course in the Humanities; Leigh SInger; Evette Soto-Maldonado; Ashley Terletzky; Florence Vigilante, professor, Hunter College School of Social Work; and Dr. Joseph Vigilante, former dean, School of Social Work, Adelphi University.

Moreover, we appreciate the encouragement given us by our friends and families, especially Winton and Noah Pitcoff; Lisa Ranghelli; George Pitt and Noreen Clark; Martha Rayner and Danny Haselkorn; Ruth Pearl; Jeffrey Krebs and Kaja Ross; Marjorie and Harold Seftel; Evelyn and Bernard Yudowitz; Lillian and Bernard Stein; Dan, Elissa, and Ken Krebs; Suzette Gerardi; Leslie Adelstein; Sharman Stein and Stuart Sherman. A very special acknowledgment goes to Gabriel and Daisy Stein. Most important, we are grateful for the support of Harriet Pitcoff and Sheldon Stein, for this project would not have been possible without their understanding and love.

Finally, we changed the names of institutions, places, and individuals for this book. The incidents and dialogue we describe present our best recollections. The stories are true. In some cases, we combined characters or incidents where we felt it made the book clearer, and where it represented what we found to be the most common experiences of our work with teens in the foster care system.

Selina rushed from her last college class of the day to arrive on time. Hurrying down the block, she noticed Gloria, a young woman standing on the sidewalk outside the imposing law school building. Gloria looked uncertainly at the main entrance doorway, unsure if she belonged there.

"You here for the graduation?" Selina asked.

Gloria didn't look surprised, but her answer seemed a bit cautious. "Think so."

"Come on, I'll go in with you," Selina said with a smile. She knew how imposing the building looked to this girl, how it represented another world, although it was not that far from where either of them had grown up. As incongruous as the situation might have appeared, a supposedly troubled teenager from foster care honored and celebrated at a famous law school, it was happening in just thirty minutes.

In the polished marble lobby, Selina asked a uniformed security guard where they should go. Together they found the correct room, which had wood paneling, glass covered bookshelves, and dark oil paintings on the walls. Gloria momentarily hesitated to enter the room, and then she broke into a cautious yet uncontrollable smile of pride. This was her graduation.

Soon two dozen teens surrounded Selina and Gloria. Most lived in temporary foster homes and group homes. They had survived the traumas of separation from their families, movement from one placement to another, and countless other painful experiences. One might expect they would be thankful to realize that they were getting too old to be in foster care, but they all knew that the day was soon approaching when they would have to leave their foster homes or group homes; they were scared. The plans for where they would live and who would help them were, at best, shaky.

Gloria and her fellow graduates had gathered to celebrate their completion of a self-advocacy seminar we offered them. The purpose of Youth Advocacy Center's Getting Beyond the System® Self-Advocacy Seminar is to empower teens by teaching them to advocate for themselves and prepare for independent futures. The seminar helps youth between the ages of sixteen and twenty-one understand how to critically analyze information for crucial life skills: making decisions, setting goals, developing achievable plans, negotiating with adults, presenting personal strengths, understanding the other party's needs, and giving compelling written and oral presentations. During the seminar, these teens learned from a facilitator trained in the Socratic method. They read, studied, and argued about the meaning of case studies, or stories of young adults just like them who were struggling to make it in the world. Each participant identified a career goal for himself or herself, and, as the final project, each conducted an informational interview with a successful professional in their career field of interest. Despite their tough demeanors and challenging pasts, all these teens had successfully completed this seminar with the hope of improving their chances of succeeding at independence and reaching their dreams of success.

Naturally, the teens were excited. They usually got attention for all the things that were wrong in their lives, not for their accomplishments. Completing this seminar was an important achievement. Each week of the semester, they had complained about the workload of homework assignments, reading, and the requirement that they attend all twelve classes. Some of this whining attempted to cover their fears that they would not survive the semester; some was ordinary teenage grousing. Their caseworkers and social workers also fretted that undertaking the seminar work might lead to students facing another devastating failure in their lives. Yet, the teens had assembled here for their graduation.

The teens in the audience stopped fidgeting and paid attention when Selina stood up to address them. She was their hero. Selina spent thirteen years of her life in foster care. Now, three years after leaving foster care, she was studying in a prestigious design college and pursuing her dream of becoming a graphic artist. The students had never met her in person, but they felt they knew her. They had learned about her struggle to make a future for herself through watching a video about her in one of their classes.

When Selina took part in our seminar she was quiet and thoughtful, yet insecure and unconvinced that she would succeed. Now she represented success, and her success was a compelling reinforcement for the graduates. Her experiences gave them hope that they too possessed the ability to make it beyond the foster care system.

As we sat back, we knew that our speeches could never have the effect of the authentic story told by Selina. We felt confident Selina would give a great presentation, even though we did not know what she would say. We remembered how the previous year Selina had been honored at an elegant fundraiser. The sponsoring organization had selected her for this honor because, despite the considerable challenges she faced while in foster care, she had kept her focus on her future and had successfully enrolled herself in college. At this benefit, Selina was supposed to give a speech about how our program had helped her. We eagerly waited for her to speak to the hundreds of wealthy and influential New Yorkers gathered at this dinner. When Selina stood at the podium, she began in a soft, almost tentative manner that contrasted with an underlying assertiveness that nothing would stop her from delivering the truth. The audience listened attentively. With great pride and anticipation, we were fairly sure she would refer in glowing terms to our program and all the help we had personally given her.

"The single most important moment of my life occurred with a remarkable person. . . ." We knew the next moment would be ours, and Selina would publicly acknowledge us for the role we had played in her success. ". . . Al Ferugi." We looked at each other thinking, who is Al Ferugi? "He was my informational interviewer, and he took the time to explain that I had what it takes to be a graphic designer and told me how I should begin my career. If it wasn't for Al Ferugi, I wouldn't be here today, and I wouldn't be going to college."

We looked at each other again and started laughing. Part of the strength of our program is that it is not about us, but about the students—what they want to do with their futures and their connection to the world beyond foster care and welfare. With great satisfaction, we recognized that Selina had learned to use her own resources to pursue her goals.

For the final project of the seminar, each student at the graduation had gone on their own informational interviews with architects, designers, nurse practitioners, musicians, sports agents, anthropologists, teachers, law enforcement officers, pilots, or any other person practicing a career in which they were interested. And each had returned with stories about how that person offered them education and career advice, books, people to call, the genesis of a network to help them. Each student in the seminar gained more confidence and satisfaction by exercising their intellectual abilities in these interviews. Through such meetings, the teens' perspectives of themselves and their places in the world changed forever.

Why do teens in foster care need this kind of outside advice? Foster care teens interact with dozens of caseworkers, mental health professionals, foster parents, childcare staff, lawyers, judges, and miscellaneous supervisors and administrators involved with their cases while they are in the system. However, they still need outside advice because even when they do establish close and important relationships in the foster care system, they always wonder: "Am I only getting help because it's their job, not because of my talents or who I am?" Further, teens recognize that relationships with these helping professionals are temporary—despite their dedication and benevolence, more likely than not, either they or the teens will soon move on. This uncertainty makes teens unable to fully believe in or utilize the help from foster care professionals. These fears explain why Selina felt the meeting with Al Ferugi was the one that transformed her life; not only had he provided sound advice, but he was also a volunteer from outside the system.

At the graduation, Selina ended with an impassioned challenge to the graduates. "I know what you have gone through. I had some really bad times when I was in foster care. I didn't know if I would make it, and I know others thought I wouldn't. I know. It's important that you decide that nothing is going to stop you." The graduates' pride was evident, as they sat a little straighter and smiled. The graduates then stepped up to get their certificates, and their teacher told an anecdote about each student's successes in the seminar. The students held their inexpensive certificates carefully, as if they were antique scrolls on the verge of crumpling into oblivion. Some talked about how surprised they were to complete the seminar and do so well.

We glanced at the faces of the assembled friends and some family members of the graduates. A few interested professionals from the graduates' foster care agencies, some informational interviewers, and a number of Youth Advocacy Center supporters also sat behind the graduates. We saw many in the audience wiping away tears. They had expected stories of challenges and hardship, and instead they got stories of hope, and witnessed dramatic transformations in the young people and in their own conceptions. At the beginning of the ceremony, some viewed the graduates as deprived kids destined for failure. By the end, these images evaporated, and ones of ambition, courage, endurance, and charm replaced them.

Watching the students intensified our own appreciation for their resilience and broad range of talents. Selina's spirit gave us energy and called us to continue our work. She had endured forced separation from family and a number of temporary foster care placements, but she still continued to work toward contributing successfully to our society. We enormously respected her and all the students assembled that day. We were proud we had helped hundreds of teens in foster care during the previous decade, and we felt driven to help many more.

We were also frustrated that we had not yet been able to change the odds for more teens leaving foster care. The graduation event reminded us how many years we had dedicated to trying to help teens from foster care escape what seemed like a prevailing sentence of failure. We had taken on what many told us was an insurmountable challenge: we were trying to both change the foster care system and help individual teens reach their potential. Despite our efforts and those of government officials, policy makers, advocates, and caring professionals working to help kids, too many young adults were still leaving foster care unprepared for work or college and without the means to build a life above the poverty line.

The federal, state, and local governments invest considerably more than twenty billion dollars a year in child welfare programs.[1] Because the federal government gives the most funding for foster care, all systems must adhere to basic federal mandates; the states and municipalities impose additional requirements. Yet, through this system, we are creating a continuing class of citizens that requires government maintenance. The lives damaged and financial implications associated with this ongoing process are consequences that affect all of us.

How can this be? If there were a simple answer, someone would have solved the problem decades ago. Our work in foster care spans fifteen years. During that time we have worked with hundreds of youth in foster care, professionals at all levels of service, administrators, government policy makers, and citizens connected to or interested in foster care. From this experience, we have come to believe that significant factors prevent the system from successfully preparing youth for transition to independence.

For example, the government did not design foster care systems to raise teens to adulthood; rather its intended goal is to provide temporary safety to children at risk of harm. Children in foster care are supposed to be reunited with their families or adopted by new families within a year or two. For teenagers, this scenario has been less than likely, and thus many remain indefinitely in care and move from one temporary foster home, group home, and institution to another, with little stability or preparation for the future. Although the law requires the system to prepare teens for independent living, teens have not found this preparation effective. Although most child welfare professionals acknowledge that the system cannot realistically expect eighteen- to twenty-one-year-olds to survive completely alone and independent, few people have done anything to create viable systemwide alternatives.

Scant public attention has focused on the issue of teens leaving foster care without the resources to succeed. Awareness of the problems in the foster care system is usually sparked by either horrible stories of a child harmed or killed, or headlining lawsuits against the various systems of foster care for egregious cases of neglect or abuse of children while in the system. The media and the public are enraged, and the foster care bureaucracy may make some adjustments as a result of these stories or lawsuits. This story, of teens insufficiently prepared for independence, lacks the drama of tragic deaths or violent confrontations. However, the disastrous outcomes will continue to play out well into the future, affect more lives, and with longer lasting significance than the horror stories in the news.

Furthermore, the ideological debates which influence foster care have tended to focus on issues connected with kids coming into the foster care system, not how they leave the system. Children usually enter foster care because the government believes they will be unsafe or neglected if they remain with their biological parents. Tension exists between those advocating for family preservation (putting more money into prevention services to keep children out of foster care) and those advocating for better child protection (removing children promptly from dangerous situations). These goals are not mutually exclusive, but they drive two competing policy interests; scholars, government leaders, and program personnel have tended to lean one way or the other. Although this debate is important, it ignores the needs of teens aging out of foster care.

From our experience, we know that a large reservoir of people supports helping all teens become productive, successful, and independent citizens. We believe that, despite the determined advocacy work of many, the foster care system will not change until the public understands the problems and missed opportunities and requires accountability. With this goal in mind, we decided to write *Beyond the Foster Care System*. We hope that our insiders' view of the system helps focus more attention on redesigning foster care so as to improve opportunities for the teens who are in the system.

Why and how did we get into foster care? When we met, our backgrounds, positions in life, and interests differed enough that we could not have predicted that we would develop such a lasting collaboration focused on helping foster care teens achieve a better future.

Betsy took a position as an attorney assigned to represent children in New York City's foster care system after graduating Harvard Law School in the late 1980s. She quickly became responsible for hundreds of cases involving children and teenagers whose foster care status was being reviewed by the court. Every case was important for her. She spent long hours preparing and fact finding, until she built the strongest case for her young clients' positions. Betsy was also tireless in visiting the agencies where her clients lived and seeing first-hand their conditions before engaging in advocacy to improve those conditions.

About that same time, Paul was starting law school. For twenty years, he had served as a filmmaker and the chair of the department of communications at Adelphi University. Paul had produced award-winning documentaries for nonprofit institutions about a wide array of social problems and solutions for improving the lives of people who were marginalized by the community. After two decades as a tenured professor and chair of an academic department, Paul wanted to try something else and was interested in legal issues related to communications. He decided to give up his tenured professorship and go to law school. While in law school, he took an internship in family court, where they assigned him to work with Betsy. Upon graduating, he accepted a full-time job as a lawyer representing children.

In family court, we grew dismayed seeing many of our clients fail after foster care, despite the intervention of countless concerned social workers, attorneys, judges, and mental health professionals. The children and families we met in family court moved both of us. We were inspired by the teenagers who, despite their continuing battles within the system, maintained a strong desire to get an education, to work, to have healthy children, to make the system better for others, and to succeed as independent adults. We felt angry that many of our clients, after being removed from parents and placed in foster care for years, suffered fates that could not have been worse had they remained with their original families.

Our friends and families could hardly believe the stories we brought home from family court about the foster care system, the families it defeated, and those who rose above it. They were concerned that the system was not as effective as they had thought, and they were appalled that foster care did not prepare teens for successful futures, especially when they learned that the public spends more money holding a teen in foster care for a year than it would sending him or her to the best private school in the country. We grew more and more frustrated with this government system that seemed to defy all notions of justice, equal protection, and individual rights that we had learned about in law school.

We founded Youth Advocacy Center in 1992 because the system displayed no sustained effort to adequately prepare foster care teens for a better future. From the start, YAC has sought to teach teenagers in foster care how to take control of their futures and learn to advocate for themselves. A vision that teens in foster care have the potential to become participating citizens has guided our work on a range of projects, including individual and policy advocacy, community organizing, research, and education programs. All along, teens have been our partners, and therefore, many, if not all of our own ideas about the problems of foster care and the potential solutions, spring from ideas expressed by the teens we worked with from our first days in family court through those presently in our seminars.

In this book, we recount some of our journey of working with teens in the foster care system. We begin with our legal work representing teens in foster care and trace our path through working with teens on education-related projects to teaching teens about their rights, policy advocacy, and community organizing. We explore our growing desire to create a model that would help teens directly, which led to the development of our Getting Beyond the System® model and trainings for professionals.

We hope our readers will benefit from our personal views of the system and some of the remarkable teenagers in that system; the challenges created by the system, and the caring individuals committed to overcoming them; the contributions by the private sector that works with the young people in the system; one organization's approaches to meeting the system's challenges by designing and implementing a program for foster teens; and finally, how these can affect policy making and the foster care practice for teens.

This book highlights our appreciation for the mutuality of our work. We hope that we have contributed to the lives of some teens in foster care, and we are certain that they contribute to our lives. The youth with whom we have worked have increased our ability to see issues and the world from different perspectives. They have provided insight into the dynamics of resilience. They have expanded our commitment to hopefulness, and they have heightened our appreciation of humor as a tool for enduring challenges. Because of the teens our work is special. We are completely confident in our sense of privilege in conducting our work.

Writing this book reminds us how fortunate we are to partner with diverse communities and connect with people from very different backgrounds and worlds. First, we are in the world of the teens; we appreciate their hardship and also their intellectual, artistic, and interpersonal talents, combined with their extraordinary courage and resilience. The more we have gotten to know the teens with whom we work, the more we realize that all of them have some strengths and talents. Often people ask us if these aren't the exceptional teens, and we answer that they are not, that all teens who have endured foster care and continue to believe in a hopeful future are exceptional. Almost every teen we meet displays individual strengths that, if supported, would enable them to succeed as participating citizens.

We are also in the world of the foster care system, a government bureaucracy that contracts with numerous institutions and agencies, many of which have existed for more than a century. The complicated and arcane laws, regulations, and policies may be well intentioned, but they allow little maneuverability for the human situation. Nonetheless, within this bureaucracy, we meet and collaborate with caring individuals dedicated to helping teens in foster care. In our national trainings for social workers, lawyers, psychologists, educators, and other child welfare professionals, and in replicating our program, we gain new insights and learn about other methods used in helping teens prepare for independence. We are inspired by these individuals, who, despite sharing with us a similar sobering view of foster care, continue to struggle to help their teens prepare for a successful independent future.

And we are in the world of the private sector, the individuals from a range of professions who give their time, advice, and wisdom to help the teens in our program. These individuals and their corporations and firms seek out and create new ways to provide support for teens in foster care. One happy surprise of our work is the number of people in the business community who are eager to find meaningful ways to help teens prepare for future success. These individuals may start out with many prejudices against foster care teens but are often the quickest to back away from these stereotypes when they meet the teens and see them as individuals with a range of strengths, rather than as one-dimensional victims or problems.

This opportunity to straddle a number of worlds provides us with the energy to continue our work and encourages us to think creatively about solutions. We are grateful for the independence and freedom to develop our ideas and program, which has been granted us by the many generous foundations, corporations, and individual donors who recognize the importance of innovation and advocacy for teens in foster care. The independent support has allowed us to both think creatively and test a program with great flexibility to meet the needs and concerns of teens in care.

From the start, we felt that focusing exclusively on policy advocacy or running an after-school program for teens would be limiting. At Youth Advocacy Center, our commitment is twofold: first, we help teens in foster care build a better future for themselves, and second, we try to change the system to better meet the needs of teens in care. We combine both policy and practice (programming) because the interplay between the two is essential to creating meaningful change. We see the need to have programs that are relevant and appealing to students and, at the same time, support the goal of successful independence for teens leaving foster care. This link between the practical and theoretical is critical for creating effective policies that work and for designing programming that goes beyond the common expectations held within and outside the system.

If the foster care system is to change in a substantial way, then the following questions must be addressed. Through telling our story, we hope readers might consider these questions in a more thoughtful way and thereby stimulate discussion about the larger issues connected with foster care for teens in the United States.

1. Should the government's responsibility for the care and protection of teenagers in foster care include preparing them for successful independence?

The government removes kids from their families and keeps them in public custody at a cost of at least $50,000 per year, per teen for the purpose of protecting them from neglect or abuse.[2] In our society, we expect parents and custodians of teenagers to properly prepare them to be participating and contributing citizens. Has the foster care system adequately met its responsibility for care and protection if the majority of teens continue to fail at independence when they age out of foster care? Does the teen hold the responsibility of properly preparing themselves for independence while in foster care? Are the majority of young adults in foster care simply incapable of ever achieving independence, no matter what preparation they receive?

2.   Can the foster care system apportion more attention to teens' futures and less to their problems?

The foster care system is based on the assumption that the children and teenagers are mentally ill or too fragile to take on the responsibility of preparing for their future. The trauma of separating from biological parents and living in foster care is formidable, and certainly teens need support from mental health professionals. But is there too much focus on a mental illness model, as opposed to a mental health model in child welfare? If so, does the presumption that teens in foster care suffer from mental illness or incapacity eclipse the fact that they need to prepare for their futures? Can the system integrate a commitment to promoting teens' mental and emotional health with a priority on education and future planning?

3.   Can teenagers in foster care successfully engage in intellectual activities for the purpose of preparing for their independence?

Are the minimal expectations that are formalized in systemwide policies warranted? Can teenagers rise to intellectual challenges? Is there a distinction between intellectual ability and educational deficiency? Can they become successfully empowered to critically analyze information and make good decisions about their future?

4.   Can citizens from the general community become more directly included in making the foster care system more responsive to the needs of teens in care?

Does the general community care about children in foster care? If so, are they willing to contribute new approaches, from their differing experiences, on ways to help teens in foster care adequately prepare to become participating citizens? Can teens benefit from more contact with members of the general community? Will successful members of the community volunteer to help teens in care in a significant manner? Can child welfare professionals prepare teens to use these contacts in a meaningful way that will advance their success at independence?

Examining and analyzing these questions are the first steps in bringing changes to a foster care system that inadequately prepares teens for the future. In recent years, we have seen movement toward addressing these questions from individuals and groups dedicated to changing the existing approaches. The experiences and ideas shared in this book are not intended as definitive answers. Instead, we offer our vision of and experience with the foster care system as a means for supporting the argument that the foster care system needs to change, that the teens can be better prepared for independence, and that the system can exchange creative, cost efficient methods for the existing failed and costly approaches.

The foster care system is about hope and despair. Every child and every dedicated professional in the system experience wide swings between the two. We offer our experiences not as a solution, but as a source to strengthen hope and to demonstrate that with the existing talent and strengths of foster care teens, child welfare professionals, and the community at large, we have endless possibilities to integrate the teens' needs into the foster care system. We have an opportunity to use the bountiful creativity and wisdom of our community of citizens to substantiate and build on the hope of every teen in foster care.

The failure of teens in foster care is our failure because they are in our custody. Foster care begins when the government, acting on the behalf of all its citizens, decides that a child is safer in government custody than living with his or her family. After the government makes this decision, we assume both custody of a child and the responsibility for protection and care—that is, essentially, we are communal parents. If we as parents consistently failed at preparing our own teens, we would feel a sense of shame, and certainly, we would not want others to repeat our mistakes. At this time we not only fail at preparing these teens in our custody for independence, but we also succeed in preparing them for a life of dependence. For Selina and the half-million other young people in foster care, this pattern must change.

While we watched the teens at our graduation and listened to individuals like Selina talk about their aspirations, we couldn't help returning to thoughts of a lofty goal we had come to embrace. Could new participants join the process of finding better ways to support Selina and all the teens in foster care by properly preparing them to succeed in our greater community? We hope *Beyond the Foster Care System* will encourage and embolden readers to create new visions of supporting teens in foster care and other teens from poor and disadvantaged backgrounds. We hope that our readers will join the debate and start new debates about how we can better help our teens. The changes we envision will not cost more, but they will require a different and more positive way of looking at teens and at ourselves.

Beyond the Foster Care System

1

First Impressions
of the Foster Care System

Teresa   To get into foster care, you have to pass through family court. To get into family court, you have to wait on a long line to go through metal detectors. The court officers proudly show off garbage cans filled with weapons, guns, knives, brass knuckles, and weapons discovered on clients attempting to enter the courtroom. Some evade the metal detectors, like the family member who brought a rock to throw at a judge.

We too first entered the foster care system through family court, when we worked there as lawyers for children in foster care. Betsy was an attorney, recently out of law school, working for a small legal services office that represented children in foster care review cases. Paul was a law student, on sabbatical from the chairmanship of the communications department at a university. He applied for an internship at the firm and was assigned to work with Betsy, who persuaded him to continue at the firm when he graduated from law school.

As law guardians (in New York the official family court name for lawyers who are assigned to every child in foster care) we were assigned by judges in the family court to represent children who were put into foster care. These children had "cases" in family court because every child in New York City's foster care system had their case—living situation, permanency plan, and any special needs—reviewed by a family court judge, not because they had done anything wrong. The children were assigned lawyers to represent their interests. Our job was to articulate the child's position in court and present evidence or argument to support that position: stay in a foster home, return home right away, move to a better group home, prevent separation from a sibling, receive preparation to live independently, or receive attention about other issues related to foster care placement. This court review typically lasted less than five minutes; but its purpose was explicit: to ensure that (1) the child was in the right place with the right sort of services, and (2) that the city was either working with the family, if that was the plan, or trying to place the child with an adoptive family.

Many of our cases were teenagers. Many had grown up in foster care, and others were placed into foster care when they hit adolescence and family conflicts escalated. For youth older than about fifteen, the judge usually approved the goal of independent living. In practice, this meant the teen would remain in foster care indefinitely, until she or he "aged out" somewhere between eighteen and twenty-one years old. We learned that for many teens, foster care became a long-term living arrangement.

Paul

On the second day of work as a lawyer, my supervisor handed me a stack of folders. "Here are some cases that you can take over," she said. "I don't think any are coming into court right away, but you can start checking up on your clients. See how they're doing. Ask their social workers to bring them in to meet you." I was somewhat confused, but I began looking through the files, making phone calls, introducing myself as the new lawyer on the case, and requesting a time to interview Brian, or Maritsa, or Lateesha. One of the first clients I saw was Teresa.

Teresa and I met for the first time in my minuscule office. There were no windows and no discernable air vent. Teresa moved into the office with little emotion and sat down. I had to ask her to stand again while I maneuvered her chair so I could close the door. I cursed the fact that both she and I had to meet in such an inhospitable environment.

Teres's face was unreadable, as if she were a captured spy preparing for interrogation. Teresa was seventeen years old with a pleasant face and well-kept short hair. Her clothes were surprisingly nondescript, in contrast to many teenagers trying to define their identity through their clothing. The few times she looked directly at me, her eyes conveyed a sense that she was aware of every action I took. I let Teresa know that the purpose of our meeting was for me to learn where she wanted to be placed. I informed Teresa that I was just starting out as a lawyer and I would need her help. No reaction. "I need you to make sure I don't make any mistakes," I said. I tried to get a smile, but whatever warmth I thought I communicated produced no response and little eye contact. "All right, then, let's get started." I quickly resorted to a newly acquired, just-the-facts, official approach.

I had been working as a lawyer for only three months. Unlike most of the young lawyers in family court, I had prior careers before going to law school. For twenty years I was the chairman of a university communications department and a documentary filmmaker. While I had produced films for organizations serving children and families and I had experience educating and helping young people develop their abilities to succeed as adults, I had never contemplated entering the unlikely setting of Manhattan family court, nor was I prepared for this awkward conversation with Teresa.

I knew from Teresa's file that she was living in a foster care institution outside the city. She had been in foster care for about three years. Apparently her mother used drugs and became unable to handle Teresa when she moved into adolescence. Once placed in foster care, Teresa was diagnosed with all sorts of mental problems, and the term mildly retarded was used more than once in her records. In most circumstances I would have found this information quite troubling, but here in family court it seemed that almost every child had some type of mental illness label. Consequently, mildly retarded told me very little about the young woman seated in front of me.

"Do you like where you're living?" I asked.

Teresa looked at me blankly. She let my question go unanswered for what seemed like a long time and then spoke to the wall behind me. "I'm going to live with my grandfather in Chicago." This non sequitur must be a delusional fantasy, I thought. The file never mentioned a grandfather. Even if he did exist, I was already familiar enough with the system to know that a grandfather in Chicago was not a likely source for placement. Despite myself, I was easily buying into the family court prejudices against fathers, older men, and out-of-staters (although I fit all of those categories myself at one time or another).

At the moment my job was to take what she said at face value, at least as a starting point in representing her. And besides, Teresa intrigued me. Whatever diagnoses and labels she'd been given, she carried herself with a kind of dignity, clearly telling herself she was above all of this. She wasn't going to fall for my lawyerly charm. I liked that. "Look Teresa, I hate this office. How about I visit you where you're living? Maybe we can talk more about your grandfather there, and I can talk with some of your staff. If you want to live with your grandfather and if he has a suitable home, I promise I'll try to help you."

Teresa acknowledged my offer by getting up to leave. We did the same awkward dance to open the door. Once I unblocked her path out of the office, she began walking down the hall. I followed in pursuit and caught up to her at the waiting area outside the elevators. Upon seeing Teresa, the staff person who accompanied her from the institution got up and followed her to the elevator. No words were spoken between them, nor did either acknowledge me. As we waited for the elevator, six eyes staring at the elevator doors, I told Teresa that I was glad to meet her and would arrange a visit soon. I reminded her that I still would need her help. As the elevator doors closed I was left without any clue about Teresa's understanding of what I was trying to do.

Meeting Teresa in my office was actually a rare luxury. Often I would meet my clients at the family court, in a small room reserved for law guardian interviews. The interview room had a few institutional desks scattered haphazardly; the stained desktops were hidden under old newspapers, dirty coffee cups, miscellaneous articles of clothing, and discarded umbrellas. Anybody who had been in the room often enough knew better than to open empty drawers for fear of finding cockroaches or mice. The only indication that this was the 1990s was an occasional phone. No effort was made to brighten the surroundings because only the transient lawyers and clients used them.

If I was lucky I would get to interview my client alone. Usually, however, attorneys and staff would flow in and out of the interview room as I met with a client. I'd be trying to get some important and often intimate facts from a child while trying to ignore another lawyer talking about her evening or weekend plans, venting frustration about a judge's order, or recounting some horrible case of another child in foster care. Most clients seemed to shrug off these intrusions. The kids know that once they're in family court and foster care they can say goodbye to privacy.

When the interviewing room was filled I'd do what the other lawyers did and interview the client in a public waiting room. There was a lot of waiting. Everyone was told to arrive at 9:00 a.m. but the individual case might not be called until 3:50 p.m. The faces of those waiting communicated fatigue, impatience, anger, and fatal helplessness. Their anxiety intensified as they overheard others in the waiting area: opposing attorneys arguing about the meaning of a court order, a social worker and attorney expressing frustration at each other's incompetence in preparing for a case, caseworkers calling their offices to warn of hours of further delays, court officers losing their patience with both lawyers and clients continually asking why their case wasn't being called, infants crying, and family members fighting with each other.

Any excuse to get out of family court was welcome, and the day I went to visit Teresa was a great day to escape. The air was brisk, and the sky was deep blue. I kept the window open as I drove out of the city to the suburbs. The range of colors of the turning leaves contrasted with the gray tones of the misery of family court, and the fresh air elevated my spirits. I felt guilty thinking of the daily ravages facing my colleagues, but I was elated, as if I was on a one-day furlough. The homes I passed in the upper-middle-class neighborhoods were cheery and ready to warm their occupants throughout the winter. This was going to be a good day. I was visiting Teresa and meeting with the professionals at her institution. I would spend the day with people who were truly helping children.

I had gotten negative vibes from Teresa's case worker. Before taking so much time away from the office, I contacted the executive director and asked for a meeting. I hadn't yet learned that this was not the protocol and that typically my communication with the agency should be limited to the case worker.

I turned into the beautiful grounds of the institution, which looked like a small college campus. Rolling lawns spread before well-kept buildings.

Unlike family court, there were no outward sounds, sights, or smells of hope-lessness. A pleasant secretary accompanied me into the office of the executive director. The office had the quiet hush of deep pile carpeting, a solid wood desk, small accent lighting with charts and reports in organized piles on the desk, sofa, side chair, and end table. The director was wearing a brown suit with the jacket hanging over the back of his chair. With his deep blue shirt he wore a silk tie with bright colors that at first seemed like ordinary business attire but on closer inspection had little children's figures dancing across it. His sleeves were buttoned at the wrists, as if at any moment he might have to pop into a board meeting.

He seemed as comfortable in his crisp clothes and polished leather shoes as the CEO of a large organization, which it took me a few moments to realize, he was. (The annual budget of an agency like this could be in the tens of millions of dollars because each filled bed represented at least $80,000 a year. I had yet to realize that maintaining the cash flow for the agency depended greatly on the disposition made by a family court judge at Teresa's next hearing.)

Somehow I felt lulled by the director's calm explanation of the institution's history and the value of the therapeutic milieu, as he called it. It sounded impressive—all these psychiatrists, social workers, teachers working together to care for Teresa. Though this was clearly an administrator in command and exceedingly busy, he also seemed eager to assist my client and me. This was a welcome surprise. My old instincts from the days before I became an attorney resurfaced. I wanted to believe Teresa was really in a good place. I had the urge to simply thank him for his time, for the care Teresa must be getting, and head back to my car. Yet I had come to see Teresa, and arrangements had been made.

Teresa was brought into a formal conference room about twenty times the size of my office. The worker who led her in was neatly dressed, with an air of self-importance for the custodial role he played. With a stern smile, he instructed Teresa to "listen to what the nice man tells you." As I witnessed this rote interchange I felt my optimism fade and my wariness return. Again looking beyond me, this time speaking to a window, Teresa explained once more, with little affect, that her grandfather lived in Chicago and was ready to pick her up. I asked Teresa more about him and learned that he was retired and married to a woman who was not Teresa's grandmother. He had visited Teresa here in New York.

My family court colleagues had advised me to assume that Teresa had invented her grandfather. If he did exist, he probably was unconcerned with Teresa. This assumption made me feel disoriented when Teresa then told me she had visited her grandfather in Chicago. "Really? What was it like? Tell me about the visits." With my questions, I figured I'd bring her out of fantasy land and back to reality. Instead, Teresa smiled for the first time, as if to herself. She then spent five minutes giving me details of a visit with her grandfather that she had before she came into foster care, describing the building he lived in, the stores nearby, and what they did together. I took notes. I asked Teresa about any other family members. She mentioned a sister who lived and worked in New York.

I had no way to appraise whether Teresa fully understood that I could help her leave the agency and live with her grandfather. I explained that her grandfather would have to comply with a home inspection and other require-ments. She acknowledged this in a matter-of-fact way. In this second inter-view Teresa remained consistent with her goal to leave the institution and go back to her family. She let me know she was completely miserable at the insti-tution, through not only her obvious discomfort in her surroundings, but also her terse comments—"It's just not any good here," "the school is ridiculous, like for babies." She was as tense and guarded as she was at my office. She smiled only when talking about her grandfather.

The worker returned and told Teresa it was time for her lunch. I asked him if he could show me Teresa's room. We walked through a dormitory type building. Open doors revealed rooms decorated with posters, stuffed ani-mals, radios, and baseball caps. One room, Teresa's, had nothing on the walls, bed, or bureau. It looked strikingly like a cell. At first I was stunned and just moved down the hall following the worker. Almost as an afterthought I asked, "How come Teresa has nothing in her room?"

"Teresa has a problem," he said. "She stays away from the other kids so they steal from her. We can't replace what is stolen so anything she gets from her family we lock up in storage."

As we walked through the lunchroom I saw Teresa sitting at a large table without any other kids. One older man sat with her. I approached them to say goodbye to Teresa and introduced myself to the man, Mr. Dobbs, a part-time child care worker. He offered to show me around the campus.

I asked if Mr. Dobbs could show me where Teresa went to school. Mr. Dobbs took me to a class that was in progress. A group of about eight students ranging in age from twelve to seventeen sat in the classroom. A young and eager teacher was working very hard to try to interest one student. The others sat scattered through the classroom gazing at a TV mounted on the ceiling, like in a hospital room. There were a few books, ragged with age and aimed at a much lower age level. I was struck by the irony of a relatively nice looking classroom that lacked anything meaningful with which to engage the students.

Mr. Dobbs let me know that he felt Teresa, as well as some of the teenagers we just saw, had greater capacity to learn, but no one placed much attention on this area. As we strolled through the institutional halls passing windows that framed bucolic fields, Mr. Dobbs freely answered my questions. He suspected that he was kept part-time because it was less expensive for the agency than the costs of benefits for a full-timer. He told me he earned minimum wage, and, although he wanted to help the kids, he felt he would need to leave in a few months. Mr. Dobbs felt that as a parent and a former supervisor in a supermarket, he had the background to help children. He noted that most of the staff were not as experienced as he was and lacked any significant training to work with children. Many staff members focused more on learning how to do reports than on helping a child prepare for schoolwork or overcome some of the traumas of living in this institution.

As I drove back to New York I was feeling far more sober than on my trip out of the city. It seemed unjust that Teresa had to endure the indignity of living in an institution that seemed so punitive and wrong that no one was helping her rejoin her family. The more I talked to her and saw the environment she lived in, the more skeptical I became of any reason to keep Teresa at the institution.

A week later I got a call from a Mr. Banes, Teresa's grandfather. He asked if he could visit with me on his next trip to New York. I agreed, though the

family court culture made me doubt that this would work out. I was suc-
cumbing to a common phenomenon in the legal world, where we take sides
before the evidence is presented. As a lawyer for children, I was being pushed
to develop a strong prejudice against parents, not dissimilar to the defense
attorneys who believe that every defendant is innocent or is being prosecuted
too aggressively, or the many prosecutors who believe that all defendants are
guilty. This grandfather would have a heavy burden to prove that he could
take care of a teenager. He would have an easier time convincing my colleagues and me that he was a child molester rather than a suitable custodian
for Teresa.

The sixty-year-old Mr. Banes arrived, wearing a simple suit and tie and a
friendly, warm smile. "Yes, I am aware of Teresa's diagnosis," he said, "but I
think it's understandable because of the shock of being taken from her family. My daughter had a difficult time, lost her job, and got into drugs. Teresa
was left unattended sometimes. But she doesn't belong in an institution."

I looked for problems with his taking Teresa. "What about your wife?" I
asked, "Does she really want this?"

"She wants to help Teresa too. We have a two-bedroom apartment and
live on a nice block. She knows people in the schools; she'll help Teresa get
the right education." I explained to the grandfather that my role was to help
Teresa get what she wanted and that if we pursued this, the agency and the
city would look at his situation carefully and that he might consider getting
an attorney. He smiled and said he didn't have enough money for an attorney
and didn't see why he just couldn't have Teresa live with him. After all, he was
the grandfather. I realized that without an attorney, this man had no idea of
how the system was stacked against him. This wasn't a Disney movie; this was
family court. I suggested that the grandfather take out a petition requesting
guardianship. In the meantime, we could send a social worker to investigate
his home. This would lead to a hearing before a family court judge where he
could present reasons why Teresa should be released to live with him. The
burden would be on him to prove he was a suitable guardian for Teresa.

As a new attorney, I had no idea what to do next. So many cases in foster
care are on endless hold, even though suspending proper resolutions damages
children and their families. My responsibility was to get a social worker to

investigate Mr. Banes's home in Chicago. With a backlog of cases and a limited budget this process would be slow. The grandfather's responsibility would be to make some definitive decisions and take the time to file a petition for custody of his granddaughter. The agency appeared unmotivated to see Teresa moved to anyone and was comfortable waiting for the court review, scheduled for eighteen months but likely to be extended beyond that time period.

I was soon swamped by the flood of other cases—babies, little children, school-aged kids, older teenagers. All needed attention, and each case had at least a dozen foster care professionals simultaneously working on it—investigative workers, caseworkers, placement workers, city workers, agency workers, supervisors, social workers, psychologists, lawyers, judges. It was overwhelming to learn about each child, much less all the various players attached to his or her case. I now understood why so many of my colleagues referred to their work as triage.

One day, several months later the phone rang. "This is Mr. Fays, Teresa's worker. You her lawyer, right?"

I quickly searched through more than sixty manila folders of open cases on my desk and floor to refresh my memory. Finally I found it. "Yes, of course, how is Teresa? Tell her I'm going to visit again soon." Arranging to have the home visit had been frustrating. In the meantime, Mr. Banes's wife had become ill, and his attention was diverted. Everything continued on endless hold.

"I'm supposed to tell you. Got some bad news about Teresa. She was raped."

I was completely unprepared for this. My client, in a prestigious institution that prides itself on maximum supervision, was raped? This was not a statistic or a news report. It was someone I knew. It couldn't be true. "Is she okay? What happened?"

"It was on campus. She seems to be okay. It was another resident here."

"What are the police doing?" I instinctively asked, while I was giving myself time to absorb and then react.

"I don't know if they were called. She seems okay," he repeated.

After hanging up and taking a few moments to digest this information, I called the executive director. I probably did not understand something. This was insane. The director explained that indeed Teresa was raped, that she was getting good medical and psychiatric attention and was doing well. She had asked for her grandfather to be informed, and a worker would be doing so. His calm tone contrasted with the magnitude of the assault. I managed to control myself for about fifteen seconds.

"How could that happen?" I screamed.

"Calm down, Mr. Pitcoff. We have many disturbed teenagers living in close quarters. These things happen. These things happen in a setting like ours."

My supervisor peeked into the office, wondering what my yelling was about. "Dickens, this sounds like Dickens, what kind of place is this? You better call the police!"

His calm tone persisted. "The police will just be annoyed and make things more difficult for us to give the care Teresa and the boy need now."

"Call the police now, or I will," I threatened. He said he understood I was upset and, that if I insisted, he would call the police; again he assured me that Teresa was in the best possible place.

At this point I was convinced that Teresa needed to get out of foster care. I was slow in getting to this position, but my faith in this mental health facility was eroding, and my sense of the injustice of keeping Teresa imprisoned there was rising. I left a message at the institution asking someone to call me about how Teresa was doing, and a few days letter found a scribbled phone message on my desk: "Teresa is fine. Sister visited." When I called Teresa's caseworker back, he reassured me, "There is really nothing for you to do!"

Teresa was assaulted and hurt. I felt connected with her even though we had such a minimal relationship. Finally, I got the agency to let her talk to me on the phone. She sounded the same and told me she was okay. When I told her that I had heard she had been hurt, she only responded, "I still want to leave this place." She hung up. I felt like I was watching a victim of a shipwreck drifting away in a barely adequate life preserver, resigned to her plight. The agency would not bring Teresa to my office, and I didn't have a day to visit her in the institution. There were so many cases.

Some veterans of the family court system tried to comfort me. They reassured me that after a little more time in the system it would become easier.

They told me of other clients who had been raped, beaten, starved, humili-ated, and abandoned. They were trying to help me maintain realistic expec-tations and aim for some incremental successes. Yet this reassurance had the opposite effect. It started me thinking that I couldn't be part of a system in which rape was an expected occurrence and even the victims had to learn to accept it as part of the environment.

Meanwhile, my colleagues dampened my enthusiasm for Teresa's grand-father as a potential guardian. They pointed out that the agency would most likely demand a series of supervised visits between Teresa and her grand-father at the institution. This would require the grandfather to make fre-quent trips to New York. This would surely be impossible for him financially. The city would have to approve an interstate investigation and supervision of a trial release to Illinois, which would take an interminable amount of time, making such a solution next to impossible. I needed to maintain hope since I believed that Teresa needed to be with her family and out of the institution.

Another five or six weeks went by, and new cases joined my older folders. During the course of a week, a law guardian may represent forty or more cases in family court and deal with forty or more outside of court. My caseload included Marc, a five-year-old with burn marks on his arm, whose teachers suspected his foster mother was the culprit. I was supposed to ask him how he got those marks. I also had John, a fourteen-year-old who was terrified of being returned to his father, who he said beat him with a pipe. Another chal-lenging case was Larissa, a fifteen–year-old girl who was present in court when the judge stated that she needed evaluation for her "borderline per-sonality disorder" and ordered the agency to refer her for a ninety-day in-patient evaluation. Larissa now threatened to run away, claiming she'd rather be homeless on the streets than in an institution. Jessie, a sixteen-year-old, was prohibited from visiting her family. The agency felt this was appropriate punishment because she had missed curfew at the group home one evening, when she stayed late for a school activity; yet Jessie was making progress toward reuniting with his family, and the home visits were important and legally required. Benito, a seventeen-year-old, wanted me to help him get back into a foster home where he didn't get enough food and was made to babysit the other kids in the house. Why? He was determined to get back to this inhospitable home because his seven-year-old brother was still there, and Benito wanted to protect him. And there were many more of these human stories lying in the coffee-stained, scribbled-over manila envelopes that represented each of my assigned cases.

One day I noticed a petition for a custody hearing for Teresa. I looked for Mr. Banes, the grandfather's name, but instead saw "Bernice Williams, sister." I was confused. What had happened to the grandfather? I called him in Chicago. He said he still wanted Teresa, but if she could live with her sister that was good, too. His wife was getting better but not fully recovered. Now I had to reconsider the plan for Teresa and see if she indeed wanted to live with her sister, and if her sister was a suitable guardian.

In difficult cases, a law guardian needs to negotiate between family members, the foster care agency, sometimes foster parents, and the city agency. The city agency at that time was called the Child Welfare Administration, or CWA. (Many in the system persisted in calling the agency BCW. In ten years, the agency name had been changed from the Bureau of Child Welfare, BCW, to Special Services for Children, SSC, then to CWA. A few years later, the agency was once again "restructured" and given a new name, Administration for Children's Services, ACS.) Working out a resolution that all parties would agree to would be frustratingly difficult. Thus this new twist in Teresa's case was not welcomed on my part. I had been working toward getting Teresa to go to her grandfather, and I wasn't prepared to change suddenly to another relative. I was not yet accustomed to the seismic shifts that often occur as families attempt to resolve their problems. Against my will, I was being pulled into this huge bureaucratic foster care system, unable to adapt to the intricacies and changes that are a part of any family life. The inability to give sufficient time or assistance to any of my clients made the introduction of the sister into Teresa's case feel like an assault on my own time and beliefs.

Two weeks before Teresa's hearing, I received a call from Ms. Williams, Teresa's sister. She told me she wanted Teresa out of foster care, and she wanted to take custody of Teresa. She said she was twenty-six, had an apartment and a job with the transit authority, and did not want to see Teresa continue to be harmed. Over the phone Ms. Williams made it clear that she felt I was part of the system and responsible for Teresa's situation. I got defensive and quickly resorted to a lawyer persona.

When Mr. Farley, our social worker assigned to the case, informed me that he had traveled an hour to visit the apartment and Ms. Williams didn't show, I was furious. I called Ms. Williams at work, although she had specifically told me to call her only at home. With some effort the person who answered found her and called her to the phone. She and I were both highly annoyed. "You missed our appointment. Where were you? You can't just not show up—this certainly doesn't demonstrate responsibility. How can I get Teresa released to you?" Even while I was talking, I was disappointed at my own hostile and adversarial manner. I had transformed into an accuser and saw everyone as the enemies of these kids and of justice.

"Why are you calling me here? I'm at work. I couldn't be home because I had to work overtime. I called your office, but no one was there. Come Thursday at 6:00 p.m. I'll be there." Her last words before hanging up on me continue to haunt me. "You have an attitude problem."

Ms. Williams had struck a nerve. I did have an attitude, and this attitude was emboldened by my knowledge that she didn't stand a chance. I told Farley that another appointment was set with Ms. Williams, but if it was too much trouble he should forget it. "We gave her a chance," I said. Luckily, Farley was more professional and charitable than I and agreed to give her another opportunity.

Farley found that Ms. Williams had a job at the transit authority cleaning subway cars. Like her grandfather, she had sufficient income so that she could not qualify for free legal assistance, but she didn't have money for a private attorney. Her home was well-kept, and she seemed to really care for Teresa. They had grown up together and were only separated three years ago, when their mother became incapable of caring for them, and Teresa went into foster care.

I was confused now and needed help. It seemed to me that Teresa's best shot at reuniting with her family was going to Ms. Williams as soon as possible, and I wanted to see that happen before Teresa suffered any more harm in foster care.

Caleb, an experienced, supervising lawyer, was assigned to help me in court. I could count on him to rely on facts rather than his own feelings. He agreed that if Teresa wanted to live with either her grandfather or sister, we needed to represent this position. Caleb, unlike most other family court lawyers, was unafraid of moving beyond the conforming expectations of the system and its players. He wore the same threadbare tie to court every day, perhaps a muted symbol of his lack of respect for the family court system.

On the hearing day my supervisor and I greeted the attorneys for the institution in one of the large waiting rooms. They in turn introduced us to the agency's executives and psychologist. Normally such high level officials do not attend petition review hearings. They were friendly and eager to demonstrate that their only concern was Teresa. I found myself wondering what if any consideration they gave to the possible loss of $80,000 of revenue for Teresa's care.

Prior to the hearing, the institution executives and psychologist talked in low voices that projected concern for Teresa. They recognized our sympathy for Teresa but made it clear that returning her to her grandfather or sister, although a noble idea, underestimated Teresa's needs.

Sitting alone in another corner amongst five empty seats was a small, young woman reading a Bible. The court officer informed me that this was the petitioner, Ms. Williams. She was neatly dressed, well-groomed. Nothing she wore was remarkably flashy or intended to attract attention. She looked young but had the eyes and expression of one who had lived more years. She sat still and erect, conveying a strong sense of control.

Perhaps the surroundings of family court exacerbate prejudices. Seeing Ms. Williams reading a Bible inside a court of law made me think she was relying on the powers of faith rather than the process of law. This reignited my insecurity about Ms. William's ability to handle real-world situations— like Teresa. She didn't know that she had to have an attorney to have any chance of winning her petition, and she had no other person here in court to give her emotional support. She was a single woman working a hard job. How could she believe that anyone would think her capable of properly caring for Teresa?

Noticeably absent in both the waiting room and the courtroom was Teresa. The judge would never see or hear Teresa. We were her only voice in these proceedings.

New to family court, I was shy about talking to the judges. This judge, however, was talkative. On several occasions before or after a hearing he would lecture me. He let me know that, while he agreed with the law that children's requests should be represented in court, we all had to appreciate that "we professionals have to make the critical decisions in their best interests." The judge's words conveyed the message that my legal role of law guardian was not to be followed or respected by the court.

. The judge asked the court officer to get Ms. Williams an 18B, an attorney who works on a panel to represent those too poor to hire their own legal counsel. A young African-American woman reading the Bible in his courtroom clearly needed her own attorney. The court officer informed the judge that Ms. Williams did not qualify. The judge was noticeably surprised. "Ms. Williams, I strongly urge you to get an attorney. These are significant and complex proceedings, and I advise you to proceed with representation."

"Sir, I can tell you what you need to know." Ms. Williams's small frame and low voice caught everyone's attention. "Sir, I mean your honor, I want my sister. I can take . . ."

Most proceedings involve legal jargon familiar to the judge, lawyers, and social workers. Rarely does one hear a child, parent, family member, or foster parent argue in plain language inside the courtroom. "Stop right there, Ms. Williams," the judge interrupted. "You will have your chance."

The judge noted for the record that Ms. Williams had filed a petition for custody of her sister. He asked the agency what their position was. The agency lawyer informed the judge that although Ms. Williams had visited Teresa, she had not done so on a regular basis. He also somberly noted that there was a prior abuse report on Ms. Williams when they both lived with their mother. Finally, he threw in for good measure, there was no evidence that Teresa had bonded with Ms. Williams.

No longer was I stunned. I had become numbed by the fact that abuse cropped up everywhere in family court. At this moment when I was beginning to be convinced that Ms. Williams would be a suitable guardian for Teresa, I learned she was abusive. "I should have suspected . . ."

But my thought was interrupted by Ms. Williams, "Your honor, I was a teenager myself then. I had a fight with Teresa and pulled her hair. A neighbor, who had a grudge against my mother called it in. You can't hold that against me. I have a job, and I care about Teresa, and I'm ready to take her home."

Ms. Williams's explanation rang true. I knew that anyone can call in an abuse claim anonymously, and the allegation will be investigated. Although this provides needed protection for children, it also gives feuding neighbors or family members an opportunity to harass each other. The judge wasn't as easily moved as I. "What about the fact that you don't visit? That certainly doesn't show a strong intent or capacity to care for Teresa," he inquired sternly.

Ms. Williams's slender frame remained the focal point of the court. In spite of the insulting and bizarre allegations leveled at her, she remained poised and focused on getting Teresa back to her family and out of harm's way. "I can't see how remaining at this place where she was raped is good for Teresa. I tried to visit, and the agency made it very difficult for me with my work schedule. I have asked for Teresa to visit with me on weekends at my home, and the agency won't let her. I have a job, I don't want any money from you, I care for Teresa, and she is my sister. She belongs in a home where there will be no danger."

The judge turned to the agency attorney. "The agency's position?"

The agency attorney asked for the psychologist to take the stand. The agency psychologist explained Teresa's emotional instability and retardation, quoting diagnoses from the DSM III reference used by mental health professionals. "Your honor, after two years of treatment, Teresa still fails to show the ability to bond with any adults, appears to manifest little affect, and truly needs a great deal of psychological counseling before she could function in home environment. Further, the agency needs time to assess whether sister or grandfather would be suitable placements for Teresa if she were released from the agency."

Then, Caleb took his turn questioning the psychologist. "Can you assess the psychological trauma of Teresa's rape at your agency?"

"Clearly it has had an effect and is another reason why she needs continuing psychological counseling."

Caleb looked to the judge to see if he saw any irony in this reasoning. "Do you know of specific reasons that Teresa should not live with Ms. Williams or her grandfather?" he continued.

The psychologist responded in a collegial manner, addressing the judge. "There has been no assessment of either placement. We would need at least six to nine months of observing weekly meetings between Teresa and her grandfather or Ms. Williams to make such an assessment."

Caleb did not accept this pronouncement. "Are you aware that the grandfather lives in Chicago, and Ms. Williams has a full-time job, which makes visits at the institution extremely difficult?"

The psychologist maintained her most professional manner and softly explained, "Our job is to help Teresa and provide the counseling and therapy she needs in a protected environment. It would be highly risky to send her to family members who have not been properly assessed, and as in the case of Ms. Williams, are known to have abused Teresa in the past."

Throughout his examination, Caleb's questions focused on bringing out the major facts that supported releasing Teresa to her sister's care. "Are you saying that you don't believe Ms. Williams when she explains the incident as a rash overreaction of a teenager that happened well in the past? Do you dispute the report of our own psychiatrist whose opinion is that Teresa can live in a home environment? Do you dispute the work of our own social worker that has visited Ms. Williams's home and found it and her suitable? Do you have any knowledge that over the past three years Ms. Williams has not been a responsible employee and member of her community? Do you have any doubt that Ms. Williams loves her sister, or recognizes her degree of emotional problems, or is incapable of providing a decent loving home?"

The psychologist managed to maintain a polite and patronizing smile. She no longer looked at Caleb but at the judge. "Your honor, we have a reputation of providing extensive care for emotionally traumatized children. I think you can understand that it is our professional responsibility to predi-cate release upon extensive observation of the family member in question. Ms. Williams may have good intentions but may not be the suitable place-ment Teresa needs."

Now Caleb addressed the judge. "Your honor, while in care at the agency, Teresa was raped. She lives in a cell-like room with no personal belongings because the agency cannot prevent other children from stealing them. The agency admits she has made no progress since being placed there. She has emotional problems and may be retarded, although there is no conclusive evidence. Yet she has two caring family members who are eager and capable of caring for her in a loving home environment. Teresa has consistently over the past six months indicated her desire to live with her sister or grandfather. Teresa can get mental health help while living with her sister. Such service may be more helpful than in an institutional setting where Teresa's safety is not even certain. I request you order the agency to allow weekend home vis-its with Ms. Williams for six weeks and then release Teresa to her sister on a trial basis to be evaluated in six months. Without any evidence that Ms. Williams is incapable of caring for Teresa, the court must move to reunite her with her family."

Ms. Williams sat with quiet dignity throughout the back and forth. She clearly felt all of us, including Caleb, who argued Teresa's case as eloquently and competently as any lawyer in family court, were against her. In her mind, we were all part of the system that was separating Teresa from her. Surely, Ms. Williams never saw family court as a system designed to support families.

The judge was baffled. He couldn't ignore the rape incident or our own psychiatrist's report that Teresa could live in the community. However, he also gave great credence to the professional opinion offered by the agency's psy-chologist. Ms. Williams did not have her own professional experts. It was our report against the testimony of the agency psychologist. The attorney for CWA supported the agency's position to deny release, even on a trial basis. The judge had a heavy docket, with perhaps thirty-five hearings that day. He had to make a decision quickly, in the next minute. The agency had not made any effort to earnestly evaluate return to family options, and they and the city were the only parties with enough funds to do so. Absent such evaluations, Teresa's release from foster care appeared risky.

Relying on the system is often the easiest way around such difficult situations. If the judge continues the status quo, situations often take care of themselves. The petitioning parent or family member gives up or eventually an agency may even release a child. However, everyone in the courtroom, including the judge, was moved by Ms. Williams's presence. For a moment, my hopes were raised. The only evidence against Ms. Williams was that when she was a teenager, she pulled her sister's hair.

The judge looked at Ms. Williams. "I am ordering the agency to allow you to visit Teresa on your day off. You must make those visits and allow the agency to assess your relationship. If those visits go well I am ordering the agency to allow home visits six months from today and then we'll bring this case back and see if we can order a trial discharge to you."

The agency's lawyers, executives, psychologist, and the CWA lawyer walked out of the courtroom thanking the judge, smiling, and complimenting each other. The agency had their position upheld by the process. The impediments for Ms. Williams would be considerable. Making visits to the suburbs from the city every weekend is not easy for someone with a full-time job. The scheduling of appointments with the case workers, arranging transportation, train and taxi, and using a full day to travel back and forth to the suburbs are impediments that often are too challenging for poor parents and relatives living in New York City. Yet if a petitioning parent or relative cannot make these visits, he or she will be denied custody of the child. During the six months ordered by the court for the next review, the agency would have time to convince Ms. Williams that Teresa would truly be better off in the agency and Ms. Williams's life would be much easier without caring for this teenager.

But Ms. Williams walked out of court appearing satisfied that she had made progress toward Teresa's release. After all, the judge had ordered something in her favor. The psychologist now acknowledged Ms. Williams and said she hoped the visits would go well. Ms. Williams was not familiar with the law or the next steps toward release. She didn't recognize that every aspect of her life would be subject to disclosure and investigation if she were to gain custody of her sister. She didn't realize that along with their stated desire to treat Teresa, the agency had a financial stake in keeping Teresa in custody.

I walked up to Ms. Williams and introduced myself. We had only talked on the phone. "Ms. Williams, I hope everything works out for you. I enjoy spending time with Teresa and know how much she wants to live with you. If you have any problems with the agency or need help, call me. I also want you to know that you were right when you said I had a bad attitude toward you. I apologize."

Ms. Williams allowed the slightest of smiles. "Thank you, and I apologize too, if I was rude to you. I just want Teresa to be in a safe place." She turned and walked toward the elevators, where a crowd was gathering, heading out for the lunch break. She was temporarily released from the interminable waiting and sorrow of the place, but the system's considerable hurdles would eventually defeat Ms. Williams's efforts to get Teresa out of foster care and into her caring home.

The visits between Ms. Williams and Teresa did not go well. It became increasingly hard for Ms. Williams to see Teresa every weekend at the institution, and the agency did not allow home visits. They treated Ms. Williams as a suspect, and I assume she finally was forced to give up her efforts to bring Teresa out of the institution. Some will use the fact that a family member gives up on their efforts to get their child out of foster care as evidence that the parent or relative is unfit in the first place. Yet there is also evidence that the system can make the burden of getting one's child back too difficult to overcome, especially if one lives at the margins of society and does not have the financial, professional, and educational resources most middle-class citizens take for granted.

I'm haunted by the image of Teresa's plain manila case folder with its pages of files, half a dozen crossed out phone numbers representing the six different case workers she had in a nine-month period, and coffee and food stains evidencing continuing handoffs of her file to those of us representing her, sinking lower and lower in the pile of the next attorney who took over her case. As other children were harmed or in need of a change in placement, their immediate needs trumped Teresa's. I better understand now Teresa's lack of affect, a common trait among teens in the foster care system. She knew the first day we met that neither I, nor any other member of the system, was going to help her. She had no reason to believe that things would change for her, and she was correct.

Pain and suffering fill the air in family court. No one escapes breathing it. The family court atmosphere changed the way we thought about all kinds of things: our work, families, government aid, and the justice system. Foster care seemed to be the least hospitable place for supporting children and families, and family court raised uncomfortable questions for us about what we were doing as individuals and as a society.

The divisions between social classes were stark and disturbing. Families that end up in family court fighting to keep their children out of foster care live in poverty. They are raising children with little or no money, with in-adequate housing and schools, with health problems and fear. In New York City, 97 percent of the children who go into foster care are African-American and Latino.[1] In contrast, most of the lawyers, and when we practiced there, all of the judges, were middle-class and white.

Entering foster care means crossing into a world of government control over children and parents. Most of us in the middle classes never get pulled into that world. In countless court cases, the behavior of parents examined in the context of charges of neglect or abuse seemed uncomfortably similar to actions of middle- and upper-class parents: keeping a child out of school, leaving a seven-year-old unattended for forty minutes, pushing or slapping a child, drinking, taking of drugs by one or both parents, experiencing serious emotional problems by a parent, and so on. While no one condones such behavior, we all recognize that parenting is an imperfect art. The difference is that middle-class families rarely have their children removed by the court. Daily we were confronted with the fact that society does this only to poor families.

Poor people find little justice in family court. Once in court, they have little practical means of overcoming the burden to prove they are competent. The child welfare system typically has full-time city attorneys with wide inves-tigative resources, supported by private foster care agency attorneys and legal

staff with similar goals of maintaining foster care as long as possible and getting children into the system as easily as possible. Families trying to keep or
regain custody of their kids may get a court appointed 18b attorney, who until
quite recently was paid only $25 an hour to work on a case, and thus had an
overload of cases that prevented him or her from devoting sufficient time to
any one. If the parent was lucky, the 18b attorney would spend twenty minutes preparing a parent's case before a hearing. If a parent works, then he or
she may neither meet the requirements for a court-assigned attorney nor
have sufficient money to hire effective representation.

The adversarial system, with the government trying to prove its case that
a child needs to be in foster care, puts parents on the defensive and kids in
the middle. It doesn't necessarily seek solutions to family problems. Each
party is against another—parents, children, the government, the foster care
agency. Too often, as in Teresa's case, the assumption is that all biological
family members wanting children released from foster care are suspect.
Lawyers for all sides adopt the stance that they, the select group of protec-
tors, will save children from cruel and sick family members.

We began to doubt that the adversarial litigation model was an effective
way either to resolve problems for poor families, to determine the truth of
what was going on in a particular family, or to implement any valuable help
to children and families.

The paradox of the family court system is that for the most part, well-
meaning professionals—the social workers, lawyers, judges, and mental
health professionals—never gain any traction in significantly helping children or their families. With dozens of cases at once, we had little opportunity
to plan strategies, consider justice, or find creative solutions to difficult and
individualized problems. In our desire and hope that we were helping clients,
we tried to ignore the reality that the system would probably wash away the
benefits of temporary assistance and carry clients off in its own haphazard
currents, regardless of a child's needs.

Gradually we concluded that family court was not a suitable institution
for helping children or their families, which requires a continuum of support
over time, with the ability to modify that support as situations evolve. The
justice system relies on finite solutions to a conflict. In a civil case, one party

may pay damages or one party may be exonerated from any responsibility. In a criminal case, a jury will find the accused innocent or guilty. In most TV shows or movies, the climax occurs with the court's decision. Using this model for resolving long-term and ongoing family issues seemed crude and ineffective. More often than not, the judge's final order brought neither resolution to a problem nor a solution to helping a family. Often the judge ordered the city to carry out some service for a family or child or be held in contempt of court; yet the city might not comply with the order. This fact reinforced the impotence of the court and naturally gave the city more room to ignore its own inadequacies. Other times, judges ordered a placement in foster care during a fluid family crisis that might resolve itself three days later, but the court calendar did not permit review in such a short turnaround and thus a child might remain in foster care inappropriately for six to eighteen months.

The legal process for overseeing foster care has a necessary function to protect rights of children and families. However, the legal process also promotes the process of disempowering children, especially teens, by making many critical decisions that can be made by or at least shared with them. Furthermore, by removing the process for formulating goals and negotiating decisions from the teens and their families, the process withholds responsibility. In the end, the teens learn that their lives are out of their control. We observed this valuable lesson and kept it in mind when formulating our program.

Between the two of us, we represented hundreds of children. For the most part, they were intelligent and courageous, with a powerful sense of humanity and the potential to lead valuable lives. Yet, with rare exception, they were put on paths that ensured failure and dependent futures. We found ourselves endlessly battling the belief that these children were so damaged there was no hope for them to have a brighter future.

Each day back at court we felt increasingly uncomfortable. More and more we felt part of the system. We realized that our own professional self-interests were linked to the ongoing existence of the foster care system, and yet we believed that system provided no real relief for the majority of children in care. As lawyers in the family court system we could not do enough to help our teen clients. At the same time, when we were effective in small ways, we were proving to the teens that reliance on the system worked, and we were teaching our teen clients to rely on the system to resolve problems.

Our continuing debates focused on how best to help the children in foster care. The answers appeared to lie in better education for both children and their parents, better support systems for families, more comprehensive legislative changes to address the real needs of teenagers preparing for independence, better trained and educated child care staff, additional alternative programs for teenagers, and more public education as to the nature of the problem and possible solutions. Although we were uncertain of the solutions, we became convinced that family court was not a suitable venue for helping, or even protecting, families and children, and it was certainly not a place to develop any meaningful foundation for helping children take hold of a fulfilling future.

No one experience motivated us to leave family court. We ended up leaving not just because we felt we could provide no lasting help for children and their families but because we began to realize that our own sense of justice, humanity, and hopefulness was being diluted each day we remained as part of the system.

Paul felt more hopeless and overwhelmed by the strength of the child welfare bureaucracy. His inability to deal with the sorrow and injustice of family court led to a desire to leave foster care permanently. Paul left his job in family court and returned to film work. Several weeks later Betsy left her job in family court. She believed that many teens she had represented had the potential to succeed and that once people learned of the challenges faced by children in foster care, new types of services would be funded. Without any experience in fund-raising, she set about raising money to develop programs that would either change the system or bring new opportunities to the children in the system. Betsy asked Paul to stay involved in her efforts, and he agreed in part because he believed in the goals. The risks of his commitment were not great because he didn't see much chance for finding funding for a new program for foster-care teens.

Betsy's knowledge of the system and her commitment to the teens helped her succeed in raising money to begin the Youth Advocacy Center.

Within a short time she convinced Paul to leave his film work and join in what would become a rich experience of successes and failures in helping teenagers establish a base for gaining successful independence.

Our experiences in family court were useful. They helped us understand the priorities of the foster care system. The court setting demonstrated how the system modeled and reinforced victimhood and the value of presenting problems. It helped us understand why so many intelligent and capable teens develop approaches to seeking help that are not useful in the wider community outside the foster care system. Although we were unsure how to address this negative pattern of seeking help, we became dedicated to finding new and more creative ways. In addition, we observed how the paternalistic nature of family court contributed to the pattern of teens rejecting responsibility for the control of their future. These insights would help form the core of our program.

In our earliest stages at Youth Advocacy Center, we decided our first initiatives should focus on education. The teens expressed interest in improving their educational opportunities, it was apparent that they were severely deficient in rudimentary skills and knowledge, and we believed that a well-educated teen would be capable of transcending the handicaps produced by separation from their families and immersion in the foster care system.

2

Education
for Foster Care Teens

| Carlos |

When we were lawyers in family court we were supposed to help our teen clients with their placement issues—that is, finding a place for them to live. But often we met teenagers who, when asked how it was going, complained about their education or lack thereof. This surprised us at first. Our prejudice was that teenagers didn't care that much about high school and that, because these teens were in foster care, they should be exclusively focused on the things we were supposed to be concerned with—whether they would be reunited with their family soon, whether they should be in a foster home rather than a group home. But many first talked about school. They imagined futures for themselves that involved education as a key component, and they were angry and scared that no one was making sure they were getting a decent education.

Our young clients knew what they needed and what they were deprived of; more than half of teens leaving foster care don't have high school diplomas.[1] We were aware of the many obstacles to high school completion and college attendance in poor communities, particularly for minorities.[2] But an overriding question loomed: shouldn't a child in the custodial care of a government system be assured of an education?

After we left our jobs in family court, we began looking for funding to work on a project to help teens in foster care. The first project for which Youth Advocacy Center received funding was production of a video. *Listen to Us* would present the authentic teen perspective on foster care. We spent several months traveling around the city and met with groups of teens at foster care agencies and community groups. We talked about the project and asked teens if they wanted to work on a video in which they could talk about their experiences in foster care and their ideas for making the system better.

The experiences of working in partnership with young people in foster care on *Listen to Us* and subsequently, other projects, increased our understanding of the challenges of changing the foster care system to meet the educational needs of teens. It also led us to understand that young people needed to be, and could be, effective advocates for themselves. Finally, through our collaboration with teens we grew to admire their resilience, ingenuity, and strengths.

Betsy

At one meeting to recruit teens for the video project at a journalism program for teenagers, I met Carlos. He was fifteen but looked much younger. Carlos had a baseball cap pulled down over the top of his face, so you could just barely see his eyes over his high cheekbones. He sat quietly listening to the other bigger, louder kids talk about the problems they had in foster care—you couldn't use the phone; one group home put everyone on house restriction if one person got in trouble; no social worker had visited them for two months; and so on.

Finally, Carlos spoke up. "Me, I just want to go to school."

I was not sure I heard him right. "Excuse me?"

"I want to go to school! I'm sick of sitting in the house all day watching TV. Staff isn't doing anything to get me in school." He sounded exasperated.

It was the last week of September and three weeks into the new school year. In New York, the law requires all children between the ages of six and seventeen to attend school full-time. How could Carlos not be enrolled in school? It seemed crazy.

"Well, I don't understand. Why can't you just go to a high school near your group home?" I asked.

Carlos nodded emphatically. "Exactly, that's what I say! My agency wants me to keep going to their school all the way in the suburbs at their campus.

But that's a special ed school, plus it's an hour and a half bus ride each way from Brooklyn. I just want to go to a regular high school."

"Have you talked to your social worker about it?" I asked.

"Yeah, I told her at the end of the last year, in June, that I want to go to a regular school, and finally she said okay, but now they keep saying they don't know when the paperwork will be done and all I know is I am losing time and credits."

"Maybe you should just go back to the agency school until the paperwork is done . . ." I suggested tentatively.

"No way, that place is a zoo!"

"What do you mean?"

"They don't care about what you're learning. You know what they care about? Sending kids to detention. If a kid breathes the wrong way, he is sent to the detention room, and that is not a pretty place to be. It's a room with high ceilings, but nothing in it, no chairs, desks, nothing. No windows, just gray dirty shaggy carpet, walls with graffiti, smells like . . ."

He finished his tirade, "Anyway I am not spending another year in special ed, I was never even in special ed before they stuck me up there. I was a straight A student!"

At that some of the other kids started to snicker, "Ooooh," mock-impressed. Carlos dropped his eyes down, pulled his baseball cap lower to hide them, folded his arms, and slouched down into his seat.

"Okay, why don't we talk more after we finish up here." I was overwhelmed by his speech, plus I felt concerned that he was upset and now embarrassed in front of his peers.

We continued the meeting for another half hour. Afterward, Carlos and I went into a smaller room with comfortable couches and sat down. Away from the group he seemed at ease talking to me, looking me straight in the eye. He gave me a little smile. "Look, I may be a runaway, group home kid, whatever, but I know I'm going to need a high school degree! Just 'cause I'm in this situation now doesn't mean I'm some idiot. I want to go to college. To do that, I got to finish high school right? And to do that I got to be in high school!"

I was touched by Carlos's focus on his education and his seriousness, and I felt compelled to offer help. I found myself liking Carlos. He was bright, sweet, and engaging. I was furious with the injustice of the government bringing Carlos into foster care and then discarding its responsibility to enroll him into a school that offered a halfway adequate education. I also was hoping that if I helped him with school, he'd join us in working on the video. His perspective and his personality would appeal to people who might otherwise turn off to foster kids.

Carlos and I made a date to meet near his group home in Brooklyn the next Monday morning. By law, the local school had to admit kids who lived in the neighborhood. Even if the paperwork wasn't finalized, Carlos still had a right to go to that school. I figured we'd go together to the school, I'd explain the situation to the office, he'd go off to class, and I could leave.

It was a sunny and crisp early fall morning. Carlos was waiting for me outside the subway stop when I got there. He was dressed in a neat white button down shirt and clean jeans, looking very fresh faced and young and ready for his first day of school. Carlos pointed us in the right direction and we started walking toward the school. We began talking a bit about ourselves. I told him I had left family court to try to help teens more directly, and I asked him how he got to be where he was. He said he'd been in foster care for two years now. Prior to foster care, he had been adopted when he was a baby, and then his adoptive family had other kids after him. He became the black sheep and ran away right after his thirteenth birthday. "I don't really like to go into the details," he said, "but it was not a good situation." After living on the streets for a couple of months, he was picked up by the police and put into a group home. He was not in contact with his adoptive mother, and said he was not interested in seeing her, though he had an aunt he did talk to.

I asked him how he liked his group home.

"Home is not really the word for it. Sure they give us a bed, but we have no bedroom doors, so we got to hang blankets or sheets up for privacy. And they feed us meals, but the refrigerator is always padlocked so it's not like you can ever help yourself to a snack or drink, and forget about using the phone. Truthfully there's not much to do there, it's a lot of sitting around, watching TV."

I asked about the kids.

"Okay, I guess, but mostly I stay to myself. I learned that's the best thing in these kinds of places. Couple of the guys are like me . . . sort of more serious, but the rest, it's like a party or free time, they don't really do anything . . ."

"Aren't they in school?"

"I guess they're supposed to be going for a GED or something. Nobody really talks much about school, it's not like anyone in the group home is telling you to do your homework. There's not even a place in the group home to sit and do homework! Nobody's asking did you pass a class, how'd you do on a test . . . so some of the kids, they're cool with that. But like I said, a couple, they're trying hard—there's this one kid in my group home who spent like five years studying for his GED. He finally passed, and no one in the house even said congratulations."

Resilience can't begin to accurately describe the strength of these kids. I asked him what the staff were like at the group home.

"Well, this one staff, Mrs. Moore, she's really nice. She always makes time to sit down and talk with me about whatever. That's not even her job. She's not a social worker, just a staff in the house. She tells me hang in there; I can make it. She knows how frustrated I've been with this school problem, but she always tells me if I want to go to college, I will one day. She's cool."

The staff are the people kids in group homes have the most contact with, day in and out. They might see their social workers every couple of months, but every day they see the group home staff, and if the staff are supportive, kind, and expect something good of the teen that can mean a lot. However, many foster care teens complain that staff are uncaring. They say that child care staff seem to resent the kids they're with, teasing them, making fun of them.

"But some staff, you cannot believe what they say. One day we were having a group home meeting, and I said, 'Why do you all have to put us down all the time, maybe you could be a little more sensitive to what we're going through here! And one staff says to me, 'You want somebody to be sensitive, go to your mommy. I'm here to collect my check.' And another staff is always telling me, 'Just drop out and get your GED—it was good enough for me. Why you have to think you're better than the rest of us?' she asks me. She doesn't get it, that I don't want to end up working as a staff in a group home. I want to get a regular high school degree, graduate with a cap and gown, all that."

The child care staff who have the main responsibility and contact with the teens are the lowest paid people at the agency, many earning less than twenty thousand dollars a year. They may have their own kids and families they are trying to support; they may be very close in background to the families of the kids in the group home. To survive, many have to hold more than one job. Not surprisingly, there is a high turnover rate. They get no downtime to reflect on the work they are doing, and little or no continuing training in child development.

Work in foster care is an overwhelmingly difficult job, and many who take it leave quickly. One child care worker complained to me, "We can't do a lot that we might want to, like touch the kids at all, even to wake them up in the morning. We can't give them a ride in our cars, even if we are going to the same place. And the kids rightfully get mad about that. But there are all these laws and policies and fears." Their job is to maintain order in the group home; they've had a good day when nobody hurts anyone or goes AWOL.

Many child care workers don't see their role as supporting a child's education; in fact, they are not given the role. The advice about getting a Graduate Equivalency Degree is common. What they don't say, or probably are unaware of, is that GED recipients are the functional equivalents of dropouts because of evidence that "the job prospects and lifetime earnings [of those with a GED] . . . [are] equal or close to that of high school dropouts."[3] It is harder to get into many colleges with a GED rather than a high school diploma, though of course if a GED earner goes on to college their prospects change. Equally important, a GED does little to advance the intellectual abilities of a student or increase their knowledge.

It shouldn't be surprising that the expectations for education at this level are low. The minimal expectations correlate to federal and local policy requirements. New York City policy at that time dictated that young people aging out of foster care (who may be as old as twenty-one) must have only an eighth-grade competency in reading and math.[4] In court cases, New York State has argued that the state constitution requires that graduates of New York City's high schools only demonstrate a ninth-grade education.[5] The lack of expectations dominates the foster care culture. If the government and the custodial guardians of the teens have such low educational expectations, then there is little likelihood that most teens will be motivated or helped to pursue an adequate education. Furthermore, children pick up clues from their environment. If no one in their group homes or foster homes makes an effort to engage in intellectual discovery, or if no adults set an example by reading and discussing books or newspapers, or if no one participates in the activities that lifelong learners engage in, then there is no reason to expect that most teens will rise beyond this environment.

"They must have an education person at your agency," I persisted, "or an IL [independent living] person who helps with school? Don't they run workshops or something to help you with school?" The independent living program at a foster care agency has the responsibility for preparing teens for life on their own.

"The workshops! Yeah, they got workshops, but hardly anybody goes, except to pick up their checks. At first I was like, great, maybe I'll learn something, but then it's like a few kids are there, and the rest walking in and out. The IL person serves up snacks, talks about you know, don't have unsafe sex, and then hands out the checks. People come when she makes a trip to Great Adventures or something, but that's it."

The IL workshops offer the opportunity for the agency to provide a structured educational program for teens. Foster care agencies and legal custodians should know the educational deficits of each child in their care. However, this educational opportunity is typically ignored or unenthusiastically applied. Rather than use it as a chance to role model what they expect from kids in school and teach them something constructive, it's typically a time for kids to pick up a twenty-dollar stipend check for showing up, have some snacks, and socialize. The administrators have too many other priorities, and the IL caseworkers are overwhelmed, underresourced, and undersupported. Facing these challenges, along with continually hearing all the unsolved problems of the teens, makes besieged IL workers naturally reach for any benevolent act to compensate for the teens' misfortunes. Rather than attempt a rigorous educational approach for which they are untrained and unsupported, they simply provide enjoyment through games and snacks. But this doesn't fool the teens and most recognize how inadequately IL programming prepares them for adulthood.

On this walk, I was struck by how odd it was that I was the one taking Carlos to school. It was a parody of a parent taking a kid to their first day of school. He must have had a dozen other child welfare professionals—that is, people paid by the system, caseworkers, social workers, a legal aid lawyer—assigned to his case. And yet I, pretty much a stranger, was, I hoped, taking him to register. Why wasn't someone with a deeper relationship to Carlos paying attention to his schooling?

Kids in foster care are at a huge disadvantage because the public education system relies on the active involvement of a parent to ensure the child is getting what he or she needs. And as most parents know, making sure your child gets a good education is a long-term planned effort that requires energy, resources, time, and often ingenuity and money. Even for teenagers, the school systems are set up to deal directly with their parents, not with the teenagers themselves. Most education laws and regulations refer to the parent's rights, not the kids' rights, to request certain services and protections.

When parents become a missing link in the process of education, the children suffer. Reports and studies confirm that foster care students fare poorly in school; they often receive low grades and do not advance to their full academic potential. Children in foster care are the most educationally at-risk population. The foster care system for the most part neglects this problem. It does not provide adequate coordination, case management, and assistance in regard to the education of children in care. The system "fail[s] to put into place the fundamental building blocks that could help these at-risk children meet with educational success."[6] Even when these students are in schools in poor (economically deprived, as one study says) neighborhoods, with a lot of other poor students, the foster care kids do worse. Compared to other youth, they are more frequently absent. They are more likely to have behavior and discipline problems, more likely to have gaps in their education because of school transfers, more likely to be in special ed, more likely to be in vocational ed, and less likely to be on a college-prep track.[7]

When kids are in foster care, it is the responsibility of the foster care system to make sure that teens are in school and to monitor their cases, which should include their education. But accountability for this responsibility remains an open question. So many caseworkers, social workers, and other professionals may be involved in one case that the responsibility is never clearly assigned to one professional. Additionally, professional and child care staff too often label the teens as mentally ill, as though that were some sort of justification that they can't or shouldn't be educated. A pervasive crisis mode exists in the system, produced by external pressures that view every child as in imminent danger, and by an internal culture that views every intervention as critical to maintaining the fragile mental health of the child. This crisis mode typically preempts attention on education and preparation for the future. Although teens' educational progress is no doubt important to the professionals, their involvement in school issues is limited because it is not one of the priorities of the foster care system.

As Carlos and I entered the high school grounds, it occurred to me that perhaps the foster care agency had valid reasons to think twice about sending Carlos here. It was one of the old, big high schools in Brooklyn, designed to look like a castle or fortress. The windows now were covered with something that looked like chicken wire fencing. Kids were hanging around in groups of four or five.

We found the main office and tried to get the attention of a woman seated behind a desk talking on the phone. Finally, she put her hand over the receiver, listened to me for thirty seconds, then said we should call the central high school office phone number and should not wait here for someone to help us. I didn't want to leave because I just made the trip all the way here with Carlos, and so we remained standing by the doorway looking around for someone who might speak with us. The woman behind the desk first glared at us and then ignored us. Half an hour passed, and another harried looking woman bustled by carrying a load of files. I asked if she could give us a minute. She turned out to be the assistant principal. After hearing what I quickly blurted out about Carlos wanting to go to school here, she started talking.

"This is the deal," she spoke even faster than I did. "We get a lot of group home kids here in this neighborhood, and you know what," she glanced at

Carlos to see if he was listening (he was). "They're a lot of trouble. I'm not saying each and every one is a bad kid. The truth is we get a lot of kids in this
school who come from broken families, all kinds of messy situations. And a
teenager is a teenager—they're always going through some crisis. Some
might say that you can't tell the group home kids from any other kid in this
school and that may be true."

"But I gotta tell you, lots of the teachers say that the group home kids are
the real behavior problems. Seems every time we have a disciplinary problem, guess what? It's a kid from foster care or a group home. These group
home kids can be very manipulative. . . ."

I was feeling terrible that she was saying all this in front of Carlos. I tried
to interrupt, "But Carlos here was a straight A student at his school in Queens
before . . ."

She ignored me and kept going, "and they basically do what they want.
Problems keeping up we can deal with, problems behaving we can deal with
usually, problems getting to school, that's the big one. These kids come, they
don't come, and we don't even know who to call! We call the group home, no
one answers. We call the foster home, the phone is out of order, or the foster
parent doesn't know what's going on. We have no idea who is responsible for
these kids! Half the time we don't know if the kid is supposed to be coming
or has moved to another neighborhood, back to their country, gone to Rikers,
we have no clue what's happened."

My attempt to break in was even feebler than before, "I see, yes, that's difficult, but Carlos has been in his group home for a while now, and he really
just wants to come to school."

But clearly she was warming up and was on a roll now. "And frankly, this
school does not have the resources to go chasing after every kid who comes,
doesn't come. We don't even know what grade half these group home kids are
supposed to be in—never get the records. They say . . ."

She paused to take a breath, and I recognized this was a chance to speak
but I was taken aback by what she had said. Of course it must be frustrating
for a school not to know who was attending, where the kids were, what grade
they should be in.

Her tirade was interesting because I had heard this story but from two other perspectives, those of the foster care agencies' caseworkers and kids themselves. Caseworkers complained that the school bureaucracy couldn't handle even the simplest logistics of dealing with foster care kids. They said the schools don't transfer records, or they lose them, or the offices move so slowly that the records never catch up to the kid. Caseworkers observed that educational problems often developed before they took on the case, and behavioral problems in school were difficult or even impossible for them to manage. They complained that parents didn't sign forms they needed to—for testing, for special ed, for field trips. They acknowledged that the kids on their cases often had a lot of appointments with them, with therapists, lawyers, and others—appointments that sometimes conflicted with school. In addition, professional burnout and frequent transfer of positions made it impossible to have any consistent educational advocacy for each teen in care.

The kids told the same story from a different perspective. They saw the moves around the school system as directly related to the problems of moving around foster care. Often it was for reasons beyond their control. Foster parents decided they didn't want or like a teen, or the agencies closed group homes or revoked licenses of foster parents. Sometimes the teens asked to be moved because they were beaten up, they were treated as built-in baby-sitters, their belongings were stolen, or the conditions were unsanitary or unsafe. Within this context of upheaval and without any support or even expectation for education, the teens naturally found it difficult to respond to all the school's rules, especially consistent attendance, and few sought extra help for educational deficiencies.

In spite of all these problems, many teens hold on to their goal for education, and some teens attempt to surmount the problems thrown in their way. Foster homes and group homes for teens are scattered throughout the five boroughs of the city. Therefore when teens move to a home in a new neighborhood, they have to either commute to their old high school or switch to a new one. The difficulty of starting over every few months in a new home and a new school can be overwhelming. Even so, some teens who have been in a dozen placements in a few years make heroic efforts to stay in a high school they were in, traveling hours a day on several subway and bus lines to attend the school. These unusually long and complicated trips to and from school are hard to maintain for a long period of time, for instance, a school year. Or they are prevented or discouraged by their agencies, foster parents, or group home staff, from continuing in a school out of the neighborhood. Those in the system seem to expect that kids will simply adapt to changing schools each time they move.

To add to these logistical hurdles, many teens who are forced to transfer to a new high school can't prove how many credits they had earned and are forced to begin at a grade they had already completed somewhere else. Of course, this makes no sense from the student's perspective.

What was more upsetting about the assistant principal's rant was the rancor in her voice. "How could someone be so prejudiced against these kids who haven't done anything wrong themselves," I wondered. "They were taken away from their parents; they're not criminals."

Teens in foster care are often embarrassed about their status. There is a stigma. Rightly or wrongly, teens in foster care believe the rest of the world thinks they are in foster care because they are bad. Many teens are reluctant to disclose to other students or their teachers that they are in foster care. Teens fear that others will discover their foster care status, which will complicate friendships or potential friendships. Many kids feel cut off from peers. They say, "I like to keep to myself," and they end up socially isolated and withdrawn, not trusting other kids and certainly not trusting adults. The classroom can be an uncomfortable environment for the foster care child.

While I was thinking about how vulnerable a child is in so many ways without a stable family to buffer, protect, and advocate for him or her, the assistant principal continued on, "Now given all I'm telling you, I should not be allowing this boy into our school without records. But if you are telling me, as his social worker . . ."

"I'm not his social worker. I'm a . . . friend . . . who's a lawyer . . . who's helping him."

"Well, fine, if you are telling me he lives over here, and his records are on the way, then I will say he can attend. Show up tomorrow, young man, and see Alice here." She glanced at the woman behind the desk, then at Carlos, then back to me. "As long as you understand, he'll have to do ninth grade again until his records catch up with him. And we are quite crowded right now. Up to fifty kids in some of the classrooms. Of course, not all the students show up every day, so you can usually get a seat and look on in someone else's book."

Carlos grimaced and nudged me, "Can I talk to you for a second?"

"Sure," I said. The assistant principal checked her watch, gave us a shrug of exasperation, and turned away.

Carlos seemed embarrassed. "Look, I really appreciate your trying to help me, and you came out here on your own time and all, but I don't think this is for me. This place is scaring me! And I really cannot take being put in ninth grade again. . . . I'm sorry, I feel bad disappointing you . . . and if you really think I should, I'll try, but . . ."

Disappointing me! I was frustrated and angry that this was the school available to Carlos and all these other kids crowded into the classrooms. I would have felt terrible encouraging Carlos to go there.

"Come on, let's get out of here," I said. Unsure where we were going and feeling like I was a little out of my mind for taking this on, I grabbed his arm, and we left the school office and grounds.

Walking back to the subway, I tried not to let Carlos see how helpless I felt, and I was silent, thinking of what to do next. "Can I ask you something?" he said. "Do you think maybe they're right, that I really should be in the agency school just for special ed kids back on the campus?"

I had no way of knowing, but if what Carlos had told me was true, that he had done well previously in school before going into foster care, my hunch was he didn't belong in special ed. Foster care kids are placed in special ed at a rate far above the average, and they are placed in the most segregated types of classes at three times the rate of other kids in the New York City school system.[8] In addition, most kids in city foster care are African American and Latino, and it has been widely documented that there is systemic segregation of African American and Latino students; a study in the mid 1990s, by the federal Department of Education's Office of Civil Rights discovered that New York City not only places "too many students in segregated special education classrooms, but also that it disproportionately classifies African American and Latino students as 'learning disabled' or 'emotionally disturbed.'"[9] Although special ed services must be offered to help some students, the services and type of class must fit the needs of the student; many feel that much of the time foster care children are unnecessarily placed in special ed. No legal mandate requires tracking or monitoring of special education services to children in the foster care system, so there is no way to know if the services are truly needed or appropriate, or if they are being used as a way to contain problem kids, or a way for the foster care agency to maintain more control by keeping its kids in its own school.

I answered vaguely, "There's no way for me to really know, but maybe you would do okay in a good school that wasn't only special ed."

"I mean when they started me in that school at the RTC [residential treatment center] I was like, what? You buggin'? I never had any problems in school and all of a sudden I'm in a school that's only for special ed?"

I began to say how that must have been hard, when he continued, "I was the quiet one, who did his class work, gave the teachers respect, and tried to get good grades. But then I noticed, nobody seems to care about the grades there . . . and if a kid gets upset in that school, forget it. Time for restraint, and I don't mean holding someone's arms. I mean two to three teachers, restraining one student. By whatever means necessary is the way they would restrain. I've seen teachers twist kids' arms, wrists, legs, then get on top of the kid and hold him down. They either put their leg on the kid's neck or their whole body weight on the kid's chest. Then they would tell the kid to calm down, but while there is this 185-pound person on him. How the hell is he supposed to calm down?"

I probably wouldn't have believed this except that I knew the residential treatment center and its school, and I knew that significant resources focused on behavior management as much as anything else. Of course it is essential to keep teens and the adults around them physically safe, but the extremes to which behavior management and modification was taken seemed overused and cruel to the kids.

"Do you know how they decided to put you in the RTC school?" I asked.

"They had one of those meetings you go to where everybody from the agency talks about you and your problems and how you need to move. That's it."

He was referring, I thought, to his CSE conference. For a child to be placed in special education, the Committee on Special Education (CSE) must hold a conference to determine the appropriate kind of classroom and services. The CSE team consists of agency employees, including teachers, psychologists, social workers, and directors, who decide what kind of educational setting the child needs.

"Wasn't there anybody to speak up for you at this conference?"

"Oh, sure, this gray haired lady who never met me and didn't say boo to me in the meeting. She lived in the neighborhood around the campus, so she was just like, great! agreeing with whatever the agency said."

To ensure that parents can obtain services for their disabled children, the law gives parents certain rights, including the right to participate in these meetings. Yet only 6 percent of parents with kids in foster care say they were invited to participate in their kids' education plans.[10] While some parents of kids in foster care are deceased or in prison and physically unable to participate in their child's education, not all are prevented from participating. And while some teens want nothing to do with their parents, others are in touch with them and would benefit from their parent's involvement in their education plans. Virtually all parents care about their kids getting a good education, even if they have failed their children in other important ways. If the parent is not there, then someone else must represent the child's interest, and that person may be someone more closely aligned with the agency or school, rather than an advocate for the child's education.

Involvement of foster parents in education, like the overall quality of foster parents for teens, varies. Some research shows that children placed in kinship (family) or foster homes improve their school attendance after placement in foster care.[11] In other foster homes, the parent may only have a second-grade education and thus have little idea how to help teens do better.

Finding Carlos a school became my mission for the next week. I called around to other schools, and through a social worker friend I found one that sounded like a good possibility. It was one of the alternative high schools in Manhattan, and I asked to come in with Carlos. This time the experience was dramatically different.

This school was in an office building on a gray nondescript block of commercial buildings. We took a freight elevator to get to the school itself, which occupied a few floors in the building. It didn't look anything like any high school I'd ever seen before. But the halls seemed relatively quiet and orderly, and, when I peeked in the classrooms, kids and teachers appeared engaged.

Carlos and I met with Joe, the principal. After our last experience at the school in Brooklyn, I was steeling myself for all kinds of excuses and reasons why Carlos shouldn't attend here and was hoping Carlos wouldn't be too disappointed. Joe surprised me. After listening to us, and after asking Carlos a few questions, he said, "Sure, you can come here. My rule, though, is you have to promise to meet your homeroom teacher every day, and let her know if you're having any trouble keeping up with the work here." Carlos agreed happily.

"What about the paperwork?" I asked. "Won't that be a problem?"

"Oh, we'll track down the records somehow. They always show up eventually, usually, anyway." He was obviously the type to bend the rules and take a chance, and I appreciated that deeply.

The experience with Carlos was not only enlightening about the hurdles teens faced in the school system, but it was also instructive in that it helped us define the rudiments of what we came to later call self-advocacy. First, Carlos taught us that to advocate for yourself you had to find the "Joes" in the system and get them to help. That simple idea grew to be an important component of our self-advocacy program, a unit that we eventually called "how to find allies and mentors." The concept is that these adults can become valuable advocates and, at the same time, that the teen has an active role to play in making that relationship happen. In other words, we teach that mentors, allies, and advocates are not always appointed by the court or matched through a program. Most often in life, you have to make some effort to get people interested in helping you.

Carlos was a star at this. He excelled at persuading me and others in positions of authority to gain respect for him and to believe that he would be successful; thus, we wanted to help him reach his goals. The more I thought about it, I saw this was a valuable skill and asset—to be able persuade people in power that you are someone worth helping. Carlos did this in part by presenting himself consistently as someone who wanted to succeed; from the start he told me he was going to graduate high school and go to college. Although he could have, he didn't play the victim role. Instead, he had articulated his goals and presented strengths, two other concepts which eventually became essential components of our self-advocacy theory and curriculum. He also made an effort to understand my needs, some of which I had told him outright (to get Youth Advocacy Center off the ground, to find young people in foster care to work on our video about the system) and some of which he must have known intuitively (to feel good about myself by assisting him with school, to get a close-up glimpse of the problems in the system). This idea of understanding the needs of the other party became another key piece of self-advocacy. In doing this, Carlos made me feel that by investing my time and effort in him, he would succeed and that this would somehow help me. And it did.

Once he was settled in school Carlos started to work at YAC a couple of afternoons a week, helping produce the video. We recruited two other teens, Kevin and Lorraine, to cowrite the script about their experiences in foster care and how they thought the system should improve. We called the video *Listen to Us*. In the video, the three teens talked about some obstacles they faced in foster care and the pressures on them as they strove to create independent lives. Paul, who had worked with college students for two decades producing films, was impressed with the foster care teens' contributions to the content and production of the video.

Listen to Us was produced to influence policy makers, practitioners, and those studying to become child welfare professionals by giving them the youth perspective of foster care life. On the screen, Carlos and the other teens were articulate, insightful, and compelling. I couldn't believe that child welfare specialists wouldn't want to change the conditions of foster care after listening to these veterans of the system.

Once *Listen to Us* was completed, we gave Carlos the responsibility of contacting graduate schools of social work, law, and public policy throughout New York City. He sent letters and made follow-up phone calls offering to show the video and speak to classes. Carlos persuaded the first professor that this would be an important educational experience for her graduate students.

Arriving at the college campus, Paul and I realized that just being in this environment was a big deal for Carlos. I watched him looking at the undergraduate students, who were not much older than he. They must have resembled the kids he knew in dress and mannerisms, but these kids seemed so comfortable in this setting—lugging textbooks, lounging on couches in common areas, talking and laughing outside the classrooms. He seemed to be surreptitiously studying them, as if he were beginning to dare to imagine what it would be like if he went there.

Entering the school of social work graduate class with Carlos, we were nervous about how we and the video would be received. The professor welcomed us and then stepped aside. Paul introduced us and briefly told the class about our organization and some of the overarching problems with the foster care system.

Then Carlos began. All the graduate students looked at him intently as he talked about the years he spent in foster care. For this presentation, he had planned to show the video and tell some personal accounts that, while not horror stories, would illustrate systemwide policy or practice problems. It worked. Carlos related his own experiences and insights to current laws, state regulations, and policies of the child welfare system. The graduate students were soon asking challenging questions about what they could do to help improve the system. They pretty much ignored Paul and me and treated Carlos as the expert. Carlos responded thoughtfully, politely, and with a sense of good humor. He relished the experience of being teacher. Carlos was outgoing about turning around their questions and refuting ideas held by the students and their professor. Clearly, Carlos' knowledge, manner, and analysis had a deep impact on the graduate students and the professor.

Buoyed by that success, Carlos continued his outreach, and soon deans and professors from Columbia University, New York University, the New

School, and other prestigious universities responded positively, and we began presenting at their classes, as well as at professional panels and conferences, on a regular basis. Because of the demand, we developed an informal training for teens on making these *Listen to Us* presentations. We then created a speakers' bureau of foster care teens to make the presentation Carlos modeled available to hundreds of professionals in the child welfare field.

As we did more and more of the *Listen to Us* presentations, Paul and I realized that what Carlos and the other teens had to say was always more interesting than anything we could communicate. This was an odd experience at first, but one we grew to enjoy. Even when we disagreed with what Carlos or the other teens recommended as solutions, we remained confident that it was important for their voices to be heard. Differences we had stemmed more from our different perspectives in life than from a fundamentally different analysis of the problems or even the solutions. They clearly had intellectual capacities to integrate different types of information into a comprehensive presentation.

We had to remind ourselves during these presentations that Carlos was literally a street kid. Before he came into foster care, he was a homeless runaway, sleeping on the streets. And now he conducted presentations to graduate students and child welfare professionals. The intellectual capacities of teens were rarely noticed in the context of a typical foster care setting, where issues of physical safety and mental health are paramount, or even on the streets where survival and peer acceptance take precedence. But in a setting that acknowledged the teen's expertise and experience and provided relevant intellectual challenges, the young person was transformed. In these contexts, we saw the dominant stereotypical identity of foster care teens—troubled youth with significant emotional and mental health issues—disappear. Intellectually curious and capable individuals with a passion to achieve important goals emerged in front of our eyes.

At these *Listen to Us* presentations, policy makers and practitioners appeared open to reforming their prejudices, opinions, and convictions about teens in foster care. These presentations were a powerful tool, if we could figure out how to use them. They encouraged us to believe that changing the system to meet teens' needs would be possible because such a wide range of individuals wanted improvement to happen. The puzzle was how to harness this individual goodwill to change an intractable system.

As the year went by and Carlos was involved in high school, in working for us, and in the journalism program where we had originally met, he grew more committed to his goal of going to college. Carlos was lucky because at his high school he had a guidance counselor and a college advisor to help him decipher the application process—something a lot of kids in foster care or in big public high schools don't have access to. Carlos applied to a number of state schools. When he got the letter of acceptance to a college upstate, he was thrilled, in part because his high school advisor said it had a good reputation for journalism.

Financial aid paperwork is a quagmire for any student, and for Carlos it seemed especially complicated. The college sent him a letter asking for proof of his financial status, about which Carlos asked his social worker. She was unsure about what information to give him, and soon he got another letter from the college saying his application would have to be withdrawn unless he completed the financial aid information request form. His high school advisor was stumped because there was no box to check off indicating his foster care status and therefore his eligibility for financial aid assistance. With many phone calls and letters back and forth, the problem was finally straightened out. More complications arose, however, when the foster care agency realized what had happened; Carlos had gotten himself into a school outside of the city. Carlos called me one day when he was supposed to do to a presentation at a graduate school. "I'm so sorry, but I can't make it. The agency scheduled a meeting to talk about me going away to college, and it's at 3:30. I have to be there," he apologized. That was the last I heard from him for a couple of weeks. When he showed up again, he related a bizarre tale that reminded me that while many individuals in the system want to help teens achieve, others seem to inherently resist allowing anyone to rise beyond the lowest expectations.

Carlos said he had been summoned to a meeting with four caseworkers and social workers—two from the city and two from the agency that contracted with the city to run the group home in which Carlos was living. When

Ms. Daly, the city supervisor walked in, Carlos thought to himself, "she is having a bad day, looks like she wants to beat somebody up."

Daly sat down and turned to Carlos first, cutting to the chase. "You are not going to the upstate college. That won't be possible. The city is not going to pay for you to go away to a school all the way upstate. You best look into the city colleges."

Startled, Carlos replied, "I did, but this one is the one I want to go to because I want to study journalism."

She replied, "Well, get over it, change your major, plenty do." Carlos felt tears of frustration welling up in his eyes. "Unless you want to be discharged, because then you can do what you want," she continued. "The city has to bring down its numbers anyway, so if you want to be discharged we can easily do that. From what I hear you don't like to follow rules in the group home anyway, and you're not even in counseling. I hear you've missed several meetings at the group home. Now why would you think you can just go to this fancy college and get us to put in money for that?"

Carlos pulled himself together to protest, "I don't have trouble following rules, ask anyone. I do all my chores in the house, and everything, plus I work after school. And I don't know what you're talking about counseling. I had a therapist, but then she left and nobody else was assigned." He was getting mad.

"You know what I think, Carlos?" She didn't wait for an answer, "I think you are trying to use the system to get what you want."

"I just want to go to the college I got into, that my high school advisor thinks will be good for me."

At that, Ms. Daly got up from her seat and said, "Meeting adjourned."

Carlos was still hopeful. He only needed the same living allowance to which he was entitled if he stayed in the city. He was looking forward to the orientation at the college, and he called his city caseworker the next day to remind her of the date. "Oh, didn't you hear?" she said, "Your agency casework said that's cancelled . . . because you are not going to be able to go to the upstate college." Carlos hung up and immediately started calling everyone he could think of—caseworkers, his lawyer from family court, other social workers. He learned the meaning of "catch twenty-two." If he wanted to have the necessary financial support to begin college, he would have to remain in foster care. It seemed that if he wanted to attend a college outside the city, he would have to leave foster care and not get any support.

This left Carlos feeling defeated. Even his high school advisor couldn't believe the runaround Carlos was getting. Together they decided on a back-up plan. He would start college in the city and then try to transfer to the upstate college second semester, or possibly sophomore year. It was not ideal, but it seemed the most expedient route to getting into his chosen college. In the end, Carlos successfully attended and completed college, but he never got to transfer to the upstate school.

Carlos wasn't unique in his aspirations. A recent federally funded study at a university found a "surprisingly high percentage—seventy percent—of teens in the foster care system have a desire to attend college."[12] Why should this be surprising? Teens in foster care understand the connection between education and a better future.

Carlos's experience demonstrated the overwhelming challenges of college admissions for foster care teens. Most teens in foster care do not have the level of self-advocacy skills possessed by Carlos. For them, college is a desirable but distant dream. In their group and foster homes, there are not enough adults who are strong role models, advocates for further education, or skilled guides in helping teens navigate the application process for admission and financial aid. Equally important is the critical support a foster teen needs during the transition to college. We know of only a few programs nationally dedicated to ensuring that, once admitted, teens from foster care receive support in finding ways to maintain their college education.

Programs in New York and throughout the country help children and teens from disadvantaged backgrounds prepare for and succeed in prep schools and in college. However, these effective programs have a difficult time enrolling qualified teens from foster care because such potential candidates don't have parents or other consistent adults encouraging and supporting their effort to pursue education. Many professionals in the system don't make efforts to enroll teens in these programs because they want to protect the teens from additional failures in their lives. They worry that college could be a devastating failure. Even if this observation had some valid-ity in some cases, it is hard to believe that anyone can predict who will fail or who will succeed.

With some support and help, more teens from the system could go to college. Group homes frequently resemble flop houses for teens to watch TV, hang out, and sleep. If group homes were designed around the format of uni-versity dormitories, where everyone's objective is education, more teens would take more responsibility to get a college or vocational education. Teens tell us that when they bring our casebooks back to their group homes, their friends show interest and want to read the cases. These casebooks have no pictures and are not intended for casual reading. The thirst exists. A group home with reading groups, homework support groups, and current events discussions would easily change the environment and promote fur-ther education. Child welfare professionals may think, "They wouldn't attend." Our experience indicates they would attend if these programs con-tinued for a reasonable duration and selected topics were relevant to the students' interests.

Efforts to help foster care teens succeed educationally have not reached a significant level. These successful efforts need policies and a strong philo-sophical commitment to making education a priority. Most important, foster care agencies need to be held accountable for making sure the teens in their custody are educated.

I thought about all this on a June day in a hot and crowded high school auditorium, surrounded by women in bright silky dresses clutching cello-phane wrapped bunches of roses and the hands of little boys in three piece suits. Joe, the principal, climbed the steps to the stage, and the ceremony began. I was half paying attention when I heard Joe announce Carlos's name. When Carlos proudly walked across the stage in his cap and gown to receive his high school diploma, as he had long hoped for, I applauded along with everyone else.

Working with Carlos and other teens during this period led us to better understand some of the systemic problems regarding education for foster care teens. First, without a parent to advocate for them, the teens have no single person with a primary interest in or responsibility for ensuring they go to school and plan for their future education. Second, many teens have the potential to succeed academically, if they are only given a chance. Third, educational success has not been a priority for the foster care system, particularly when it comes to college preparation, probably because there is no expectation, commitment, or accountability for education; the agencies are neither penalized nor rewarded based on their teens' failures or successes.

The foster care system's inadequate approach to education shifts more responsibility to the individual teen. Carlos was an inspiration because, in the end, his efforts, more than mine or anyone else's, got him through high school and into college. However, most teens in the system are neither prepared nor permitted to take on the necessary responsibility. We felt compelled to help teens learn to take on more responsibility rather than wait till the bureaucracy perhaps helped them or ignored them and crushed their chances of successfully preparing for adulthood. By readying students to take control, they might create greater educational opportunities for themselves, opportunities individualized to their needs. We began to imagine what it would be like if every teen could advocate for himself or herself, to somehow mold the bureaucracy's rules and regulations to fit his or her needs.

But we weren't yet finished with attempting to directly change the system. If we could organize around the advocacy talents, as evidenced by teens like Carlos, we still held out hope that we could change laws, policies, and regulations to meet the needs of teens. Although education still remained the most compelling problem, we felt that its scope was too complex to make meaningful changes. Thus we looked for issues where a simple change in policy could have dramatic results in the lives of teens in foster care.

3

Teaching Teens Rights

Jenny Most teens in foster care are intently focused on their rights. This makes sense because they live in a government system that has countless mandates and regulations. In an effort to protect children, control behavior, and assure compliance by staff and clients, the government's child welfare bureaucracies proscribe by law and scrutinize for conformity most activities. The government has rules for every decision about raising these teens to prevent them from being treated too arbitrarily by foster parents or group home staff. Everything—from how often you can see your siblings or call your parents to how much allowance you get—is spelled out in a web of federal, state, and local laws and regulations.

One who hasn't grown up in such a system would find it hard to imagine the infringement on one's life and individuality. Most of us don't walk around pondering what our rights are until we are desperate. Not until one has a conflict with a government agency or a dispute that might require legal action do we usually consider our rights. If people have to think seriously about what their rights are, then they are probably in a less than ideal situation.

Rights become important and necessary when one is overpowered by the majority or a larger force. This is what happens to children and teens in foster care who typically lack any say in the decisions made about them. They live without what we take for granted as part of childhood: their families, physical safety, their own bed and personal possessions, and a consistently decent education. The sense of powerlessness that accompanies being removed from one's home and put in one strange placement after another is terrifying and disorienting. Once they settle in, if they do, the system still makes hundreds of decisions about them that they have little or no control over. Every day becomes a struggle to maintain one's sense of control, and for many their only recourse is grabbing on to their partial understanding of rights. In this context, it makes sense that kids tend to focus on rights that we may find insignificant (for example, arguing for a better clothing allowance) when they lack so much.

Of course, kids living in intact families of any class live with rules, often ones they argue are terribly unfair, imposed by their parents, relatives, schools, and so on. The difference is that these rules are designed with particular children in mind and are enforced or not enforced by the adults who presumably have a long-term interest in their children's well-being. Most important, in families these rules tend to be negotiable. Becoming an adult requires the skill of negotiating and resolving disputes with other adults. Many teens learn this through engaging with their parents. Sometimes they lose and sometimes win disputes, but they learn a process for resolving disputes. Teens also gain understanding of the process by observing their parents negotiate around some conflict or tell a story about some self-advocacy they are engaged with at work. Most parents instinctually hold the value of this skill equal to or higher than the objective of the negotiation with their teenager.

Teens in foster care typically lack rudimentary self-advocacy skills. Teaching teens to negotiate and advocate is not a goal in the foster care system, where teens rarely get a chance to negotiate with adults or advocate their position in an environment that would teach them these skills. At the same time, teens' rights in foster care are continually denied. The laws provide for the right to an adequate education, a range of basic human needs, and preparation for independence; too often, however, what the law states is not provided to the teens—and they know it. In trying to assert their rights or merely trying to garner appropriate support, teens in foster care have observed and learned that acting out and presenting themselves as problems and victims has a better chance of getting attention than just about any other method.

Although this behavior brings attention, it rarely helps the teen in any long-term, substantive way.

We came to appreciate the fixation foster care teens had with their rights and felt compelled to help them secure rights that they deserved, rights that were essential for their well-being. While many teens demonstrated an unusual knowledge of the range of their rights, this knowledge alone was not enough to secure those rights. And even when teens had adequate representation, they needed skills to guide the process toward securing their rights. To be effective, the teens needed to transition from being passive observers of rights abuse to being effective advocates.

Betsy

Jenny knocked on Youth Advocacy Center's door one day in the middle of the afternoon when I was writing yet another letter to a foundation seeking money. She was short and wiry thin, wearing baggy jeans, white sneakers, and a big red t-shirt that made her look tomboyish and even smaller than she was. She had delicate features, long dark shiny hair, and huge, almost black eyes. She was beautiful. "Can I help you?" I asked.

"I'm here for the internship?" she said tentatively, and I invited her in, somewhat confused. Carlos had been working with us on and off for a year, doing the presentations with the video and helping us develop ideas for how YAC could be more of a resource for foster care teens. But he was pretty busy with school, and we needed at least one more teen working with us on a regular basis. I had posted an internship opportunity at a nearby high school, figuring it was a chance for a teen to get some hands-on experience and for us to get some free help, but I hadn't heard anything, until Jenny showed up.

Sitting down, she was nervous and jittery, bouncing her knees up and down. "My advisor sent me over?" I asked her why she wanted this internship. "Ummm, I don't really know. My advisor said it would be good for me. . . ?" She had that way of ending sentences as though they were all questions. She paused. "Since he knows I'm living in a group home and all? I guess he thought it would be good to work for you, seeing as you're a lawyer?" She shrugged and gave me a big smile.

"Okay then, what are you interested in doing?" I asked her.

"Well, you being a lawyer and all, I thought I could find out about my rights?"

Though states like New York have designed an entire legal bureaucracy to provide all foster children with attorneys to protect their rights, this free and useful service can handle only a fraction of the rights violations faced by the thousands of teens in the system. When I was a lawyer I always had a huge caseload, but some kids got my attention through a combination of persistence and appealing to me by presenting themselves in strong, positive ways that got me thinking these were good kids. Like Carlos, they were the ones who successfully navigated the foster care system by getting people like me to help them. After the experience with Carlos, I was curious if we could teach teens to advocate for themselves in the various situations when they didn't have professional advocates. I was now hoping Jenny could help us figure this out.

While I was becoming interested in this advocacy idea, I knew it was somewhat complicated and abstract, but I also knew that rights were the hook to get kids interested in advocacy. Pulling a fat, dark green loose-leaf binder off a shelf, I started telling Jenny that a lot of her rights were expressed in these state social services regulations. They were densely written in tiny print on thin paper. Dragging a chair close to Jenny's, I showed her the sections that pertained to youth in foster care and marked those pages with post-its. "Okay, if you're interested in rights, why don't you take a look at these," I said, really having no idea if she could make heads or tails out of it. She sat at a desk with the heavy book open before her on a table, and I turned away to go back to working on a grant proposal.

Three minutes into it, she looked up. "Excuse me?" she said. "I'm a little confused. Who writes these things? Who decides on what rights we have? I mean, who exactly is in charge of this all? I thought it was the judges in court?"

I saw this was going to be more complicated than I had first thought and started to explain that she, like tens of thousands of other kids in New York, was in the state's custody, and so government officials, social services commissioners, and such decided her rights. She interrupted me before I got to the part that other rights were decided by judges in court cases. "Custody of the state? Damn, sounds like I'm under arrest. Or are you saying, like, I'm a 'ward of the state?' Whatever that is? 'Cause I've heard of that, but it doesn't really make sense because my mom's still my mom and all. I mean, I know she can't take care of me but . . ."

She went back to studying the green book and for the next half hour she was quiet. At 4:00 I told her, "Look, it's time to go." I thought that she must be bored out of her mind, daydreaming or counting the minutes till she's free.

"I can't believe this is in here," she said. "How much clothing allowance we're supposed to get! How we have the right to privacy! And all this stuff about preparing us for independent living. What I'm thinking is that if it says we are supposed to be prepared for independent living, then they should be letting us work at jobs and whatnot. Of course, I know there are those laws about how many hours you can work when you're still a kid, but that should be part of what we're learning. . . ."

Now I was stunned. Jenny had muddled through the complicated bureau-cratic language and figured out what it was saying? She had started to draw inferences from the regulations and was thinking about the implications of labor law on child welfare regulations? This was a girl from a group home who went to a city high school with a so-so reputation, and she was poring over the law books and understanding the arcane language.

"Oh, man, what if all the kids in my group home knew this shit? 'scuse my language—this stuff. Can I make copies of this? Is this book in the library? Can anybody take it out?"

We talked for another half hour about what the state laws entitled kids in foster care to, and she kept remarking that other kids should know this so they could "stand up for themselves." We then talked about possible projects she could do during her internship; we decided to write up a booklet and per-haps some pamphlets for foster care kids about their rights according to these state regulations. We would work together to translate the "regs" into language that was easier for kids (or anyone, really) to understand. At the end of the day, I was thrilled that Jenny had found me and I had found her.

Throughout the next two months, Jenny and I wrote and put together a booklet for teens called the *Rights and Advocacy Guidelines*. It addressed every conceivable right teens in foster care have, starting with Allowance and going alphabetically to Weekend Visits. Kids in foster care had been looking for a guide like the rights booklet because it had the information they wanted in a format that was easy to read. They could use it to urge their caseworkers, lawyers, and others to help them. I suspected that it would be a revelation and a valuable instrument for the caseworkers as well. We were proud of the booklet and excited to get it into the hands of teens across the city.

Jenny had a quick wit, a bubbly personality. She seemed savvy about many topics and incredibly naïve about other areas of life. The vast gaps in her knowledge were striking because she was obviously bright and could read and write fairly well.

As I got to know Jenny, I learned she was living in a group home because her mother was 'upstate' (in prison) on a drug charge. She took the bus to see her a couple of times a year, but the prison was far, eight hours away. She wouldn't say more about her. She was not in touch with her dad, who lived in Puerto Rico. She had one older sister she looked up to, who had her own apartment, but Jenny wasn't allowed to go stay with her that often.

When I asked her about friends she shrugged. "Acquaintances, you know? In my situation, I don't really like to get too close. Things happen, you know?" I asked her what she meant. "Look, I'm not about to go around telling kids in my school, yeah, mom's doing time so I got to live in a group home. And the girls in my group home, they alright, some of them, but how long are we all gonna be there? You know foster care, here one day, gone the next to a new place—what's the point?" She didn't sound bitter but matter of fact.

Her internship was ending. I called her high school advisor to thank him once again for referring Jenny to us and to let him know how incredible she was and all she had accomplished. We had been immersed in the challenges of researching and writing the booklet, and she had been so good at it, that I took for granted her intellectual ability and apparent comfort with focusing on completing it with me. The high school advisor was pleased but sounded surprised and a little skeptical. "You mean to tell me Jenny was interested in reading law books? She just doesn't come across as someone interested in academics," he mused. I could understand his surprise somewhat because Jenny had told me how boring she found high school.

Gillian, Jenny's social worker, upset me more when I called her to report what a great job Jenny had done in the internship. She was silent. Finally, she responded, sounding affronted by my praise for Jenny. She started with a half laugh, "Oh, yes, Jenny can behave if she's in an unfamiliar environment, trying to make a good impression, but you should know she is a real problem." Gillian told me this as if to be helpful, but she was clearly trying to send me the message that she knew Jenny better than I did, and she was not "all that," as the kids say.

"Maybe she didn't let you know this, but Jenny is quite a storyteller, shall we say? Smokes way too much and has a nasty habit of borrowing things and not returning them, if you know what I mean. I constantly have to keep an eye on her or she will be out the door here." This set my blood boiling. It was demeaning to Jenny and, in a way, to me. I became angry because this attitude seemed to be a frequently recurring thread in the dynamics between the kids we work with, their social workers, and us; the workers were always trying to show how the kids were trouble.

Because her semester was over and I didn't want to lose her, I offered Jenny a part-time job after school a few hours a week. Carlos was still working, so they would be in at the same time, once a week on Wednesdays. I was nervous about how they would get along. From Jenny and other teens, I knew that kids in foster care resisted forming relationships with other kids, an understandable defense to their foster care status. My suspicion was correct; at first they barely acknowledged each other in the office. When they did have to refer to each other, they said "that kid" or "that girl" in referring to the other, though they obviously had not forgotten each other's names every week. They also aggressively competed for my attention and my approval.

One Wednesday, I decided I had enough of this; they had to work together. I told them that, given their mutual interest in helping more kids learn what they already knew, they should begin putting together a workshop to teach kids about their rights and a little about advocacy, a program that we would eventually bring to foster care agencies.

Jenny, Carlos, and I discussed an agenda for the workshop. We struggled, but Jenny and Carlos finally decided that the workshop agenda would cover what it meant to have rights, what the word advocacy meant, how the system was set up, and an example of what teens could do if they thought their rights were violated.

I left them working for another hour and overheard them talking with each other and arguing about how to get the kids interested in the workshop. In their discussion, they decided to use skits and assign kids different roles to act out in various situations where they either had to advocate for themselves or pretend to be someone in authority. They wrote down what they wanted to do and began making up skits. Hearing their laughter was exhilarating, as their first attempts failed, and they struggled to perfect a useful skit. They worried out loud about what they would do if teens were disruptive or bored. Near the end of the afternoon Jenny pointed out that they needed to call themselves something. "What do you mean?" I asked.

"You know, like peer leaders." Carlos added.

"No, that's played." Jenny's face lit up. "How about Youth Advocates?"

They liked that, and so did I. From that afternoon on, they began to work together as a team.

A couple of weeks later, I realized how far their relationship had gone. Carlos needed a winter jacket. His old one had been stolen from the group home. Jenny saw him coming in, shivering in his sweatshirt jacket and commented, "Yo Carlos, you got to get your agency to buy you a warm coat, like a Columbia or Timberland."

"Trust me, I've been telling my worker, but she hasn't gotten approvals. . . ."

"Look, the laws say you have a right to 'appropriate clothing' right? And you're freezing your butt off! You're a freaking Youth Advocate, write a letter!" she teased him.

Then Jenny sat down with him to help him write a letter asking his social worker to go to her supervisor to get money approved for the jacket. She opened our rights booklet to the regulations on clothing allowances, so he could quote that in his letter. Carlos was a great writer and persuasive with adults, but I was still a little surprised that the next week he got the approval and a check for fifty dollars. Jenny and I were as excited as he was. Carlos asked us to go with him to pick out the jacket.

By working together on this project, the relationship between Jenny and Carlos turned from one of wariness to one of admiration, understanding, cooperation, and respect. A friendship developed. I got the sense that it was a big step for both of them. Over time we saw this happen again and again with the teens who attended programs and worked at Youth Advocacy Center. Often the system will label kids with "has difficulty making relationships." Yet the system rarely questions whether part of this inability to make relationships stems from the foster care or group home environment rather than the teen's natural personality. Throughout our work, we find that teens in foster care demonstrate the capacity to make close relationships within the context of seminars and advocacy projects where they work together on assignments that have recognizable and appealing goals.

To get the rights booklets into the hands of teens, Jenny began calling all the foster care agencies and asking if they would like to have Youth Advocates present a workshop. Somewhat to my surprise, the agencies were interested. I was sure that if I called asking to come talk about kids' rights, they would have hung up pretty fast, but they were interested in the Youth Advocates coming, maybe seeking a good influence over what they thought were their own rowdy or disinterested teens. The first workshop was set up. "It's in Queens at a group home!" Jenny was clearly excited by this first positive response. "Great, I'll come too, just to watch and help out if you need it." I couldn't wait to observe her presentation.

The group home was at the last stop on the subway line, more than an hour away. That part went quickly enough, with Jenny insisting on rehearsing her presentation twice, then filling me in on the latest electronica hip hop artists. For many adults one attraction of working with teens is that you get the chance to feel you're not as out of touch with youth culture—the latest clothes trends, slang, and music—as your age might lead you to be. While I admit to liking this part of my work, I was more motivated by the fact that in these conversations the teens and I could learn from each other in an informal way.

These informal interchanges often have a profound effect in creating a sense of empowerment. The teens understand they have something to offer in a conversation, and therefore they are more prone to learn from the adult. Adults who enjoy talking with teens and are open about sharing their own insights and experiences can provide a rich and natural learning situation.

After waiting for a bus and taking a long walk, we finally reached the group home, a three-story nondescript red brick house, indistinguishable from the other houses except for the iron bars over the windows and front door—a welcoming touch.

A staff person with a jangle of keys on a string around her neck walked us downstairs to a common area in the basement, where a stationary exercise bike sat in the corner, next to some board games with torn covers on a bookshelf. I smelled cooking mixed with mildew. She gestured to a couch with soiled orange fabric. "The young ladies will be down when they finish supper," she said. "It'll be about ten minutes. Would you all like me to fix you plates too?" she asked pleasantly enough.

"Oh, no thanks," Jenny sounded enthusiastic as she was reviewing her agenda and assembling the booklets. "Think I had enough of that group home food," she whispered as the worker turned away.

Half an hour later, we were bored with waiting when finally girls started to wander in one by one, wearing unlaced sneakers and slippers on their feet. They looked like they hadn't been out of the house all day. One with a bathrobe tied loosely over her big belly, sweatpants pulled down low below it, spoke to no one in particular, "Who you all?"

"They are the ones to tell you about your rights, remember?" reminded the staff person who brought us down.

"Don't look like no lawyers, especially her. She looks like a girl in my last group home." Jenny rolled her eyes. I was irritated that no one at the group home had prepared the teens for our presentation. The responsibility had fallen on this staff person to introduce us, but clearly no thought went into preparing the teens or providing an environment conducive for learning.

I realized this was a maternity group home, for pregnant girls in foster care. Why hadn't Jenny told me? She probably didn't know or think it was important. I figured the presentation would be a disaster. The pregnant girls probably wouldn't be interested in this workshop because they had a lot more to worry about than advocating for their rights.

They sat down on some folding chairs that the staff person dragged out of a closet, and I was focusing on moving my chair to make room for one of the girls near me when all of a sudden I heard, "Good evening, everyone."

Jenny stood up and smoothly started, "Thank you for coming. My name is Jennifer Santana, and I am a Youth Advocate, here to tell you about your rights and what advocacy is." She struck the right note of authority. She got their attention.

Jenny's enthusiasm was apparent despite her formal introduction. "Listen up! Me, I been in the system for eight years now? And I have to tell you the group home I'm in now is cool, but it hasn't always been like that—some of the people I dealt with were off the hook! And all the time I been in care nobody told me I have rights! Not until I started working at the YAC that I found out all this stuff about what we're supposed to get when we're in foster care, and . . ."

Jenny continued. She explained how we had researched the rights teens have and put them together in the booklets we were going to give them. But first she wanted to tell them about advocacy and its importance. She asked them if they knew what advocacy was, and they shrugged.

Jenny was unfazed. "Let me give you an example." She then told the advocacy story she and Carlos made up. "Listen to what happened to my friend Jose. He bought one of those CD player walkmans from this store on 34th? And it stopped working the first day he got it. He changed the batteries three times, and the dang thing was broken. So he asked me what he should do. What do you think I told him?"

She looked around the group for answers.

"Bring it back, tell them that's wack, give him a new one."

"Report the store to the better business whatever."

"Call my lawyer."

"Okay—those are some good ideas. What about the second, reporting the store, what are the good things and bad things about doing that?"

"Could take a lot of time, still won't have your CD player . . ."

"Right, that's what I told him, bring it back to the store. But he's a little slow, if you know what I mean? So I got to be real specific with him. What should he do when he brings it to the store, I mean who should he bring it to?"

"First person he sees in the store!"

"Oh, you mean the security guard? Cause when you go into those electronics stores on 34th they always got those security guards saying, can I help you? You know, making sure you don't walk out of the store with too much stuff."

The group laughs, "No, not the security guard! The cashier?"

"Yeah, I thought that too, but she is real busy and tells you she can't take it back because the box is opened."

"Customer service? Returns?"

She got them to the right answer playfully, in a way they enjoyed, while also getting them to see they could figure things out. From there, it was a short jump to move them over to thinking about how they could get what they need in the foster care system. "Now if you got a problem in your group home, say, like you need a winter coat, and your social worker is taking her sweet time getting you one and you're freezing, what are you going to do?"

"Call my social worker every day."

"Not me, I call my legal aid lawyer."

"I go right to the top, to the director."

"I just AWOL. Go get one from my boyfriend."

"How do you know which of those is right?" Jenny was leading them into a discussion about the pros and cons of these different strategies, including AWOLing. When I entered the foster care world, all these paramilitary terms struck me as inappropriate when talking about children in a social services setting, but everyone so frequently used and accepted them that I too learned to accept them.

The girls talked about who was responsible at their agency for making these decisions and when was the best time to approach them—when they were in the middle of a meeting with someone else, when they were on the phone? She got the group to take turns role-playing the parts of the kid without the winter jacket and the social worker.

While this didn't seem radical, it markedly differed from many independent living workshops, which were either lectures or games. It also differed from the mental health interactions the teens usually had with adults in the system. Jenny was imparting important independent living skills and concrete information, but she did it in a way that engaged the teens in intellectual debate and at a level with which everyone was comfortable. She was not getting into therapy issues. Her presentation presumed that the teens had had their share of bad luck but that they were hopeful things would get better. We didn't explicitly articulate all this, but the message was embedded in what we were doing: educating the teens, taking them seriously, and respecting their intellectual abilities. Jenny was teaching this group a new way to think and solve problems rather than preaching specific rules.

Although we hadn't planned it specifically, these peer-led Youth Advocate workshops became the genesis of YAC adopting the Socratic method to teach teens. The agendas the Youth Advocates used were in the format of questions. They didn't lecture, but asked the audience, "Where do you think rights come from?" "How many kids are in foster care in the city?" The skits they composed, the scenarios of various rights violations, were essentially case studies that provoked discussions about questions: What would you do in this situation? What are your options here? How can you think about the situation broadly? What is the other person thinking about? How can you meet his or her needs?

In this first workshop, I saw Jenny's potential as a leader and a gifted teacher. Jenny asked about some things the group might want to change, and the teens fought to speak over each other.

"I want to find out where I'm going to go after the baby is born."

"They're telling me I lost my high school credits, and I should just get a GED."

"The food here is terrible."

"What if I want to go home to my own family?"

"You get no privacy around this place."

"They tell me I'm not allowed to have a job while I'm at this place."

The group of young women brought up some of the big issues: where will they live when they have their babies; their education; their job prospects— side by side with day-to-day quality-of-life issues such as bad food, limited phone priviliges, cheap clothing allowances.

Yet, I sensed that the pregnant girls were concerned about their future in a way different from other teens. They knew they had more to risk and to lose without a place to live, a family to support them, an income, or an education. At the same time, what could they do? They clutched the booklets that Jenny passed out, paged through them searching for answers. I desperately wanted to help these young women but didn't know if there was much to offer them besides our booklets and phone number.

On the long trip back to Manhattan, Jenny was elated with the workshop's success. She was also scheming about what to do differently next time. "You know those girls don't know nothing about the foster care system. I'm gonna talk to Carlos about us making a big chart to show these kids what's what, so they understand this better."

At some point the Youth Advocates began calling the system chart "the chain of command." They loved it, just like they loved talking about how it's important to go to the top when you have a problem. They were intrigued with power issues, and perhaps, because the chart illustrated the fact that they were on the bottom, they became students of power.

During the next weeks I was busy looking for funding so we could rent a bigger office. I sent Jenny to the library to research foundation grants. I told her to take one or two afternoons on this, depending on what she found. The agency social worker Gillian, who said Jenny was a real problem, probably would have laughed at me and told me I was foolishly wasting my time and also taking a risk sending Jenny somewhere new without supervision. If she knew, Gillian might have predicted that Jenny would skip the library and use the subway money I gave her to go back to her old neighborhood to get high. But I had no time to think twice about it. Worst scenario, she wouldn't come up with anything, in which case I figured it would still be a learning experience. Plus I needed help from wherever I could get it.

The first day Jenny didn't come back to YAC at the end of the day. The second day she didn't come in at all. I became uneasy—what happened? I was relieved the next day when Jenny showed up with a long list of foundations, some I'd heard of and some new ones. Jenny went on nonstop about all the people she saw at the library, the interesting notices on the bulletin board, the proposal writing training that was coming up that she wanted to attend. "I think I can get us in for free if I write a letter on our letterhead," she assured me. When I asked Jenny why she thought she could take the proposal writing training, she said, "I asked the librarian? And here's her card? She said I should call if I have any more questions." Continually Jenny impressed me. She took initiative and was interested in not just what I asked her to do but also this new experience, in a neighborhood where she hadn't been before, with people she didn't know.

After talking with her and Carlos about how we wanted to build on these workshops, we developed a proposal and mailed it to fourteen foundations. Only one was interested. Not a bad rate! We were lucky to get a meeting with Victor, who worked for a progressive foundation. He wanted to visit us, but because we literally didn't have room or chairs for all of us to sit, we borrowed a conference room for the occasion. We needed a grant urgently. I had to get a regular paycheck soon. I wasn't sure how he would react to meeting with the teens and me. What kind of impression would they make on someone who was considering giving us tens of thousands of dollars?

I prepared a presentation about the importance of both educating foster care youth about their rights and advocacy (what Jenny had been doing) and also about including the "youth voice" in the child welfare system (what Carlos had been doing with the video presentations at graduate schools).

I was nervous and just got to the part of my speech about why adults shouldn't be controlling the dialogue of reform when a loud, impatient, real live youth voice interrupted me. "Hey, can I say something? I don't know if you understand what it's like for us living in the foster care system? Sure they give us a bed and something to eat, but we need more than that. And what Betsy's trying to say is that we are the people who know what's what, and we should be able to tell more people about the facts. We are learning about the rights and the laws and how to be advocates, and we have to tell other kids about this. It's only fair!"

I was about to break into the conversation again to clarify Jenny's outburst (I wasn't sure if it made any sense or not) when Carlos chimed in. "Another thing is that the social workers and the people in schools learning to be social workers, they need to know what the system is like for people like us. It shouldn't be all about book learning. It should be about what it means to us when they say, you should stay in special ed, or no you can't have a winter jacket. They got to realize we're people with rights and feelings!"

I was smart enough to shut up and let Victor talk directly with the Youth Advocates. He was charmed, but, more important, he was impressed. Victor asked the Youth Advocates about their experiences and then about what our strategies were for the year to come. It was clear he was seriously considering what Jenny and Carlos presented. The only questions he directed toward me were to confirm that we had our nonprofit status and to ask how often our board met. On the way out, he gave me a handshake, smiled, and said, "I think we'll be able to help you out." After he left, the kids jumped up and down with excitement. I sat elated but dazed, marveling at what had just happened: the Youth Advocates took the meeting right out from under me and got us the grant.

Carlos and Jenny were unusual, but over time I came to meet many young people like them. They possessed intellectual abilities to analyze and consider complex issues, exhibited abundant energy, felt a passion for justice, and hoped for a better future. Carlos and Jenny were typical of numerous teens who have early on suffered tremendous life hardships, traumas, and experiences that are too painful to rationally understand. They clearly possessed one element that characterizes the majority of teens in foster care—resilience. Working with them during YAC's development expanded my expectations for teens in foster care. I came to realize that foster teens had a vast, untapped resource of inner capabilities, no less than possessed by teens with more fortunate backgrounds, with perhaps a bit more resilience.

With the new grant we rented a small office—still one room, but a bigger room where we could fit more than three of us comfortably. It was on the second floor, above a drugstore. Jenny, with a bandanna tied over her hair, but otherwise in her uniform of baggy jeans and t-shirt, coordinated the move, and all the teens helped carry stuff in and arrange the little furniture we had. I truly felt we had accomplished this together. This was their place as much as mine. We celebrated by having pizza and Cokes, sitting on the floor of our new office.

The demand for our workshops grew. Jenny set one or two up a week now. We heard the same questions over and over again. "How often can I see my siblings?" "Shouldn't I be able to live with them?" "My clothes are too small—can't I buy some new clothes for school?" "Am I allowed to change schools?" "Can I be forced to change schools?" "How much allowance should I get?" "Is it okay if I get a part time job if I want to earn money?" "Is a grown up allowed to use physical force to punish me?" "Can I be forced to take medication?" "Do

I have a right to use the phone to call my family?" "What about to call about a job?" "To call a friend?" "Am I allowed to open the refrigerator to get a snack after school?" "Don't I have a lawyer to help me with all this?"

Some questions related to significant life decisions; some seemed minor, but they were incredibly important to the teens at the time. If teens faced these assaults to their daily living, how could they be expected to prepare properly for successful independence? As YAC met with many more teenagers, we became increasingly frustrated with the repetitiveness and urgency of these questions and with being unable to help teens resolve the large number of problems related to their foster care placements.

We were torn between helping individual kids protect their rights and trying to change the system. We decided to try to work more intensely with a group of teens to help them develop a youth council, through which they could better advocate for improved conditions in their foster care agency. Jenny made a contact with Lisa, a young social worker at an RTC. Lisa was responsible for teaching boys independent living skills, and she readily admitted to feeling overwhelmed by what was going on at the agency. She thought our program could be helpful in her work with the boys. She thought they were great kids, but with their many complaints she had difficulty teaching them anything.

Lisa agreed to start a youth council advocacy project in which Jenny would visit the RTC campus once a week to help a group in a cottage organize to improve some policy or practice at the agency.

On the day of our first meeting at this agency, we were leaving the office to catch the train when Jenny said, "I just gotta get something from the drugstore." I waited on the corner outside for her. Next thing I knew Jenny walked out with the drugstore owner, who was also our landlord, right behind her, not looking happy.

"Betsy, we got a problem. Your kid here is stealing from us."

"What are you talking about?" I asked.

At the same time, Jenny protested, "I did NOT!"

"I saw her peeling the price tag off this deodorant."

"I was NOT!" Jenny was upset. Words just spilled out. "I was just LOOK-ING at it, I wasn't taking it."

"I saw her peeling the price tag off. You gotta understand, shoplifting is a big problem for us, and we know the tricks people do."

Jenny kept protesting and looked at me beseechingly to believe her, which at that moment I really wanted to do but was unsure. I put my doubts aside. "Look, if she said she didn't do it, she didn't do it, okay?" I wanted Jenny to see that I was standing by her.

"I don't want the kids from your office back in here if this is what we got to deal with," warned the landlord.

"All right, I understand this is a problem, but we're late for an appointment," I told the landlord. "Can we talk about this later?" We ran off to the subway.

"I'm just so embarrassed," said Jenny nervously. "It's so hot today, and I didn't have any deodorant left, you know they are so cheap about that at the group home. They never give us enough toiletries . . . so I wanted to buy a new one before we went to this workshop. . . . . I was just comparing prices." I was silent. I wanted to believe Jenny and at the same time suspected she might be playing off of my trust. The odds were high that she was trying to steal, but I had a lot of reasons to want to believe her.

A week later we sat down with Jenny and the four other Youth Advocates working with us. We talked about the incident at the drugstore. If it was true, then there was a lot at stake. I explained to the teens that we needed to have a good relationship with our landlord and that this warning was very useful, though I never mentioned who did what. As we talked, the teens became aware that their actions no longer represented themselves as individuals but as a group. If someone got into trouble, that person could jeopardize our entire mission of helping teens in foster care. The question was whether they had enough commitment and self-control to stay out of trouble for the sake of the group and the work we were doing.

Unanimously, the group of Youth Advocates made this commitment. They actually appeared proud to be part of a group in which their actions mattered. From that meeting forward, we never had any similar problems. I was impressed with the teens' ability to analyze a situation and make clear decisions. It seemed almost too easy, especially having heard so frequently how troubled these teens were. Yet, if presented with information, they could and did make good decisions and act upon them.

Like most of the RTCs that house New York City foster care kids, this one was in a wealthy suburb. When we got to the train station near the RTC, we took a taxi to the "campus." The big, old houses shaded by tall maple trees reminded me of where I grew up, not that far from here, and now I saw the appeal of the beautiful homes with brilliant flowerbeds in a way I didn't as a kid. Jenny had quieted down too, unusual for her, and I figured that she was either contemplating what she did wrong or maybe appreciating how nice it was here compared to the hot noisy city in the summer.

"Yo, what the hell do people do up here?" She broke the silence with the exact opposite of what I imagined she was thinking. She made me laugh, and for the moment, I totally forgot about the alleged shoplifting. I asked her what she meant. "Come on, you can't walk anywhere, nobody's hanging out, it's dead! I need some action, too quiet around here."

Jenny did have a point, it was quiet. Passing through the stone and wrought iron entryway of the RTC, the cab drove through woods up a winding driveway, which crossed over a little bridge and stream. Suddenly the cab driver cursed and slammed on the brakes. Two girls and a boy, ten or eleven years old, jumped out of the bushes into the road, almost in front of the car. "Take us out of here, please! Help us escape!" they yelled, and it was hard to tell how much of a joke their screams were. They ran away fast, disappearing back into the bushes. I almost thought I imagined it, but Jenny shook her head and laughed, "Oh my God! See what I mean!" The taxi started driving again and at the end of the driveway dropped us off at a walkway leading to the main administration building.

The building looked like a mansion and probably once was. Arranged around a big circular lawn were three-story houses, updated with fire escapes, and mixed in with some 1980s era low brick dorms. These were the cottages, where the kids slept. No kids were around outside, just some geese. Jenny and I walked up to the front door, which was very tall, dark carved wood with an ornate decorative metal knocker, as well as a regular doorknob. "Ooooh, spooky," said Jenny "like a haunted house, right?"

Most of the residential treatment centers circling New York City take kids from the city foster care system. They all have long, similar histories. Originally they were country estates. Many became orphanages in the late nineteenth century, taking in real orphans without any parents and kids who simply came from very poor families or were living on the streets. The orphan trains, which shipped these kids out west for adoptions and to become laborers on family farms, were connected with many of these institutions. From there, they evolved into training schools, vocational programs, or preparatory-type schools for poor children, readying them for apprentice-ships or higher education. Until the early 1940s they served mostly immi-grant European children from city slums; during this period social work began developing a professional identity, mental health advocates grew more powerful, and, at the same time, more African-American children were being placed into the foster care system. By 1962, the system became in-voluntary, with recognition of the battered child syndrome. The most com-mon reason for placement became neglect due to substance abuse. Children may have been previously abused and neglected, but these situations became less acceptable than in the past; now there was a different thresh-old for removal. Families once seen as simply poor and incapable of provid-ing for their children were now also labeled dysfunctional, and those who were in earlier years described as orphans, homeless, and destitute were now deemed in need of treatment. Very quickly, the institutions that for years provided care to the orphans, homeless, and destitute now became residential treatment centers.

The children and teenagers in these residential treatment centers were coined the most damaged, the most emotionally disturbed, the most diffi-cult. Many teens were sent to an RTC for behavior problems because no more foster homes would take them. It seemed that child welfare professionals had difficulty distinguishing the problems kids enter RTCs with from those issues that being in a foster care institution caused. Many RTCs claimed to operate on mental health principles, when actually the system seemed to possess no overall philosophy as to what promotes childhood mental health. For the most part, RTC staff focused on pathology and mental health disorders. In short, regardless of the reasons the teen entered the RTC, the institution was designed to immediately describe the teen and any family he or she had in mental disorder terms. I had spent a lot of time with teens who were placed in RTCs, and many seemed capable, intelligent survivors, who were almost all angry about the circumstances of their lives. (The official diagnosis of oppositional defiant disorder can be a good, or at least sensible, adaptation from a psychological perspective.)

At the time Jenny and I visited the RTC, there was no consensus that residential centers worked. Government and private studies had consistently found little effectiveness for kids in long-term care. Periodically, RTC environments produced scandals and crises such as staff attacking kids, kids attacking staff, kids attacking kids; these incidents resulted in public hearings and outcry for reform. Then business would return to usual.

The social worker Lisa walked us to the cottage where we were to meet the boys. On the way, we saw two kids run out of another cottage and begin to fight. Others followed and jumped in, and ten kids were quickly involved in a small brawl. Staff ran over and peeled bodies off. Lisa explained that this was unusual because the kids were supposed to be escorted from one building to another; they were not supposed to walk by themselves around campus.

In the cottage living room, which was clean and furnished with bright and sturdy dormlike couches and tables, we found twelve teens, boys ranging from thirteen to sixteen years old. They were sitting around finishing up a snack of donuts and juice. Lisa asked them to turn their chairs into a circle, and Jenny began the rights and advocacy workshop, going through the agenda she had developed and practiced, asking questions to get the boys involved. Then she told them we wanted to help them learn advocacy so that they could change something they felt was unfair.

They were more reticent than most groups. Unlike some kids to whom Jenny had presented, these boys seemed intimidated by her—shy of her shiny long black hair and red lip gloss, of her mastery of words like *advocacy*, and of the fact that she had the guts to stand up in front of them, a group of teenage boys. But she was undeterred by their lack of response. "C'mon, yo, you're tellin me that everything's just great up here—no problems?"

A boy named Jeff, who had been sitting silently in the corner with dark sunglasses on, holding a paper cup over his mouth and making noises like rap beats into it, suddenly dropped the cup and said, "We get our clothes from their warehouse." He picked up the cup again, his eyes watching Jenny over the rim, to see what she would say.

"For real? What do you mean?"

He put down the cup slowly now and explained angrily, "We all have to wear the same clothes. Don't you notice? We go to the storeroom and pick out the same jeans, shirts, and sneakers. It doesn't look proper, everyone having the same clothes. How would you feel if everywhere you looked people were wearing the same stuff you had on? No individuality."

Another kid sitting a couple of seats away chimed in, "And it's all ugly shit. Cheap quality—when you wash them, they fade and rip and shrink." That, for some reason, made them all start laughing, which got Jenny laughing, too.

Jeff caught my attention when he spoke up again. "Anyway, ain't they supposed to be teaching us how to budget money and all that? Don't they want us to get jobs when we get out of here, so we can buy our clothes in a store like regular people? It's not like we're just going to be able to go to a big warehouse and pick out what we need. They should be teaching us things that are gonna help us when we leave."

He was smart, intuitively connecting the clothes issue to what the agency's responsibility was (or should have been): teaching the kids how to be independent when they leave. Jenny got them to start discussing how the boys could make an argument to the administration. She began the process of teaching them advocacy.

"What is the agency's mission? You know, what are they supposed to do?"

"To make money."

"To help us."

"To make themselves look good," they guessed.

All had a point, Jenny acknowledged. The agency did need to make money and to help kids, and it had a reputation to protect. "How does this fit in with them changing the clothing policy?" Jenny asked.

Arguing it out, the boys, led by Jeff, roughly articulated that it would be in the agency's interest to help the boys feel better about themselves. In addition, if the boys learned practical skills that would help them succeed after care, the agency could elevate its reputation.

The pitfall to this argument, I saw, was that perhaps the agency didn't have an investment in the kids' futures. Maybe the agency didn't regard the boys' abilities to budget or shop as high priorities. Or maybe the agency leaders thought on some unconscious level that the children in their care would never achieve independence.

The kids then turned the discussion to complaints that they had no closets, only lockers, and they weren't allowed to put locks on those. Their stuff went missing all the time, leading them to suspect each other and the staff of stealing. Jenny asked them to think about the reason for this rule.

"So's we don't bring drugs here," said one boy.

"They want to check up on us."

"So they can go through our stuff. . . ."

"Keep us from having anything nice."

Some of these seemed on target, and Jenny encouraged them to talk about whether they could think of any solutions to accommodate the agency's needs. "They can have regular checks of our locker, they could. . . ."

They talked about the action plan, the next steps they could take, such as setting up a meeting with someone in the agency's executive office. Lisa, the social worker, appeared pleased with the way the meeting turned out and participated in the discussion about whether they should write a letter first or just stop by the office. Jeff was studying our booklet about rights and advocacy with a serious expression on his face. When they decided to write a letter, Jeff volunteered to draft it and give it to Jenny to look over.

At the end of the meeting, Lisa asked Jeff to give us a tour of the cottage where the teens lived. Upstairs there were no real bedrooms, no walls or doors, just partitions separating sleeping areas. Most of these cubicles were decorated by the kids with posters, some stuffed animals, snapshots of boys, girls, and family. One cubicle was bare, with no sheets on the mattress, nothing on the walls or shelves. "Oh, they have an empty bed," I commented, meaning that the agency had a vacancy.

"Nah, he went AWOL home to his mom's," shrugged Jeff, "so they stripped his bed and locked up all his stuff so it won't be here when he gets back," as if this was an everyday happening. How sad. A teen without a home and parents can't deal with these losses and misses his curfew. Then he will return to this RTC and find all his belongings are gone. What purpose does that serve? Does it prevent him from missing curfew again? Does it help him deal better with the pressures of foster care?

The excitement that I felt when the kids were engaged in thinking about how to change the clothing policy started to leave me as I heard this. Clearly, Jeff and some of the others were bright enough and angry enough to fight to change their agency, but I was overwhelmed by the difficulty or even futility of trying to empower teens by teaching them their rights and how to advocate in this kind of setting. Were we giving them false hopes that they could change anything?

Soon after this meeting Jeff faxed Jenny this letter, neatly written in script, addressed to the RTC director.

Dear Mr. Arthur,
We are writing you in concern of the clothing program. We believe we are responsible young adults. We also believe we should be able to shop for the appropriate attire. We would also like to request that we get permission to put locks on our lockers to prevent some of the stealing. We would like to schedule a meeting to discuss these issues.
Sincerely,
Jeff Rogers.

Jenny typed it up and included other points the boys had brought up at the meeting. Lisa, who genuinely was on the teens' side, eagerly helped them with this. She promised to deliver the letter to Mr. Arthur. She reported back, with some surprise and pride, that he said meeting with them now might harm their treatment plans. However, he changed his mind once Lisa explained how such a meeting could play an important part in their in-dependent living skills development. She told him that they were really look-ing forward to it and that YAC had been helping them prepare. I wondered if the possibility of outside scrutiny moved him at all.

Jenny went to meet with Jeff and the other boys two more times to pre-pare and practice for the meeting. Jeff was going to be the main spokesperson. Lisa got permission for Jenny and me to attend the meeting too. We met in a conference room with a U-shaped table set up. Lisa, Jeff, and two other cottage kids sat on one side of the room and far on the other side was Mr. Arthur. Before Jeff or the other kids could say a word Mr. Arthur began, "I have your letter here about the clothing program, Mr. Rogers," (sounded condescending rather than polite to my ears) "and is there something you want to say about it?"

"Uhhhh. Yeah." Jeff mumbled. "Y'all should be letting us buy our clothes. We got to get the experience of doing that otherwise how we going to later on?'

"I'm sure you understand I can't have you spending your clothing allowance on a one hundred dollar pair of brand name sneakers."

Jeff acted differently from the time I heard him speak at Jenny's presentation. There he was fiery, angry, now he seemed not just shyer and quieter, but a little out of it. "Yeah, uh-huh, but you don't trust us. . . . That's the problem. . . . Y'all think we stupid and wasteful and you don't give us a chance." He spoke slowly, and his words were almost garbled, making them hard to understand.

I knew this wasn't what they had prepared. Jeff was going off in another direction, not talking about the agency's role. Jenny noticed too and broke in, "Look, what he's trying to say is that your agency should be teaching the boys independence and that should include things like picking out their clothes. So maybe they should be allowed to, you know, learn how to do some shopping, compare prices and all, you know what I'm saying?"

"Yes, young lady, I think I do. But you have to understand that these are very troubled teens with no experience being responsible. We cannot let them run loose in the mall or down in the city."

"Well, how are they going to learn if they don't get a chance?" asked Jenny.

"That's why our agency is fortunate to have Lisa, our IL specialist. She teaches them budgeting and exactly what you are talking about—price comparisons, etcetera. And in the cottage, they learn to take responsibility step by step, by staying in our program. Now we will consider your proposal, but I have to be honest, I can't promise you anything. That's the way we do it here."

No one spoke for a long moment. Mr. Arthur looked at his watch. Glancing at Jeff I saw his eyes at half-mast. I nudged Jenny and whispered, "You better take over with the agenda."

"Umm, so what about the locks?" Jenny asked, not at her best. She too was surprised by Jeff's passivity.

"No, I'm afraid that violates our procedures to allow locks. Jeffrey and the other young men know the problems we have here with young men bringing back illegal substances from the city."

The meeting was going nowhere fast. Jeff seemed to be falling asleep, Lisa appeared helpless, and it was coming down to Jenny arguing with Mr. Arthur.

"Anything else?" he asked.

Out in the hall, the boys left to go back to the cottage, and Jenny went to the bathroom. I stood with Lisa, and we agreed that the meeting was not what we hoped for. I asked her, "What happened to Jeff? Is he alright?"

She shrugged and nodded vigorously, "I know, isn't it awful!? I think it's the new meds he's on." All of a sudden I got a sick feeling. Many kids I used to represent in family court complained about being forced to take medication at RTCs. They told me how they hid or tried to spit out the pills that were supposed to calm them down but made them ill with side effects of nausea, dizziness, and sleepiness. Some were obviously groggy while we were talking, and, when I asked them if they were tired, they explained, "The pills make me like this." Medication isn't in itself good or bad; it can be useful if it improves functioning and harmful if it doesn't or if the side effects outweigh the beneficial effects. However, its use purely for behavioral control has significant ethical and long-term health questions. I worried that was what happened here; perhaps our encouraging Jeff to be an advocate had something to do with these new meds and his seeming disorientation.

During the following weeks we talked about what to do next. Lisa felt like we gave it a good try, and she didn't see much point in continuing to advocate for the clothing policy change or the locks. She was honest in her assessment. She just didn't think it was going to happen. I agreed with her that the administration didn't seem to have much interest or incentive to change the way they were handling the kids. She put a positive spin on it by claiming that it was a great experience for the boys and that they learned something.

Jenny talked to Jeff on the phone. She reported that Jeff had an attitude of "what's the difference what we do." She called him a second and third time, leaving messages, but he didn't call back. She was frustrated, and so was I. This project took a lot of energy on the part of the teens and a great deal of YAC's resources as well. What were we doing, I wondered? What would have been the best outcome? That the boys would have won the chance to get some better clothes, the chance to shop, the chance to prove themselves responsible? If we were going to try to help kids advocate for change at their agency, was this the most important thing we could do with them?

One day Jenny called in to say she wouldn't be able to work because she had an appointment. The next day she came in, "I got some good news and some bad news," she began, sitting next to my desk, bouncing her knees up and down with the nervous energy I had seen the first time I met her.

"What's up?"

"I got a full time job! That's the good part! The bad news is the hours will keep me from coming here . . . but you know, I'll help you out whenever I can, doing workshops, whatever, meeting with foundations. You know I'll be getting out of care pretty soon, and I want to have more work experience and put away some money in savings. . . ."

I tried to hide my disappointment. I told her that was great and that she should get other experience. Of course, I understood that she had to figure out what she was going to do with her life—it couldn't always be about foster care. I also told her I was sad because I would miss her.

I was ashamed because part of me was fantasizing that Jenny would stay at YAC, working full time, indefinitely. But that wouldn't be right. She shouldn't have to spend her life engrossed in rights violations for foster care teens. She was making a rational decision because she had to consider her own future.

I did feel upset that she wouldn't be going to college. Her intellectual abilities were sharp, and she had a strong sense of hope and ability to build for the future. She would benefit from exposure to different worlds. She was so likable and absorbed everything quickly. I was sad that no one—and here

I had to include myself—had sufficiently prepared her for seeing college as an enriching and useful next step. Getting work experience and earning money was critically important now. In fact, these goals should have been high on Jenny's agenda a few years earlier in order to prepare for leaving the foster care system. Focusing on them now was important, but it wasn't necessarily enough to help her long-term well-being.

Working with Jenny to teach kids throughout the foster care system about their rights and encouraging them to advocate for system change was meant to be the answer, but these experiences ultimately raised more questions. First, they sharpened our belief that telling young people about their rights was not enough; they also needed advocacy skills. Seeing how much power the system had over teens, was it realistic to teach teens to advocate for their individual rights? Was it unrealistic to ask them to take on the chain of command in their own agencies? Because teens had to put so much effort into every battle, was it worth the struggle? Each battle took away energy from something else. How could we expect an individual teen or even a group of teens to fight the powers in their agencies?

However, we saw the teens as effective advocates, inspiring in their drive to change the system for themselves and their peers. With our limited resources, we needed to focus. Our next step was to choose one issue with teens, to help a group of them try to change the system.

4

Policy Advocacy with Teens

| *Xaranda* | Teens seemed to encounter so many immediate prob-
lems that were endemic to the system. Even with our
growing interest in preparing teens for their future, we felt compelled to make life more manageable for teens while in care. But
the system wasn't going to change because we were teaching foster teens about their rights and the rudiments of advocacy. We often felt
unsatisfied working at solving individual and small group problems. We
would resolve a problem, but the system never changed, and the overall
future prospects for the teens remained dismal. This made us want to find
other ways to improve conditions for teens. If we could change system policy,
then teens who aged out of care might be prepared for independence. Thus
we turned our efforts toward policy change.

We needed to focus on one area or issue facing teens. Through the workshops, we came into contact with many girls and young women who were pregnant or had children. The system treated them in a manner that assured their
failure to become independent and to become successful parents also failed
and to prevent a new generation of children from being raised in foster care.

We explored different approaches to advocating for changes that would
make the system more responsive to teen mothers' needs and would give
their babies a more stable and better start in life. At the time, other groups
were ignoring this issue. We had a chance to establish our reputation as
experts on this issue. The density of the issues these girls faced—foster

care, babies, pregnancy, welfare, education deprivation—appealed to us as a substantial challenge. We believed that the ways in which the system was failing—for example, holding these babies in the hospitals for weeks on end because of a shortage of foster homes—would engender support from a wider community because of the obvious unnecessary costs, human suffering, and wasted potential. Additionally girls' and women's foundations might be willing to fund work in this area. We had to consider this funding issue if we wanted to stay in business.

After considerable deliberation, we developed a Teen Mother Youth Advocacy Project to prevent young mothers in foster care from being unnecessarily separated from their babies. The project also tried to make sure that the teen mothers received services to support them and their babies. The project had several components: legal advocacy, educational workshops, and policy advocacy. In all these aspects, we involved the teens as partners in deciding strategy and actually doing the work. We thought their involvement was necessary to bring some rational solutions to the problems in foster care.

Betsy

A girlish, almost babyish voice came over the phone in a rush, "Miss Betsy? You don't know me, miss, but I was told to call you because I really need help. See, I'm going to have a baby, and I need to get out of this place."

From what I could piece together, her name was Xaranda. She spelled it for me, "X like x-ray, a like apple . . . but you can just say it like Sheronda." None of her brothers or sisters was in foster care, but she told me that she and her father didn't get along, and he signed her into care. At seventeen she got pregnant, with her boyfriend Luis who also lived at the RTC. As soon as she figured it out, six weeks into the pregnancy, Xaranda told her social worker.

Xaranda was practically yelling at me, "You know what they told me? 'Okay, don't worry about it. We have everything under control. We'll make sure you get to a maternity shelter,' 'Maybe I better call Pam, my family court lawyer?' I ask them. 'No, no need,' they say."

Xaranda took no time to pause or even breathe as she continued her story, "Three months later, I'm still sitting in here, and I'm like, I got to move!

I called my caseworker. I asked her about my placement, 'What's going on with my placement for a maternity shelter?' And she was like, 'I cannot speak with you because you are the child. I only speak to the social workers.' I just felt she was a fool. Meantime my real social worker, she is on her own maternity leave so nobody got my case. I'm wondering, can you help me?"

Maybe it was a sign that I had already been doing this too long, but I was easily following Xaranda's convoluted story. I had heard it before. When I first started as a lawyer for kids one of my clients was Marlisa. I spent hours that turned into months on Marlisa's case, making sure she got a suitable mother-child placement. I devoted much time negotiating with the city so she didn't have to unconditionally give up custody of her son, as her caseworker told her she must. The rules at the time were clear: a girl in foster care who gave birth had to sign a voluntary placement agreement, a boilerplate contract prepared by the city, in which she gave custody of her child to New York City and State. Legally and ethically, it was improper for a minor to sign away custody of her baby, without legal counsel and representation, and I got the city to agree to rewrite the placement contract.

After Marlisa, I had represented and helped more than dozen other girls who were in foster care when they became pregnant. This was the source of numerous heated arguments with my friends and family members. "Why is someone who is still a child bringing another child into the world?" they asked. "We thought long and hard before having a baby, and we waited till we could afford it! Why should taxpayers foot the bill for their kids when they can't support them?" "Don't they know they're just keeping up the cycle of broken families? Kids need good parents, not teenaged mothers!"

Should poor teenage girls get pregnant and become parents? Clearly, teen pregnancy can be prevented or diminished. Ample evidence demonstrates that if teens received good education, birth control advice, and counseling about their options, they might make other decisions. Ideally, society should encourage teens to believe in a vision of the future that they can hold on to as a reason for not having babies so young. Those who harshly judge teen parents probably have much more education and knowledge than these teens and probably should acknowledge our shared responsibility for these teens' inadequate education. The fact remains, however, that some teens in foster care have children, many of these teens have the capacity to be good parents, and both they and their babies can have a productive life if given proper assistance while in care. Regardless of whether teens should or should not have children, the fact remained that a small percentage did, and, if society truly wanted to end the cycle of poverty, then these babies needed their mothers, and the mothers needed the system's support.

Based on the time I had spent with teen mothers in foster care and with their children, I knew that those young women who do decide to have babies were fiercely determined to be the best parents they could. In getting to know them, I saw they were loving and cared about education, nutrition, and health. Most of all, they wanted their kids to live in safe homes. Like all parents, they hoped that their kids would have better childhoods than they did, and they wanted their kids to grow up with them. Miraculously, most girls I knew summoned their courage and inner resources to overcome the hurdles set before them and kept and successfully brought up their own kids. Some didn't succeed and lost custody of their children, but that was not for lack of trying.

The criticisms and prejudices about teen mothers and their babies were magnified a hundred times in the foster care system. Instead of supporting this new family unit, as required by law, and trying to help the girls learn to be good parents, the system set up many hurdles for girls to jump: maintaining custody of their own babies; finding placement in a home with them; and then obtaining the support they needed to thrive. Because the foster care system had a shortage of homes for young mothers and babies, the girls faced a strong likelihood that the foster care system would take away their babies.

The majority of caseworkers in the foster care system were terrified of being blamed for something happening to babies of teen mothers, and thus they tended to take the babies and put them in separate homes. They didn't worry that this was against the law, which permitted removal only in cases of imminent risk. For them imminent risk was synonymous with teenage mothers.

One of our first steps in beginning this project to help a group of teen mothers change the system was legal advocacy. Our strategy was both to help individuals who were facing these common problems and also to determine whether the teen mothers would be interested in advocating to change the system for them and their babies.

Over the next few months, we worked with Xaranda as well as Kathryn, a pro bono private attorney, to help her get into a foster home with her son. The obstacles were numerous and predictable. The main issue that Xaranda faced was that she wanted to know, reasonably enough, where she would go after she gave birth. She wanted to visit potential mother-child foster homes or group homes. Kathryn spent days on the phone with child welfare administration workers.

Eventually, with the advocacy of Kathryn, the system placed Xaranda in a foster home with her son James. Xaranda was just one of the teen mothers Kathryn and other pro bono lawyers helped during this period. Although we had some successes, we saw that matching teens up with lawyers had pros and cons. In some instances, it was good for the teens to have representatives in dealing with the foster care system, when they were so angry and frustrated. If they blew up at their caseworker, then the worker could use that against them—and when they had babies of their own, the stakes were especially high. I commonly read in the case records of young mothers who had lost her children to foster care, "Kim is unable to control her temper and so is a risk to her child." Despite the advantages of legal representation, child welfare caseworkers sometimes grew infuriated with dealing with a lawyer, whom they saw as interfering and making trouble. The lawyers had to master the intricacies of the bureaucracy, while the young women were expert in the acronyms and procedures because the system was their life. The young mothers felt frustrated that lawyers were restricted to focusing on discrete problems and couldn't help them in a more comprehensive manner.

We decided to try to start affecting policy directly by organizing a group of teen mothers to become involved in advocating for policy and practice changes. Because we were committed to involving youth in everything we did, we decided to first meet with groups of pregnant teens and young parents in foster care to get their ideas and their feedback on our own thinking. Our first group met on a Saturday morning in September. Nancy, a social worker at a hospital, who had a big caseload of teen mothers in foster care, and I invited a group of young women and hoped they would come.

As I was walking to the office from my apartment, the Greenwich Village sidewalks were still empty. I passed a girl with long braids and a baby in a carrier on her chest, who was walking in the opposite direction. Five seconds later, I paused and turned around to look at her. She was squinting at the doorways, as if searching for street numbers. Something told me this was someone looking for us, and I retraced my steps to catch up with her, "Excuse me? Are you looking for Youth Advocacy Center by any chance?"

"Yeah I am, but I don't know which way I'm going in this neighborhood."

"I'm Betsy. . . ."

"I'm Xaranda!" It was the first time we'd met in person.

That morning, six other girls showed up. Between them, they had three infants and two toddlers. The teen mothers sat in chairs arranged in a circle, which took up most of our small office. The little babies sat on their mothers' laps, drinking bottles or sleeping. The couple of toddlers played in the middle of the circle with some plastic blocks and looked at picture books the girls pulled out of diaper bags. The girls didn't know each other, and they were shy, barely acknowledging each other, instead focusing on their kids or talking with Nancy and me.

When everyone seemed settled, Nancy and I introduced ourselves and said we were concerned about what we'd seen with girls in foster care and wanted to try to work on a project to change these policies. We'd asked them here to listen to their experiences and ideas. We asked each one to go around and say a bit about herself.

Kim started. She was the only girl there without a child. She had beautiful, smooth dark skin and a big smile that revealed gaps between her teeth. She was disheveled though, her hair was coming out of a ponytail, and she seemed as if she hadn't bathed or changed her clothes recently. Nancy had met her through the hospital and referred her to YAC for help.

"I been in the system my whole life, from group homes to foster homes to hospitals, you know, when things got too tough for me. They say I got problems and who wouldn't, going through what I been through! Been in about twenty something places since I came into the system. But I've been in therapy, and I know what was done to me and that it doesn't mean I'm a bad person." Kim smiled. Clearly therapy can be useful to teens in care, and in Kim's case, it was important to helping her cope with the traumas she'd lived through.

"Anyway, the whole time I'm pregnant I'm living in a group home, and I keep asking what's going to happen after the baby comes. They kept telling me I'll be in a mother-child foster home or group home. Then I gave birth last October. Ms. Moto, this CWA worker who I never met before, came by my hospital bed acting all nice. 'Here, honey, sign these papers here if you want us to find you a place with Darryl.' So I sign. The next day she comes back to the hospital and says, 'You got to go to a group home, cause they need the bed here for another girl.' 'What about Junior?' I ask, afraid of what she's gonna say. 'He's going to have to stay here until we find a place for him.' 'That's crazy! He could catch something in here, and he needs me.' She tells me he'll be fine, and I shouldn't worry because she personally will make sure I can visit him every day. She says, 'I will come with you to the visits.' Liar.

"She put me in this group home in Brooklyn, with retarded kids who are all younger than me. The house rules is that you can't go out for the first two weeks. You think they care that I got a baby in the hospital? One social worker there does, but he can't do nothing about the house rules, so I'm stuck until I just decide to break the rules to go see my child. What's more important? Following the rules or seeing my baby?

"They say they can't find a place for us together so they put him in a foster home in Manhattan and tell me I have to visit him at the agency, which is like one and a half hours on public transportation from Brooklyn. The visits are for an hour every other week. I get real upset at the visits, 'cause they're so short, and also I worry about him and if he's getting taken care of. His clothes smell all stinky, what with the foster mother puffing on cigarettes all the time. And I'm still waiting for a mother-child. 'Kim, you know we don't have a lot of places for nineteen-year-olds who have your history.'

"Anyway, Nancy gave me the number for YAC, and they been helping me, got me a lawyer through this law school down here. And they have brought my case to court. But that do not make up for being separated from Junior all this time."

Kim's eyes welled up, and she wiped tears away. I felt horrible that she was still separated from Darryl, and I knew how painful it was for her to be here with these other babies and their mothers. I squeezed her hand and continued holding it while the rest of the girls talked.

Sondra went last. In contrast to Kim, who looked depressed and seemed beside herself with anger, sadness, and frustration, Sondra was poised and looked like a model. She attended with Ashley, her two-year-old daughter. Both had pale green eyes and a quiet manner. She looked down at her hands in her lap and then began in an unexpectedly strong voice:

"Me, I was never in the system until I got pregnant, and my mother kicked me out. I didn't have anywhere to go, and so I ended up in a shelter, which called CWA and got me placed in a maternity residence. It was not a very pleasant experience, to put it politely, but I could deal with it for a few months. Then I gave birth to my daughter, and the real nightmare started."

"Same as her," she said, gesturing toward Kim. "While I was lying in my bed in the hospital with Ashley one morning, two CWA workers came and said we were going to be placed. I was real excited, you know, and signed the papers they gave me. Then they tell me they don't have a placement for us together cause there's a waiting list. I go nuts, 'What do you mean?' 'You'll be placed in the next opening,' they tell me. I was at my wit's end, but really, what could I do? I had no control over the situation. I imagined grabbing my daughter and running, but I knew they would call the cops on me. So in a daze I put on my clothes and get the baby dressed.

"We all go to the elevators, and one of the caseworkers says to me, 'You better give her to me now. I got to talk to the nurse before we go.' And so I give her my daughter and get in the elevator with the other caseworker. We get in a cab, and I can't see anything I'm crying so hard. 'Where are we going?' I ask between crying. 'To Staten Island,' she tells me. 'To a nice group home on Staten Island.'

"Don't you know they put my daughter in a foster home in Queens? You know how far that is from Staten Island? I was never so depressed or upset in my life as I was for that two weeks. But I was mad too, and I kept calling every caseworker I could think of ten times a day to say I wanted my daughter.

"Finally, one day they tell me they're moving me to a mother-child in the Bronx, with her. Thank God. Over the next two years I have some problems in the mother-child, mostly because they don't allow you to make decisions about your child's life and treat the mothers like babies too. But I deal with it and eventually leave. Now my daughter and I have our own apartment. I'm in my second year of college. Believe me, I consider us lucky to have made it through the system."

Their stories were disturbingly similar. In both, the mother had no control over whether the government would separate her from her baby and was never properly informed about any of the arrangements that child welfare workers made affecting her and her baby's life. Sondra's story at least had a better ending.

Murmuring sympathetically and tsking in indignation throughout the mothers' stories, the young women were impressed into silence when Sondra told them she had her own place with her daughter. Then they quickly jumped in and began talking over each other, complaining about their foster homes and group homes.

"At least you don't got a foster father who drinks and beats up the mother," said Xaranda.

"Oh please, you know what the staff did in my group home? They called the cops on us, just 'cause we were dancing in the living room. At 8:30! Now was that really necessary?" said Sondra.

"They don't trust us. They lock us out of the kitchen and dining room, and we have no bedroom doors," said Missy.

"The foster parents just want to take over and be the mother to the baby," said Julia.

" . . . or else they want us to do everything, and they just collect the checks."

" . . . not enough homes for bad girls like us. Nobody wants teenagers— they just want our cute little babies." Laughing, "And let me tell you, some days I feel like, fine, you take him and change his diapers all day. I need a break!"

The complaining morphed into a conversation any group of new mothers would have about babies and children, a combination of bragging, worrying, comparing products, and sharing shopping tips.

"Diapers, don't get me started. Can you believe how much they get for diapers? And never mind how much they charge for formula."

"What kind of formula you using?"

"What bottle does your baby like?"

"You had regular delivery or c-section?"

"Shanice is growing out of those three-month clothes already."

"Terrell never crawled, just pulled up and started walking at ten months."

"You know where they have good prices on onesies, Kiddy City. There's one on Fordham Road."

As the meeting devolved into several cross conversations, I was pleased that at least they were talking to each other and letting some of their defenses down. I had difficulty getting them to focus on changing the system, but I was excited that they possessed enthusiasm and real concern for their kids and that in their stories, they were identifying important, common issues concerning foster care laws, policy, and practice.

I thought about how to refocus them or whether to give up. I interrupted, "Listen, obviously you all have had a lot of problems in the system that a lot of other girls have had too. Can we talk a little about what you want to do with this group—if you want it to be just kind of a support group where you share your experiences? Or if you want it to be one in which we talk about problems with the system and your ideas to change them?"

Suddenly shy again, they looked at each other out of the corners of their eyes while busying themselves with the kids.

Then Xaranda spoke up, "Hell, yes! We have problems, and we got to do something about them. I mean, I do not want to think that I went through all this, and then the kids coming up behind me in the system are going to have it just as bad. I don't know what this group can do, but we should do something, I know that."

This was a phenomenon I saw time and again in foster care—teens who had been through so much, who were barely keeping their own heads above water, who had so little resources themselves, were concerned with making things better for others in their community. It was moving and humbling.

"Okay," I said. "So, let's talk a little about what we want to do with this group. Does anybody know what advocacy means?" By now I was confident the teens would give me some response.

Quiet again, then Sondra spoke, "I'm not sure exactly, but I think it's like acting like a lawyer or something? Like speaking up for yourself."

"And I guess doing something about it when you feel like you're not getting your rights protected . . . ," jumped in Xaranda.

I nodded, "Right, one thing this group could do together, if you want, in addition to talking about the problems you all have is taking some action to try to change the way things work in the system. You could learn about advocacy, how to use it to make things better for your kids and other people in your situation. How does that sound?"

Shrugs, and murmurs of "Okay," "Good."

"So the first thing we need to do is figure out what we want to change. So let's try to put together a list of the problems you all are identifying in the system."

Sondra tacked up some big sheets of white paper to the walls, and I stood up to write what they said.

Xaranda started, "Well, what I would like to know is why don't they have homes for us and our babies when they're born? They say the problem is they don't have enough homes, but why not? I mean, how many of us are there anyway, in this situation?"

"And why can't they plan where we are going to go? It's not like they don't know we're going to have a baby in nine months. Can't they find a place while we're pregnant?"

"Why can't they just let us know where we will go with the baby? Why can't we visit placements? I wanted to see who I was going to live with, you know, check it out."

I started writing.

Xaranda continued, "And they need to train these foster parents . . . can't just dump us in their house and be like, okay here you go, meet Ms. Jones. This is it—goodbye and good luck."

"I have another problem; they make it so hard for you to finish high school. Why do we always have to lose credits every time we move? Why can't we stay in school when we're in a maternity residence?"

"Yeah, how do they expect us to become independent or whatever if we don't have a high school degree?"

"You know what bugs me," said Julia, "Why do they act like our baby's father can't come? Do they want to make us stay all single mothers? It's hard enough without telling the fathers they can't come visit."

"They treat us like we're still babies, like we can't even make the smallest decision about what kind of bottles to give, when they should be teaching us and supporting us instead."

"They don't even want us to know what our rights are."

"The food, put down the food stinks."

"We should get more allowance."

"Why can't we spend more than ten minutes on the phone?"

"We can't even get into the fridge."

In fifteen minutes, under the heading Problems/Questions I listed:

> Not enough homes?
>
> Don't know how many pregnant teens/teen mothers?
>
> Separations from children while waiting for placement
>
> Can't visit placements, first come first serve—Wilder
>
> FPs need training
>
> Education—mat. 'res. schools, lose credits
>
> Fathers of babies not allowed to visit
>
> Treat mo's like babies
>
> Can't make decisions about own children
>
> Don't know rights
>
> Not enough $$
>
> Allowance/job problem
>
> Can't use phone
>
> Not enough phone time
>
> Food stinks
>
> No access to fridge

Scribbling down their comments confirmed my conviction about the problems in the system. The teen mothers were identifying issues we had seen over and over again that were very important—whether they were with their kids, whether they were receiving the kind of support they needed to be good parents, and whether they could break the cycle of foster care. Obviously they were interested in more immediate concerns, which I considered to be the more mundane problems of foster care—the food, the weekly allowance that every teen complained about—that for me, at least, lacked import and seemed to distract from the larger problems. At this point, I decided it wasn't the time to draw a distinction. They were the teens' issues, not mine, and so all made it onto the list.

By this time, three hours had passed. Some babies were sleeping, some fussing. Some of the girls were walking the babies around the office to calm them; others were still focused on what we were writing. I was hungry and figured everyone else was too. It was time to quit for now.

"So what do we think of these problems? Can we try to come up with some ideas of what you all think should be done to fix them? Do you all want to meet again another time or not?

They agreed they wanted to meet again but not on a Saturday morning. Instead, they chose a Thursday evening, a couple of weeks away.

While the girls began to pack away the bottles and sippy cups and strap their babies into the snugglies and strollers, I went over to Xaranda. "Do you think you could stay for a couple of minutes? I want to talk to you about something."

She sat down next to my desk, holding James on her lap, murmuring to him, "Do I have to change you again already, mister?"

I tried to catch her eye, but she was focused on him, so I gave up and just began talking. "I really like what you said at the meeting today and how you spoke. You know we're thinking of turning this into a project where we try to reach a lot of girls and try to convince the city to change what it's doing. I think you'd be great at giving workshops to girls and also talking to social workers and maybe some government people about this. What do you think about coming to work for us part time?

She finally looked at me, "Whoa, this wasn't what I thought you were gonna say! I thought you was mad I was talking so much today."

We smiled at each other. "Well, why don't you think about it. I know you have a lot going on with James and getting yourself back in school and all, and we don't want to slow you down with this, but we'll be flexible and work with you on a schedule and all that."

"No, I don't need to think about it. Definitely, I'm interested—just have to see if I can get someone to watch James, but that shouldn't be a problem."

The rest of that fall, every other Thursday night we stayed late. The buzzer would ring. One by one, young women would bump up the steps with their strollers, lugging diaper bags, carrying babies, and holding their toddlers by the hands. Over the course of a couple of months, they became a cohesive group.

One night in early December Xaranda called the meeting to order. "Okay ladies! Kids go in the other room with the babysitters, we have work to do!" Kids parted from their mothers, and a sense of purpose took over. When we met two weeks before, the teen mothers had been debating what we as a group could do to try to change the way the foster care system was handling their cases. They had been going back and forth, and tonight we hoped to make some decisions about what action to take.

One of the things we had talked about was bringing a class action lawsuit claiming that the teens and babies had the right to be placed together in a safe home, with services if necessary.

Xaranda began with a report: "Now, we have been talking about this lawsuit. This week I talked with Liza, the lawyer from the firm Winston & Camp, who has been working with us. I've also been taking calls from girls who are interested in being part of it. If you want to be in a lawsuit it's called being a plaintiff, and we have to have all the plaintiffs sign papers called affidavits saying what happened to them."

"Liza wrote up a memo, which is a legal way for saying researching the laws and whatnot, and she is trying to figure out if or when we can file this lawsuit. Problem now is the girls we're trying to get to be plaintiffs are hard to keep track of because they move around a lot, and we are not having a good time keeping in touch. So that's where we are."

I knew from talking to Liza that she had had difficulty convincing the partners at her white shoe law firm to let her take on this case as a pro bono matter. She felt completely sympathetic to the teen mothers and outraged at the violation of their civil rights, particularly their right to raise their own children. She thought separating mothers and babies was clearly illegal, and she was eager to bring it to court. However, her firm was skeptical about getting involved with teenagers living in foster care who became pregnant. Liza delivered them a lengthy memo detailing how the city's policies and practices violated the U.S. Constitution as well as various federal and state statutes and finally got approval. But now we were having problems getting plaintiffs who would stick around, and I was getting worried.

"Why do you think these girls aren't staying in touch?" I asked.

"You know how it is," Xaranda shrugged, "you get moved, you got all these appointments with your caseworker, worrying about your baby, you trying to finish school, get a job, whatever. They want to do it, but also they're probably thinking big deal, another court case, how's this going to help me now when I need it? And this is all taking so many months, their situations are changing all the time."

She was right that the system did keep one from focusing on a long-term, big-picture change because of the day-to-day focus it encouraged.

"Are these plaintiffs, whatever, girls gonna get some money out of this?" asked Julia. "Because my cousin had a lawsuit when his car got hit by a bus. Brought the city to court and got a whole lot of money."

"For real? That's what we should do! Take them to court! Oooh, I can't wait to see my caseworker swear to tell the truth, and nothing but the truth— that'll be a first!"

They all burst out laughing, imagining their caseworkers on the stand before a judge and jury.

"Do you all want to go over what a class action lawsuit is?" I asked. "Probably none of you are going to see any money. This lawsuit is asking for the city to change its ways."

"Well," said Julia thoughtfully, "if it's not like my cousin where you get the money, you really don't have a lot of . . . what do you call it . . . to be a plaintiff."

"Incentive?" I asked, "But we've talked about this before. This class action lawsuit is not to win you money now; it's to change the laws or policies so the government treats everybody better. So we need to decide whether or not to keep trying to find plaintiffs and work on it or what."

I had mixed feelings as I asked this question. I was excited about us filing a lawsuit like this. As a law student, I had learned about how class actions were tools for social change. The treatment these teens and the babies suffered was truly outrageous and appeared to violate their rights in many instances. Also, I felt pressure to be involved in a "big" lawsuit, which could bring us some media attention, prestige, and funding. Many experienced advocates advised me a suit like this would force the city to change its policies, but I was less sure about that than they were.

Xaranda answered first, "I don't know if this lawsuit is a good idea. I mean, to find girls who want to go through this process is way too much. They got enough on their plates if you know what I mean. And we're hoping it's going to change the policies, but what's the chances of that happening. Look at the *Wilder* case—supposed to help us by preventing discrimination, but look, now it caused more problems by bringing on all these rules that just screwed us up." She made some good points.

Wilder was an example of a class action lawsuit that had unintended consequences over the years. The ACLU Children's Rights Project (now Children's Rights Inc.) brought the landmark lawsuit *Wilder v. Sugarman*. The suit attempted to ensure that the Catholic and Jewish foster care agencies, the agencies with bigger endowments and better services, did not discriminate against black Protestant children. The name plaintiff, Shirley Wilder, herself became a teen mother while in foster care.

Twenty-five years later the *Wilder* decision seemed to have little relevance. Now almost all the kids in the City foster care system were African American and Latino, including those at the private, wealthier agencies. Yet the laws established by *Wilder* prevailed. To comply with *Wilder* and prevent agencies from discriminating on the basis of race, the city forbade agencies from interviewing children, and on the flip side, teens could not visit agencies or potential placements. The city gave this as the reason it could not plan placements for teen mothers and babies. *Wilder*, despite its good intentions, had become part of the bureaucracy, creating more policies and rules that people followed but that hardly helped the kids. The city had even set up an office for something called the Wilder Panel, to oversee compliance.

As a lawyer for kids and then at YAC, I had seen that despite the big lawsuits against the system, kids and families still seemed trapped in the system. The hydralike system adapted to each lawsuit filed against it, sprouting a new bureaucratic head if one was cut off. Class actions became part of the static of the system or at least a force with which the system knew how to reckon. Suing the foster care system was part of the fabric of the bureaucracy. I had seen little improvement in the system as a result of these suits. In fact, many said the system was worse than ever. When we considered Xaranda's situation and the circumstances of the other teen mothers, we saw that the *Wilder* results, intended to remedy one problem, led to another. Populations and problems change over time, and court orders are fixed. Few actually blamed lawsuits for making things worse, but few credited them with great improvement, at least not the people most directly affected.

We held this discussion with the teens to involve them, the supposed beneficiaries of the lawsuit, from day one, and we hoped that their input would lead to seeking remedies substantially connected to their needs. Usually plaintiffs are little more than a name in a lawsuit, and the lawyers bringing the lawsuit consult only perfunctorily with those intended to benefit from it. Lawyers make the strategic decisions, and often these decisions, rather than the plaintiff's goals, control the eventual outcome.

Involving the teens as the prime players of the suit was undoubtedly a good idea but inevitably complicated the decision process further. Their individual interests were distinct from each other and certainly distinct from the lawyers' interests. For example, we had to explain that they probably wouldn't get any money out of this. In fact, we couldn't guarantee, even if successful, that the policy changes would occur in time to have any affect on their lives. They weren't being selfish or greedy in asking about this, simply practical. They had to plan for their own futures. The teens were interested in things that policy changes could not easily address: they wanted higher quality foster care placements; they wanted more respect, more freedom, better food, more time on the phone. They cared about these problems in addition to the constitutional right to be placed with their child.

In working toward bringing a class action lawsuit, we started to sense a conflict of interest. Increasingly, we had qualms about focusing these young women's energy and resources on a battle that was both bigger than them and trivial to their lives. They needed to focus on challenges like finishing high school, applying to college, finding work and apartments, taking care of their children. People like me and the other adults involved with YAC, who were in relatively secure positions in life, were not dealing with these problems as urgent day-to-day matters.

After a brief silence, the teen mothers jumped in.

"Yeah, well, we want to protect our kids and our rights and make the system better."

"Don't want other people have to go through what I been through, that's for sure."

"Is this the best way to do it, though?" I asked, feeling more confident that they would figure out the right thing to do.

"You know what I think," said Xaranda, "We got to get our stories in newspapers, on TV, in the magazines, for people to hear about."

"Or we should invite the people from CWA to dinner or a party or something and tell them what the problems are, then they'll change them."

"We should go on the subways and hand out papers. Ask for money too!"

"Write to Hillary Clinton and Congress!"

They were getting a little punchy, and we couldn't follow through on all their ideas, but some were solid. During the next month, we debated and hammered out a strategy: survey more teen mothers, collect information, develop some policy recommendations, and present them to CWA in a report advocating for change. Together, we decided this was a reasonable approach to trying to help the teen parents and their babies.

Working together throughout the next few months, the teen mothers transformed themselves into activists, organizers, and advocates. Led by Xaranda, they came together as a group, learning new skills, and honing their natural instincts as advocates. They were writing letters, collecting data, making phone calls, and giving public speaking presentations. To confirm that the problems the teen mothers faced were indeed systemic as we suspected, we wrote and distributed surveys to approximately eighty young women who were pregnant or had babies. We did research that included the group's own stories, along with dozens of interviews and surveys with young women, front-line caseworkers, professionals, and administrators in the field.

The group decided to call their report *Caring for our Children: Improving the Foster Care System*. We were proud of the report; it not only documented a need and made solid recommendations, but, unlike the typical policy report produced by professionals writing about the teens, it offered the point of view of the young people caught up in the system.

Child welfare policy reports are regular publications of the foster care industry. Year in and year out, government officials—mayor, commissioners, comptroller, public advocate, borough presidents, and legislators—issue reports about foster care. Most follow a pattern: history of the issue, anecdotes, statistical analysis, and policy recommendations for change. The report's release often warrants a press conference or an article or two. Sometimes an ad hoc coalition or task force forms to work on or monitor the issue. This report gave the teen mothers a chance to highlight what they had been through and what they thought should change.

Now they were ready to present themselves and their work to the world. For all their efforts, we were unsure who would listen. We were in a conference room in the Empire State Building, where we had invited dozens of people such as community leaders, supporters, and the media to learn about the young women's experiences and their ideas for change. The teen mothers had reached a milestone by learning methods of the establishment to reach their own goals

"Close the shades, please!" said Missy. "I'm going to be sick, you know I can't stand heights."

"You're in one of the tallest buildings in the world. What do you expect?" laughed Julia.

"Would someone grab the end of that banner? The tape isn't holding it up!" complained Xaranda, pointing at the Teen Mothers Task Force banner hung on the wall.

"Ooooh, look, it's the person from that TV show," whispered Viviana.

"Okay, everybody, take your seats, remember to speak loudly and in the microphone!" said Xaranda, in charge now. She smiled at the audience and started, "Good morning, and thank you for coming. We are going to begin by reading some quotes from young women who filled out surveys we gave them last year."

Missy read, "The problems I had are really bad. I had to leave my child in the hospital until placement was found. I feel mothers should know ahead of time exactly where they are going with their children."

Julia continued, "I was told it would be hard for them to find us a placement, so they kept putting me in temporary foster care. This was emotionally troubling for me because I was already uprooted from my regular home environment and now they was sticking me from house to house with people that couldn't relate to me."

Viviana said, "The most difficult thing about planning for my future and my child's future is wondering where my next placement is going to be. Things would be better if I knew where my child and I were going to be placed."

They started out with their voices a little shaky, but as the meeting went on, they sat up straighter and began talking more forcefully. They reported on the problems we had identified and their recommendations for changes. The city should keep data on the numbers of foster care teens who become pregnant, streamline procedures to allow new babies and mothers to be placed together, allow pregnant girls to visit placements, avoid disrupting their education, allow them to hold part time jobs, and so on. All these recommendations were reasonable and seemed feasible as well as cost effective.

When the teen mothers concluded their presentation, their relief was palpable, and the audience applauded long and loudly for them.

As they had hoped, that evening, the local TV news featured their presentation and report. The program showed Xaranda playing with James, as the reporter talked about how the teen mothers organized to try to change the system. The New York Times ran a piece about the teens, with a big photo. The teen mothers were thrilled, except they were insulted by a line that referred to them as "hardscrabble Cinderellas secretly waiting for a prince." As usual, they were quick to spot the cliché and resist being typecast. They were aware of the stigma they faced and the challenges they had to overcome. They wrote a letter to the Times to criticize the stereotyping.

All in all, the report appeared a success. The next step was meeting with CWA administrators to get them to implement the recommendations for change. We set up a meeting to talk to the city about the problems we found and the recommendations we made.

"Well, let's see . . . oh yes, your report, is this it?" said the assistant commissioner, picking up the copy Xaranda slid across the table to her. She, Nancy, and I were sitting across the table from assistant commissioner Betty Johnson. The conference table was a series of smaller tables pushed together so twenty or more could sit down, but it was just the five of us in the office that seemed coated in a layer of brown dust and gray grime. The light filtered dimly through dirty windows. We were at CWA headquarters in downtown Manhattan, and I felt depressed that a government agency responsible for fifty thousand plus children was in such a state of disrepair.

"So what you're saying," Johnson quickly interceded, after we were allowed to give a two minute recap of our purpose, "is that we need more placements for these young ladies and their babies. Well, it's just a matter of funding you see. You know there's been a freeze on the budgets, and we have many positions unfilled and let go. We have applied for approval to open one hundred more beds and are communicating with OFCS and ACF and DFYS and have tried going through TASA and those are all pending. But you see there are different FYs, and when we get the tentative approval, we can issue the RFP for comp bidding. But of course that depends on the rates and who is eligible under HRA regs and . . ."

I felt a headache coming on, and the overheating and closed windows suddenly seemed unbearable. I felt my eyes glaze over until Xaranda's voice jolted me.

"Excuse me one moment. I do hate to interrupt, but you understand we're talking about newborn babies separated from their mothers here? I mean, I'm sure what you're saying is very important, but we would really appreciate if you could just explain what are you going to do about this. . . . Now, do you even know how many teen mothers there are? Because y'know that's one thing we're saying, if you kept better track of who is waiting for a mother-child . . ."

Everything we had done up to that point was worth seeing Xaranda take charge. Even if nothing changed, I felt we had accomplished so much by empowering Xaranda to speak to authority figures like that. Meanwhile, the assistant commissioner seemed oblivious.

"Our coding doesn't allow us to look at who is a teen parent in the system. We just know there are babies and mothers, and we wait for the social workers to request placements. It would take an overhaul of the mxyplyx system, and jumbly mumbly department has to go . . ."

Could they possibly be any more bureaucratic? I wondered who was crazier—them or us for thinking we could do anything here.

Xaranda pushed forward. "Look, we just think it would be really helpful if y'all sitting in these mmmm nice offices up here at the top floors could hear from the real people, you know, us teens, once in a while. So would you consider that? You know, setting up a group to meet with you every month or something?"

While we had discussed our strategy for the meeting before, I was still impressed with how Xaranda was using her advocacy skills to present a reasonable solution and not be deterred or thrown off track.

Checking her watch, the assistant commissioner said, "That's a fine idea. You can set it up with my scheduler. Okay, is that it?"

Clearly, the assistant commissioner thought that was it.

Six months later, I was in the ballroom of a midtown hotel filled with round tables, each with flowers in the middle and baskets of croissants and muffins. Xaranda was late, and I was annoyed. This morning, one of our funders for the teen mothers project was honoring Xaranda for her work at YAC, for organizing young mothers in foster care. The program had started—where was she? For the past year, she had been incredibly reliable, but lately something seemed off, and I was worried she wouldn't show.

The emcee was a newscaster in full makeup and a red jacket, announcing the awardees from each group. I saw in the program that we were next. I kept looking around toward the entrance, and with relief, I saw Xaranda walking in. I stood up and in a rushed whisper said, "Thank God, I was getting nervous. Are you okay? James okay? Why are you so late? I told you 8:30. Did you have trouble finding it?"

"Xaranda Powers!" the emcee said, and I grabbed Xaranda's jacket off her back and gave her a little shove toward the stage. "Go get your award!"

Xaranda, as usual, composed herself. She smiled and gave a nice speech about how she had such a rough time and wanted to help other children in foster care. To applause, she accepted her framed award and left the stage to come back to the table where I had sat back down. She picked up her coat I had hung on the back of a chair.

"What are you doing? It's not cold. You were great up there! Come on, sit down. Here, have a muffin or something. There are some of the people from the foundation I want you to meet."

"No, I don't really feel like it. I got to go."

"What do you mean you have to go? Is James okay?" I was perplexed.

"He's fine. I have to go, that's all. I don't really have time to stay."

I could hardly believe it. Here was this amazing event, and she was an honoree, and she wouldn't sit down to eat a blueberry muffin? Was it too much for her to say hi to the foundation people who just gave her an award? Where was she running to? I knew I should be sympathetic, but I was feeling annoyed. I had worked really hard to get this grant and had put in a lot of time helping Xaranda and also in nominating her for this award. I stood up to talk to her so others couldn't hear our conversation. "What's up, Xaranda? I mean, are you upset about something?"

"No, no, I'm just going now. See ya." And out she walked.

I just watched her go out the entrance, then quickly followed her. In the lobby outside the ballroom, I caught up with her. "Are you okay?"

"Yes, Betsy, I'm fine. You want to know the truth, I'm better than fine because I'm done. I got my award certificate here, and you got what you need, and I'm done."

"What do you mean, what I need?"

"You got what you need, the grant, and whatever else you're trying to do with YAC. You have used me and my name to get it, and that's fine, whatever, but now I'm going. I really don't need this any more."

"What are you talking about? You've been part of this whole project! You've been the leader of this project, and we've bent over backward to make sure you can do things you want to do."

"Whatever. If that's how you want to think of it, I think different." She walked away again. I watched her go. I was stunned, hurt, and angry. I felt like I was going to cry.

I should have seen this coming. Obviously I got a lot from these relationships with the teens, and they got something from them too. I thought about the power imbalance. From observing and listening to teens talk about their relationships with other adults working in the foster care system, I knew the power struggles could be complex and fierce. The adults have control over decisions about the teens' lives, and the teens are struggling to get control. Once Xaranda told me, "I used to mess with my social workers' heads, telling them, 'you know the only reason you have a job is because my mother couldn't take care of me.'" When she told me this, I told myself our relationship was different because I was the lawyer for the kids, their advocate. But now I wasn't sure it was different; after all, our jobs at YAC did depend on the teens being in foster care, and they knew that.

In many of the early relationships I had with teens at YAC—such as Carlos, Jenny, and Xaranda— what happened followed a pattern. They came to me or were referred to me for some help with their court case, with changing school, with finding a new placement for school credit. I helped them, and then I asked them if they would help out at YAC, working but also sharing their experiences to promote what I was interested in doing—creating a rights book, producing a video, giving workshops. The YAC and I benefited by getting a lot back and also by building our reputation in the community as a place that involved kids, that provided high level help to teens, and also engaged them as equals. I built on their stories and felt good about myself and YAC. The kids who worked with us for a while knew they had struck a bargain. They were willing to stay with YAC as long as they were getting something back—new skills, a sense of pride and community, a paycheck for helping out, awards, and recognition.

In more than one instance, a teen got angry and acted out. Xaranda had reached that point. When this happened, I couldn't help but realize that we were in such different situations. I had choices they didn't have. I had a college degree, a law school degree, an apartment, a family supporting me in many ways. They didn't. Many also didn't have the resources or skills to cope with making a positive change from working with us to leaving and going on to something else.

I was also conscious that in these relationships, I was in some way working out my own issues, especially about having children. Sooner or later everyone working with kids in foster care (or probably kids in any setting) realizes it brings up a lot of personal issues—how one feels about one's own parents, children, homes. At this point in my life, I didn't yet have kids and neither did most of the women working with me at YAC. Through the teen mothers project, we not only worked with these young mothers, but we also hung out with them, going on day trips to the beach, inviting them out of the city on the weekends. We held their babies, played with their toddlers, and learned from all of them. For all their troubles, we were in awe of the teen mothers, who appeared terribly competent to us as they changed diapers and gave bottles and read books to their children. We had relationships that crossed the line from being purely professional to satisfying other needs—to learn something and to feel good about our own lives.

Painful as the ending with Xaranda was, I knew it had value. She accepted that she had to continue on the path to independence and break away from YAC and from me. She had to move on, and though that hurt, I had to see it as a sign of strength on both of our parts. For Xaranda, I wished I could have helped her make the ending with YAC in a way that celebrated her accomplishments here and her ability to make meaningful relationships with us. This painful incident reminded me that many foster care teens, like most of us, had a difficult time making transitions and endings, something we would address later on in our work at YAC.

I briefly tried to reach her, leaving her phone messages and sending a note, but she disappeared from my life for the next six months. Then, out of the blue, she called one day, as though nothing had happened. She was back in school and had a part time job at a fast food restaurant. James was fine, walking and saying a few words. The foster home was okay; she was hanging in there. She was friendly but a little distant. I was relieved and happy to hear from her.

In the meantime, after a few meetings with CWA, the teen mothers' group started to fall apart. Like Xaranda, the original group of young women was beginning to move on. They were busy figuring out how they would survive post–foster care and couldn't afford to spend their time changing the system. We would have had to recruit and cultivate a new group of teen mothers. The more we examined the issue, the more our hesitancy grew. These mothers had many issues in their own lives and in planning their futures. Involving them in policy battles could be a costly diversion from focusing on important educational, economic, and career issues.

Observing the young mothers' strength, talents, energy, endurance, and commitment to goals was valuable. With so many challenges in their lives, they continued to move toward objectives of independence, good parenting, community strengthening, and personal fulfillment. At the same time, we knew that a majority of teens, whether they were young parents or not, were continuing to fail at achieving successful independence. The cost in wasted lives and government support during their adulthood remained disturbing. We could keep trying to force change on a resistant system, not established or conducive for preparing teens for independence, or we could develop a program that would empower teens to take control of their futures and prepare for independence. If we succeeded in demonstrating that caring adults could educate teens to achieve their goals, perhaps we could embolden the many professionals in the system who wanted to take action and rise above the bureaucracy's inertia.

We recognized that this would be risky and that others might view it as "Pollyannaish." Yet, after observing the system deny countless teens with extraordinary strength and natural intellectual and creative ability an opportunity to even come close to their potential, and in considering the immense waste in community resources to support these individuals for the rest of their lives, we felt we had to take a risk. Perhaps our positions as outsiders to the system, perhaps our skepticism toward the mental illness approach, and perhaps our refusal to accept the pervasive low expectations for teens in foster care might work favorably for us in trying a different approach.

One unexpected outcome of organizing and eventually disbanding the teen mothers' group was that we developed new understandings about prejudices and expectations. Probably no other group of teenagers in foster care is more stigmatized and engenders the lowest expectations for success. In working closely with this group, as well as all the other teens, we realized that we wanted to maintain the highest expectations possible and provide every opportunity and support for them to reach those expectations. We would not prejudge a teen to failure or substandard possibilities because of his or her past. We set this standard not because we didn't recognize that some teens would fail but because we saw no conclusive way to judge who would fail and who would succeed.

Prejudices are hard to eradicate, and I've tried to be conscious of my own. Although I stand by my belief that young women who have babies while in foster care are capable of achieving significant goals, it's easy to focus on the problems rather than the possibilities. For example, last year we ran a self-advocacy seminar for foster care teens, and I learned that Alicia, one of the girls registered for the class, was pregnant and due to give birth in a month. Despite or perhaps because of my work with teen mothers over the years, I said, "Forget it, she's never going to be able to finish the program! You can't imagine how insane her life is going to be."

She was facing the same problems Xaranda and the others did. Her mother put her in foster care, after which the city moved her from group home to RTC and then placed her in special ed. She got pregnant in an RTC, moved to a maternity residence that held up her paperwork till she gave birth, was separated from her baby for ten days after giving birth, and went into one home after another. Nonetheless, she wanted to enroll in our self-advocacy program because she was sure it would help her reach her goal of eventually working in journalism.

Because we couldn't and wouldn't discourage her from signing up, Alicia started the class. She missed one class to give birth, came back to class the following week, and completed the twelve-week seminar. She's graduating high school now and applying to college to study journalism. What if we all held to our prejudices and diminished expectations and discouraged her from planning and working toward her future?

Like many foster care teens, Alicia would love to make the system better and sometimes daydreams about how she would run an agency. We know she faces a myriad of problems in foster care, and we don't discourage her thinking about how to change those, but we strongly encourage her to focus on her own goals for the future—going to college, providing for her daughter, start-ing a career in journalism. Alicia learned her self-advocacy skills to help her plan a path out of foster care and be a good parent for her baby girl. Unlike the work we did ten years ago at YAC with the teen mothers, we are now help-ing Alicia and other teens focus on their future.

In trying, and admittedly failing, to change the foster care system for teen mothers and their babies, we took an approach that was unusual, at least in New York City at the time. We strongly believed in the value and importance of involving youth in every single aspect of our system reform projects. From the outset, we believed that the real child welfare experts are the children and parents caught up in the system; they have first-hand knowledge of poverty, of how families are broken up, of how overloaded and undertrained case-workers are, of how isolated the bureaucrats can become, and of how infuri-ating and sometimes cruel the legal system can be. Since we started YAC, it became more acceptable for professional advocates to include the clients (children, parents) in critiquing and reforming the system. Child welfare pro-fessionals invite them to participate in meetings and conferences, speak on panels, and so forth, so real people can voice their needs in the dialogue about child welfare policy and practice.

When we involved the teen mothers on policy advocacy (similar to other projects we did at the time, such as advocating around issues of HIV testing for kids) we saw that the teens were thoughtful, analytical, and insightful about both problems and solutions, and they could be effective advocates. The young women's interest in helping their peers and their community demonstrated a strong commitment to issues beyond themselves. They were living in precarious situations, putting their energy into a collaborative pro-ject that probably would take so long it wouldn't even benefit them directly. They dug into the project with zeal, and they learned something from it. Their natural skills navigating a system, the foster care system, were devel-oped in the policy arena. We saw that teenagers, even those in stressful con-ditions, can

- master intricacies of laws and policies;
- think analytically and apply that to their own situations;
- problem solve using new concepts and skills, as opposed to

resorting to the methods that the foster care system usually responds to;

- engage in a group process based on hard work, not fun and games; and

- commit themselves to a future goal.

The teen mothers' project ultimately was useful, as we furthered our understanding of the importance of self-advocacy for teens and learned methods to teach self-advocacy. It became increasingly apparent that teaching self-advocacy skills was an excellent strategy for helping young people as individuals and eventually changing the community and the system for the better. When young people understand and use self-advocacy, they can reach their personal, educational, and professional goals. They will then act as role models for other young people. They will be in a position of more security, and perhaps they will have more power to affect change in the system. Adults' perceptions of young people in foster care will change as they realize that many of these young people can and will succeed one day.

5

Preparing
for Independent Living

| Leonard | Through working with teens like Carlos, Jenny, Xaranda,

and others, we began to see that the system's greatest failure was not that it sometimes mistreated teens, but that it failed to prepare teens for either college or employment. The system consistently failed to provide teens with meaningful skills to succeed as adults. Throughout our work representing teens in the legal system, educating child welfare professionals, teaching teens about their rights, or organizing youth to advocate for policy changes, we kept coming back to this central problem—too many teens failed after foster care. During this period at Youth Advocacy Center, we observed that even kids who appeared to be doing well in foster care struggled once they left the system.

The foster care bureaucracy clearly was designed not for teens, but for the temporary protection of infants and small children at risk of abuse or neglect. It was not intended to raise adolescents to adulthood. Policies and practices that served short-term goals, primarily daily maintenance and behavior supervision, were not suitable for managing the lives of tens of thousands of teens in the system for extended periods of time.

By law, the system was supposed to prepare teens for something called independent living. The federal and state governments passed well-intentioned laws, meant to remedy the problem of foster care teens becoming homeless and welfare dependent. However, these laws and policies had not translated into successful programs,[1] as we judged from the numbers of teens who were still leaving foster care without a place to live, a way to support themselves, or a set of relationships with people in the community who could help them. In New York, foster care agencies were required to offer teens a total of sixteen hours per year of independent living training. This provided a total of two days, only one half percent of a year in foster care, which reflected the low priority this was given by the foster care system.

Through our work we saw that many dedicated professionals in the foster care programs received inadequate training and supervision to provide consistent and meaningful programs to prepare teens for independence. Administrators and policy makers supported present independent living programs as a mandated responsibility, but rarely as a priority or with conviction that such services could produce significant results. We didn't know what caused this lack of support: was there an underlying belief that foster care teens were destined to a dependent life no matter what help they received? Or did promoting safety, managing behavior, and finding suitable foster homes simply overwhelm all other initiatives?

We began to focus on the independent living policies and programming as an area that needed change. If we could offer a new concept and effective model of preparing teens for successful independence, then we could help individual teens and simultaneously demonstrate to the system that it could prepare teens for lasting independence.

Betsy

We first met Leonard at one of these independent living workshops, where Jenny and I were presenting a rights and advocacy program. Carly Nostrand, the independent living worker at Leonard's agency, invited us to present after her workshop on finding a job. Paul and I respected Carly's commitment to teens and her desire to see them succeed after foster care. We had become acquainted when she attended meetings we ran for foster care agency staff to learn about our work. Carly was in her early forties, mature, and funny. She empathized with the teens. She had shared with us that she was in foster care as a child and relished the opportunity to help teens who are "going through what I've gone through."

Carly expressed frustration with all the impediments in her way as she tried to prepare teens for independence. She was charged with ensuring that none of the one hundred or more teens at her agency aged out to homelessness. The agency focused on preventing negative outcomes rather than supporting positive outcomes, such as initiating a career or pursuing additional education or training. Teens picked up the nuance of the agency's focus, and it added to their sense of discouragement and self-defeat. Carly felt she was competing against the agency's other priorities—continuing crises, doubling up on staffing responsibilities given problems in attracting and retaining qualified staff, fulfilling mandated reporting, urgently finding beds for teens, and so on. Child welfare professionals accepted that the goal of preparing teens for independent living was near the end of a long list of mandates and other priorities. As if this were not enough, Carly was overwhelmed by many of the daily crises faced by teens. Since Carly was a resource and advocate for them, teens came to her with the endless day-to-day problems they faced while in care.

To educate or train teens for independence, Carly's agency, like most others, offered workshops to teens, usually once a month. For these workshops, Carly had to follow detailed government mandates about what to teach—essentially a long list of topics from housekeeping, to budgeting, sexual safety, to finding an apartment. It would be virtually impossible for anyone to cover all these topics effectively in two days of workshops, and few (it seemed to us) attempted. Moreover, most professionals conducting independent living (IL) workshops were never trained for teaching job skills or, more important, how to relate the process to the lives of the teens in their care.

Throughout the years we had visited dozens of agencies and observed their IL workshops. Typically, teens that attended were either inactive—eyes glazed over during lectures—disruptive, or engaged in some type of group game. Some staff assigned to conduct IL workshops simply read out loud from pamphlets or brochures. More often than not, the IL presenter lectured teens about drug abuse and sexually transmitted diseases. While these are undoubtedly important topics, we were frustrated by the lack of attention to planning for higher education, careers, employment, and housing.

Turnout for IL workshops was spotty, with perhaps only 20 to 50 percent of eligible teens attending workshops regularly.[2] The agency offered teens cash (from fifteen dollars to twenty-five dollars) to attend each session, but some were paid even if they didn't show; such payment sent the message that young people were not required or expected to attend independent living workshops. Some would stop by at the time the workshop was offered just to get the money. Teens often wandered in and out of workshops well after they had been scheduled to begin.

Universally, expectations for the IL meetings were low, a feeling that contributed to the teens' disinterest and lack of engagement. Workshop leaders rarely expected teens to participate in any intellectually challenging way. There was a pervasive belief that teens were so brittle they would crack under any pressure. Many IL leaders, assigned an overwhelming challenge and fearing teens' fragility, diverted them to programming that would make the stay in foster care a little bit less devastating and more pleasant. So, many IL workshops were devoted to playing games, eating pizza, and planning an annual outing to an amusement park.

We knew Carly was seriously trying to engage teens in preparing for the future, so I was interested to sit in on her jobs workshop. Carly's presentation was being held on a Saturday morning, at the main office of the agency, located on prime Manhattan real estate (a not unusual phenomenon because these agencies have been around a long time and have built up substantial assets). I had instructions to knock on the gray metal service entrance door. A guard talking on the phone let me in and said, "Conference room, fourth floor," pointing to the elevator.

The fourth floor had the depressing quiet of deserted administrative offices on the weekend, with silent copiers, coffee machines, and computers. The filling out of forms and budgets and reports was suspended, to be continued on Monday, to be continued indefinitely, for perhaps another 125 years.

I wandered through halls until I found the conference room, a large space with industrial carpet and accordion divider walls. Bagels, potato chips, and liter soda bottles were laid out on a folding table. A dozen colored balloons lay on the floor not far from the tables, as though a three-year-old's birthday party had just cleared out of the room. I couldn't imagine how this setting could be conducive for educating teens about the world of work and independence.

The foster care system consistently ignores the possibility that some, if not all teens, have some intellectual curiosity and capacity. One day Jenny told us they used encyclopedias in her independent living workshop. Paul and I got excited, thinking, oh great, they teach them to do research, how interesting. When we asked what they were researching with the encyclopedias, Jenny said, "Research? What are you talking about? We walk on them."

"Walk on them?" Paul asked, sure he had misunderstood.

"Yeah, you know, they spread them out across the room, and we try to hop across on them without touching the floor."

I caught the eye of Jenny sitting against the wall. She smiled and raised her eyebrows and chin to gesture to me, patting the empty seat next to her. Like many teens we worked with, she was still wearing her black puffy down jacket in the warm room. Attachment to jackets often covers up the fact that teens are wearing the same clothes as the day before, or it expresses an unwillingness to commit to staying.

We sat together, looking at the eleven teens sitting at the tables arranged in a U shape. They appeared to be between fourteen and twenty years old, a wide age range. They seemed surprisingly awake for a Saturday morning. Many, traveling at least an hour from distant parts of the Bronx, had walked through deserted blocks to wait shivering on outside platforms for trains. They were dressed in a neat and careful teen style, clean Nikes or construction work boots, baggy jeans and cargo pants, sweatshirts. Girls' hair was braided or straightened, boys' hair cut close to their heads.

Two teens sat at a table separate from the group. They were acting out a job interview. The girl, about seventeen, leaned forward on her elbows and concentrated on the paper in front of her, and the boy, about eighteen, sat with his legs straight out crossed at the ankles. "So now, let's see. What experience do you have for this position?" she asked him officiously.

"I'm the star center on my team, and I also have an agent to sell my beats," he replied and laughed into his hand.

"Okay," broke in Carly, getting up from her seat. "Thank you Desiree, thank you Robert. Any comments?" She addressed the group.

Silence, blank stares, and cuticle examining. Finally, Leonard, a roundish boy with a small gold earring raised his hand and answered. "He shouldn't have said ummmm so much."

"That's right!" Carly said, walking around the middle of the horseshoe like Oprah. "No 'ummms' or 'likes.' Make eye contact," she demonstrated holding out her hand as if to shake Leonard's hand. "Say 'How do you do, my name is Carly Nostrand!' not (looking down, talking softly) ummm my name is ummmm Carly.' Show enthusiasm!"

"Anything else? What about how you look?" Carly seemed used to getting a weak response to her questions. "No hats, gentlemen, and ladies, earrings smaller than a dime. Remember, the first impression is the best impression!" This kind of advice, typical in foster care, might be correct (or not), but IL coordinators present it as a fixed rule to memorize; they often do not convey the significance or reason for such rules. Furthermore, this approach distracts from the most fruitful means of making a positive impression—that is, demonstrating an understanding of the employer's needs and presenting one's individual strengths to support those needs. Finally, such an instructional method ignores the natural resistance foster care and non-foster care teens have to being presented with just rules and dictates from and of the adult world, without any understanding and appreciation for their purpose.

A girl spoke up. "Can I say something? I've been to so many classes like this, and this is what they always tell us—dress nice, look them in the eye. We hear this over and over. What I want to know is, when they ask you about experience, I'm like, I've never had a job before. That's why I'm here, to get experience. So my problem is, how do I get experience without a job?"

"Excellent question," said Carly. I thought, good, this girl had raised a real issue. I was glad Carly wasn't brushing her off. Carly walked over to the middle table and rifled through some papers till she found the one she wanted. "These are suggestions for getting work experience without holding a job." She read from the paper, "You can volunteer at a hospital. Work in the family business . . ." She paused as if to say something else but didn't. This suggestion seemed to catch her by surprise, as if she were at a loss as to how to translate this into the world of the kids in this room. She cleared her throat and continued, "You can join a club. You can teach a Sunday school class or be a camp counselor. You can clean a park."

Carly was doing her best, but clearly the students found little relevance. I wondered if it was because she was resorting to what was typical in these workshops—lecturing the kids from some outdated manual, instead of confronting the question with thoughtfulness or using her own considerable life experience in the workforce. A boy with a dark green bandanna tied on his head half laughed at her. "I can't volunteer because I need money. I'm going to be on my own in a few months! Anyway, shoot, how'm I gonna get to a job without carfare." He stared at her for a moment, and then looked away in disgust, mumbling something that sounded like, you crazy.

Carly considered the situation. "Well then, you should try temp agencies. They put ads in the papers." The boy rolled his eyes.

Leonard raised his hand again. "Ms. Nostrand, I quit my last job at McDonalds. I was upset because I can only work in the afternoon, and they put me on the late night shift, and the group home won't even let me work then. So should I put it on my resume?"

Carly responded, "Well it's okay to say you quit a job, if you tell them why."

Leonard looked puzzled. From experience, I knew that he and the others understood they needed help with jobs, schooling, housing, and so much else, and they were trying to pick up the clues, make some sense of the rules of the world. Presenting IL skills in this fragmented, rule-oriented approach made it almost impossible to develop a coherent understanding of the employer-employee relationship, let alone the process of applying for and getting a job. The students' efforts at engagement, although minimal, suggested that they understood they had a lot to learn, but that the approach and content clearly had little resonance or relevance to their lives.

Analyzing the existing IL workshops and comparing them with approaches we were using with teens sharpened our understanding of the methodologies that we needed to properly prepare teens for the successful transition to independence. This understanding helped us in developing an approach to our future self-advocacy seminars. High on the list was the necessity to elevate expectations, for both teens about themselves and staff about the teens. We also became convinced that teens needed to be more fully engaged in the learning process; they needed to become active, not passive, learners. We needed to shift more responsibility for learning to them. In addition, it was vital that the curriculum material coincide with their lives to allow students to see the real possibilities for them. Independent living programs needed to expose teens to more real stories and information about the outside community. Finally, teens needed to have some primary experience in interacting with a respected member of the outside community, completely unconnected to their lives in foster care.

Toward the end of her workshop, Carly warmly introduced Jenny, who gave a presentation about the importance of advocating for oneself. The teens, as usual, were interested and seemed to want to know more. After Jenny's presentation, Leonard approached and asked if he could become a Youth Advocate, too.

He began coming by the office about once a week, occasionally co-leading workshops and attending meetings with us. Carly had told me that Leonard was considered one of the good kids in foster care by just about everyone, and I soon saw why. He had a winning smile and a cooperative attitude. He just didn't seem like a troubled youth, though he had been through his share of problems that landed him in foster care. For the past three years he'd been living in a group home where he had been doing everything he was supposed to—just finished his GED at a community program, applied to college, got a job working part time at a video store.

A couple of months later, Leonard disappeared. When he stopped showing up, we called Carly, and she said he had not been in to see her either; she wasn't sure why. When Leonard eventually came by the office after several months, I was glad to see him, but I was concerned. He didn't look quite right. His brown eyes were a little bloodshot, and his skin looked ashy. His hair, usually neatly cropped close to his head, was shaggy. The navy t-shirt he was wearing had a stain on it. I wondered if he was sick.

I asked him where he'd been and told him we'd missed him. "Yeah, I've missed you guys too, but it's been a lot for me being on my own since I got discharged on my birthday."

I felt like kicking myself. I'd been busy with so many other things that I didn't pay attention to the fact that Leonard was hitting his twenty-first birthday; he had to leave foster care to go on his own. A lot of people would say he was lucky because in many other states this happens at age eighteen. I apologized for missing his birthday and asked him what he'd been doing and where he had been staying. He answered in a monotone, with his eyes down.

"I had no idea it would be like this. Right before I left care, I found an apartment, a studio. It was really important to me to have my own space after all these years. The agency was cool about helping me sign a lease. They even gave me a few hundred dollars discharge grant to buy some furniture and pots and stuff. You're going to laugh, but my first night there I just turned up the music, and took off my clothes, and danced around! I was like, it's mine, all mine! For the first time I got a place of my own!" After allowing himself a small smile, he gave a big shaky sigh signaling a sense of defeat, feelings of being overwhelmed, and the likelihood of tears.

"I had a little money saved up, but I guess it wasn't enough. After two months I couldn't pay the rent, and I had to leave. So then I ended up staying with whoever, aunts, cousins, friends, but nobody really has room for me, and I can't really pay them anything now, so I'm just doing whatever to get by."

I was frightened to ask what "whatever" was. I thought of the kids, now young adults, I knew who left foster care and called to tell me that they had gone down south to find a long lost relative and were now living in an abandoned car, or those who stayed around New York trying to make ends meet by stripping to make money. I was sure some turned to other, less legal ways, to make money too, feeling they had no other options to survive. Every professional working with teens in the foster care system knew of these experiences. Then I thought of myself and my family members and friends, and tried to imagine how any of us would have made it if we were cut off from all support at eighteen, or even twenty-one. If you come from a relatively intact family and a middle-class background, it is hard to appreciate how difficult it is if you have to start from scratch with everything.

I tried to find something positive Leonard might be doing. "What about school? I remember you were so excited about attending college. Are you going now?"

"Well, I started, but . . . I fell behind in the rent after two months, and the landlord sent me these letters . . . finally changed the locks on me. I need a place to live to go to college! And how am I going to afford it? The video store won't let me come back. I missed too many days with everything going on. And now how am I going to get a job looking like this, with nowhere to live?"

I asked him gently if he had someplace to stay, at the same time thinking of the best shelters I knew for single young men and whom I could call to get him a bed.

"I'm okay for this week, but my aunt is not going to put me up forever, she already made that clear, got her own troubles without me sleeping on the living room floor." Now he seemed angry on top of confused.

Who could blame him? Leonard had run headlong into the problems teens faced leaving foster care. They become overwhelmed by attempting to achieve all the intertwined necessities of life at once—a place to live, a way to pay for it, education in order to get a better income, family and a community to count on as a safety net. A wave of complications from poverty had engulfed Leonard and knocked him down. He had to put aside his dreams of success to survive day to day.

I was especially sad because Leonard had had a lot going for him before he left foster care. He was at a group home that was helping him as best they could. He was admitted to a college. He even had some family members who were somewhat available to help him and a legal system that should have provided some protection.

"Called my legal aid lawyer," he said with some disgust. "She told me she had to close my case 'cause I'm too old. The judge who used to hear my case, I know he really liked me, but guess that doesn't help now." The family courts had not been much help for teens aging out of the system. The court could only review a teen's case until he turned eighteen years old. At a family court hearing sometime before the teen's eighteenth birthday, the judge would ask the agency representative what the plan was and the caseworker would reply "03," which was the city code for independent living. The judge would nod, and if the teen were present in the courtroom, he or she might inquire briefly about how he was doing in placement and then wish him luck.

I asked Leonard if he had gone back to his agency for help, which seemed like a good option since he had been a star in the group home. "They feel bad, but said they can't give me a bed because I'm over age. They gave me referrals to other places, like shelters or something, and you know, said they'd keep me in mind if they have any job openings or anything like that . . . ," he trailed off. "The thing is," he explained, "they have a lot of other kids who are going to be aging out soon, and they got to get their papers ready and all." The harsh reality was that more young people were always going to be leaving care.

Leonard was a serious person who had always been interested in ways to make the system better, so I took a different, less personal direction and asked him what he thought the agency could do differently to prepare kids for aging out of foster care. He thought a moment. "At my group home it was really easy for me not to do anything to prepare for the future. No one was on my back to do anything because I was one of the good kids, not a squeaky wheel. Then I get out, and reality hits, and I have to start paying my own bills and doing everything on my own all of a sudden. It was like a set up."

The typical foster care home life does not encourage teens to take on personal responsibility for planning their futures. Unlike parents, who ordinarily accept some responsibility for their child long past the age of twenty-one, the foster care system's responsibility is temporary and short-term, ending by, at latest, age twenty-one. The system is not accountable for young people after they leave foster care. An agency can release youth to homeless shelters or to four-year colleges, and the government doesn't penalize or reward that agency. In a family, independent living skills are conveyed every day because parents have a long-term interest in helping the teen to live independently and take on responsibilities.

"I know they taught us about budgeting back at the agency, in a workshop or something," continued Leonard. "But the truth is it didn't mean much to me until I got out and had to buy groceries, pay rent. I'm embarrassed, but really the first month on my own I felt like Mr. Big Shot. I ended up lending a friend at work some cash, then I went out partying one night, and next thing you know, where's the rent money?" I knew some agencies tried to give teens real-life experience while they still had the safety net of foster care, by providing supervised apartments and allowing teens to try and fail at things like grocery shopping. Teens should be given these structured, well-planned learning situations to obtain the skills they need to survive and thrive after foster care. They should be able to test their abilities in their individual situations as a means of reaching personal and career goals. Dead-end, subsistence jobs should not be the final goal or expectation for teens with a long life ahead of them.

We worked with Leonard over the next month or so to get him back on his feet. We guided him in preparing to meet with his foster care agency to acquire some emergency assistance and cash, which, though not readily available, was accessible if one was persistent. That allowed him to pay his aunt a bit of rent. The agency also gave him some work in their administrative office. We convinced Leonard to go back to the college and talk to someone in the financial aid office about a work-study position. These efforts settled him somewhat for the time being, but they seemed like band-aid solutions that were too little, too late. Leonard was lucky to have advocates such as Youth Advocacy Center after he was discharged, but most teens in this situation have to rely on themselves. Even with us helping him, he still needed to negotiate countless new situations that required a degree of resources and self-advocacy skills with which he wasn't armed.

The experiences of feeling relatively helpless with Leonard and witnessing the current independent living workshops amplified our theory that independent living was a broken or poorly conceived program. Around this time I attended a conference about independent living. I felt frustrated as the national experts sat on the stage and spoke proudly of their success stories in which one foster care graduate was holding down a job at a fast food restaurant and another was working at a group home. Was this the best these discharged young adults could do? Was it right that independent living essentially prepared kids for subsistence living? Yes, it was good that these young adults had jobs and were not in prison, but was that all we should expect from them and from the system that raised them? And if child welfare professionals expected this outcome for the most successful teens, what did that mean for those with less education and assertiveness?

In response to the foster care system's strategy for handling teenagers and preparing them for independent living, we began to articulate our own philosophy about independent living for teens in foster care. A foundation generously supported our work in thinking about this, and eventually we published a report, *The Future for Teens in Foster Care*, about our vision for teens in the foster care system. Our philosophy was based strictly on the work we had done with teens and professionals in the system. For us, it served not just as a summary of what we thought teens needed and deserved to succeed, but it also provided a blueprint of how to develop an alternative sort of independent living program for teens. Countless professionals, even ones who had resisted change, commented on *The Future for Teens in Foster Care*'s accurate appraisal of the system and our recommendations. We outlined our philosophy in the report:

1. All teens in foster care have the potential to succeed as participating citizens and reach their personal and career potential.

Teens in foster care, like any other young person, have dreams for a better future. They want to participate in society in a meaningful way.

When the state takes over custody of a child, it has both the legal and moral responsibility to fully prepare that child to become a successful, participating citizen. Anything short of this is a miscarriage of that responsibility. If a teen who has been cared for in the system is forced out of the system without the power and resources to become independent, then all participants lose—the young person loses the chance to be productive, and society loses a potential resource. We all usually end up paying for it in either increased dependency services or, in the worst case, incarceration and costs of crime. A democracy should demand that every individual be given a fair chance to achieve his or her potential.

No empirical evidence proves that the trauma of foster care is so irreversible that once in the system, a child has lost their opportunity to succeed at independence. And if such evidence did exist, then society, knowing these teens could never fully participate as independent citizens, would have to recognize the fact and establish institutions for the long-term care of foster care graduates.

2.   Every foster care teen must be treated as if they have the capacity for future success.

No fail-safe evaluations can predict which teen will thrive and which teen will fail to become successful, participating citizens. Within all classes of individuals, including the wealthiest, some people fail to become independent, successful, participating citizens. Teens in foster care are just one such class. Prejudging potential success is impossible to do with certainty. Yet, when youth are treated with high expectations, they achieve at a higher level. Foster care professionals must expect great achievements from all teens in foster care, without exception.

3.   Teens in care must prepare for their future while they are still in care, not wait until after they are discharged.

We have met more than a thousand teens in foster care. Many gulfs exist between our experiences and theirs and certainly it can be challenging to find mutual areas for conversation. While we have run the gamut of conversational topics, we have been most successful in creating connections with teens when we talk about their futures.

Most teens in foster care understand that their stay is temporary and that they will leave the system to some uncertain future. Many teens repress these thoughts and discussions, but not because they don't want a better future. Although it might seem difficult, all teens in foster care can and should engage in talking and thinking about their future; we are not doing them a favor when we ignore it and focus exclusively on past traumas and present crises. Instead, if we can make a better future seem relevant and achievable, future preparation then becomes an alternative to constantly dwelling on the despair of the system.

Preparing for a future outside foster care by actively involving the teens and placing more responsibility with them serves two important purposes: first, it increases the chances of successful transition to independence, and second, by placing the teen as the responsible decision-making agent, the system increases the teen's opportunities to utilize his or her own intellectual abilities.

4.   Because education is crucial to life-long fulfillment for foster care teens, it must receive as much attention as does mental health counseling.

The issues around childhood poverty, abuse or neglect, separation from one's family, the uncertainty of the future, and the trials of living in temporary homes certainly create significant emotional issues. Teens in foster care should get counseling and attention to their mental health needs. However, many experts feel that mental health counseling for foster care teens is deficient because services focus too much on pathology rather than on mental health. Regardless, this should not be the total focal point of the foster care system. Professionals should address with equal vigor other dimensions of each teen.

Most teens recognize that much of the professional attention they receive while in foster care is oriented toward mental health. When teens feel that this focus excludes other developmental areas such as education, creative development, sports, community involvement, and so on, they reflect this focus back to themselves and may unwittingly increase their sense of emotional weakness.

An emphasis on education in programming not only provides essential support for developing intellectual abilities but reinforces the idea that students are potentially capable of empowering their lives. An education approach emphasizes learning and new understandings that are essential complements for making emotional changes.

Education is arguably as vital to future success, sustaining independence, and emotional fulfillment as is good mental health. Education must become the primary focus of foster care because it is essential to help teens succeed as independent, fully participating citizens. Furthermore, it may help teens achieve more personal satisfaction as they develop intellectual skills that can be applied to all aspects of life.

Foster care teens should be expected to graduate from high school and prepare for college, if they wish. Anything less must be considered unacceptable. All involved with foster care teens should provide support to enable them to achieve these goals. Programs designed around an academic model for teens in care will encourage intellectual development and confidence; they will support a teen's motivation to more actively pursue education as an important goal.

5.   Teens in foster care need to hear stories and see role models of individuals engaging and succeeding in the world outside foster care.

Most teens in foster care have a disadvantage of not hearing stories from adults or even older peers of the struggles and successes they have faced to achieve and maintain independence. Many teens come from communities in which a large portion of the population may not have gone to college or achieved meaningful and well-paying work.

Teens in foster care are interested in the world outside of foster care and their immediate communities, but they usually have few real live role models to guide them in exploring this world. Instead, they get their ideas about the adult world and develop their goals based exclusively on what they see on television, movies, and maybe an occasional magazine or book. They may want to become veterinarians, musicians, television journalists, or judges, but they have no idea if these dreams are realistic or how to pursue them. The route to success seems mysterious, either beyond their abilities or overly simplistic.

Anyone teaching, working with, or mentoring foster care teens can do them a great service by sharing stories of struggles and successes in the world outside foster care. If these stories are carefully selected for their relevancy to the student's own prior and future experiences, they can have a dramatic impact.

6.   Intellectual empowerment is essential for achieving independence.

Teens while in foster care, and eventually as independent adults, must be able to process information, analyze that information, and develop solutions for a dynamic range of situations in their lives. No one path or prescription suits all similar situations for all individuals. Developing and strengthening intellectual skills to confront the variety of life's challenges and opportunities is critical.

Our society's values coincide with the observations of Socrates: every individual, no matter his or her background, has intellectual capacity. The system is responsible for providing every teen in foster care with the opportunity to develop his or her innate intellectual abilities.

The learning process must strengthen the student's sense of intellectual empowerment. As in sports, exercise is fundamental to developing skills. Using active methods for learning exercises the student's intellectual abilities. Learning experiences are not restricted to the classroom. While in the foster care system, students meet with countless learning opportunities. Professionals must use these experiences as opportunities to exercise teens' minds. Currently, the system takes over too many challenges faced by teens in foster care, owing to either bureaucratic necessity or individual benevolence on the professional's part. As long as this practice continues, teens will never fully develop their intellects.

7.   Intellectual self-authorship, the process of developing understanding that is relevant to the individual's life experiences and understanding, must replace the knowledge dispensing system of independent living training.

Intellectual self-authorship requires the students to employ critical thinking skills to obtain and understand knowledge for themselves, rather than try to absorb information pre-packaged by someone else. Teens in foster care, like any students, respond to active learning situations. They also learn best when they can connect new knowledge with their individual life experiences. They report greater satisfaction when they develop the answers rather than when a teacher prescribes them. While the student's academic achievements may be deficient, they have the ability to analyze, make abstractions, and deal with new facts at a normal level. These intellectual abilities make them good learners in the context of self-authorship.

8.   An independent living program must be interesting for the teacher to teach.

A continuing principle for us is recognizing all teens, and those professionals serving teens, as individuals. An effective program would allow both the student and teacher to bring their individual strengths and creativity to the learning process. Essential to an effective program is the ability to excite the teachers and fully engage the students by being flexible enough to relate to the individual's specific learning needs and future goals.

Students quickly perceive the teacher's authenticity, interest in the subject, and enthusiasm for teaching it. If the teacher is forced to disseminate specific knowledge, the process is prone to become mechanical and uninspired. The teacher can look for entertaining ways to break up the repetition and monotony, but then the entertainment becomes the primary element rather than the learning. The curriculum and methodology must challenge and excite the teacher as well as support and encourage use of the teacher's creativity.

9.   Students need a significant positive experience in the outside community to test their new understandings and acquired skills.

Although there is value to providing services in the teens' neighborhoods and communities, learning how to prepare for independence must include concrete experiences in the larger community. Teens in foster care have typically had so few meaningful and positive experiences outside the foster care system that they are prone to a wide range of misjudgments and insecurities.

We found teens eager to learn about worlds beyond those with which they were familiar, and realized that the larger community can share vast resources with the teens. It is essential that before leaving the foster care system, teens learn to interact with individuals, particularly career role models, in the greater community. For the best impact, these interactions must be authentic and individualized. Such experiences help the student understand that they have the necessary strengths and potential to be treated with seriousness and respect by a successful member of the community who is not paid to be interested in the teen's foster care experiences.

10.   The system should give foster care teens an opportunity to have their achievement in the learning process evaluated and recognized.

Because independent living programs have not traditionally been held accountable for the success or failure of teens, the system has put forth few, if any, efforts to measure what teens learned in the programs or how they were using the information they were supposed to have learned.

Teens want to know when their efforts to learn have paid off. It is important to have some type of evaluation device that measures student achievement and demonstrates to both student and teacher significant accomplishments and areas that need work. To maintain respect for each student's individuality, evaluations should measure both individual achievement and look toward students achieving benchmark goals.

———————

We were still seeking a way to directly educate teens for independence and simultaneously change the system to embrace the full responsibility of this goal. Although we knew it was hard to do both, we remained convinced that direct interventions with teens were necessary at the same time as trying to change how the system implemented practices and policies. As we evaluated YAC's direction and services, we returned to the conclusion that the only consistent individual foster care teens can rely on during their period in foster care was themselves. Even teens who have exceptionally good social workers or foster families find those relationships unreliable, as the worker could get transferred or the placement could change. We returned to the need for teens to advocate for themselves—the concept we first saw with Carlos, then developed further with Jenny, Xaranda, and many other teens.

We thought about creating a new model that could be used to complement, be part of, or even replace independent living programs. This model
would truly empower teens by teaching them the many components of self-
advocacy, namely the importance of gaining information, understanding the
needs of the other side, presenting one's strengths, combining personal
needs with organizational goals, as well as using communication skills to successfully navigate the hurdles and challenges of independence. This model
could be the basis for supporting a teen's preparation for future independence, but the model still would depend upon the system providing specific
independent skills education and supporting students taking advantage of the
multitude of community resources available for developing a successful plan.

In our first attempt in testing this idea, a precursor to our current Getting
Beyond the System® Self-Advocacy Seminar, we offered more structured
classes to teach teens self-advocacy. In these classes, we showed teens how
to look up their rights and then taught them to construct an argument to use
with their agency. These self-advocacy classes challenged students for a number of reasons. First, we were teaching something very conceptual, although
we tied it to the students' concrete goals. Second, it required a good deal of
writing and reading. Students who supposedly could not write began to com-
pose simple but effective self-advocacy letters. They learned about the chain
of command and to whom they should direct their requests. They learned to
conduct a more formal meeting with decision makers at an agency. They
became skilled at focusing on the issues and not personalizing the situation.
They also gained knowledge about the importance of presenting their
strengths and educating the agency about how a certain action could benefit
all parties, including the agency.

In this approach, we encouraged the teens to purposefully identify the
problems they wanted to tackle. Our experiences with giving rights workshops
and organizing teen mothers around policy advocacy convinced us that teens
needed to learn how to prioritize and focus on what they identified as important to them—getting a placement with their child, transferring to a more
appropriate high school, or obtaining a more generous clothing allowance.
Because it was important to make the self-advocacy education relevant to
their lives, we passed no judgment on what they deemed worthy of their

effort. We believed that the experience of learning to develop an advocacy argument was transferable to numerous situations, and thus, understanding and applying self-advocacy would benefit them for a lifetime.

We saw that teens not only pursued worthy goals, but that they often impacted policies at their agency through their own advocacy efforts. For example, Danielle wanted to get her driver's license and selected this goal for her self-advocacy project. (For teens in most places in the country, getting a driver's license is a rite of passage and an essential to get anywhere. But in New York City, most of us rely on public transportation, and for teenagers in the city who don't have access to cars, getting a driver's license is not a priority.) Danielle figured a license would help open up different, better paying job opportunities for her. Danielle's foster care agency professionals put her off, letting her know they were more focused on managing daily living in the group home than arranging or paying for any type of training, including driving lessons. In our class, Danielle looked up the statutes and found, not surprisingly, that the law did not require driving lessons. However, she argued that driving was important for jobs she wanted and that the law stated the agency was responsible for providing job readiness skills. Danielle convinced her agency to provide her with driving lessons. Interestingly, after that, the agency began offering the lessons to other teens as well.

Teens successfully advocated for more home visits, better placements, and even more flexible rules about working part-time. Danielle, as well as other students, demonstrated the enduring passion teens had to develop a meaningful future life. This passion led them to seriously approach learning new skills and apply them in difficult situations to achieve specific goals.

The success stories of our initial students convinced us even further that self-advocacy was a core independent living tool. We imagined that if every teen had the chance to learn and use self-advocacy, it might help the teens directly and also result in new expectations, attitudes, policies, and practices in the system. While the system was a naturally good opportunity to practice self-advocacy skills, it wasn't the same type of system typically found in the outside community. We wanted to shift the focus from foster care to learning skills specifically applicable to the wider community, where teens would hopefully live their entire adult life beyond any government system.

We discussed this approach with the teens working with us at YAC. They at first came to no clear consensus; many felt conflicted because they passionately desired to remain focused on foster care issues and change the current practices. The injustices they faced every day corroded their ability to attend to the need to plan for their futures. They so intensely sensed the system's injustices that they resisted the idea of YAC abandoning its efforts to help teens fight their individual present struggles in the system. At the same time, they understood the idea of prioritizing struggles and came to realize (as we did too) that the system might win if we simply continued to engage in every individual's rights abuse skirmish. Focus on the bigger picture—long-term success for the individual teen and the undermining of the low expectations that dictate policy—might, in the end, have a more important and lasting impact for all.

Finally, we began to understand a clear connection between our self-advocacy work with teens and creating successful independent living skills. Self-advocacy is essential for success in the community at large. To join the community means being interdependent with others. Self-advocacy, negotiations, and problem solving that include all parties' needs are essential. If people understand or have facility with self-advocacy, then they can adapt to changing situations and need not depend upon learning new rules for each situation.

By focusing the development of self-advocacy skills on preparing for independent adult life, we would serve an obvious need of teens in the system. Most child welfare professionals, the greater community, and foster care teens themselves agreed that self-advocacy is an essential and, for the most part, an underdeveloped skill for teens in foster care. If we could teach self-advocacy to teens preparing for independence, we could address a known and significant problem and greatly increase the likelihood of teens successfully transitioning to independent adulthood.

6

Creating the
Getting Beyond the System®
Self-Advocacy Seminars

We had traveled many paths in the foster care system, engaged in many problems faced by teens, and considered a range of solutions. During this time we had observed many worthwhile program efforts fail. We believed that the combination of our work, in both policy and programming areas, positioned us to develop an effective curriculum that would actually work for the teen, be suitable for meaningful replication, and eventually promote a positive change within the foster care system. We focused in on one overarching problem: the system failed to prepare teens to reach their potential as individuals and citizens.

However, we faced a risk by basing our program on the premise that teens in foster care could take on more personal responsibility for preparing for their future, engage in intellectual programs to advance their understanding of independent living, and become empowered through skillfully applying self-advocacy techniques. Transferring this responsibility to teens could potentially be disastrous by confirming the system's low expectations, threatening teens by requiring more from them, threatening professionals with a perceived loss of control and power, and being effectively resisted by the foster care bureaucracy. However, our experiences suggested we could and should attempt this program, and few other options seemed realistic.

We concluded that the stronger forces of inertia would continually defeat our efforts to force change within and on the system. Instead, we would openly attempt to undermine the premise of diminished expectations through creating a successful model that would gradually attract resources and policy change for wide-scale adoption. In addition, we would develop a method that would empower equally professional and student to benefit from the potential of all participants in the learning process, rather than focusing exclusively on either the student or professional.

We analyzed the source of diminished expectations. The rationale for inadequate programming, passivity regarding inadequate high school education, and absence of college or career planning stemmed from the theory that teens in foster care were too traumatized to significantly achieve anything in their lives. The government presented traumatization and victimization as reasons not to challenge teens to higher achievement and more rigorous education.

We wanted to prove the trauma theory wrong. Some literature, coupled with our experience, suggested that trauma could spur a person on to greater achievements. Thus we wanted to replace, or at least balance, the prevailing trauma theory by highlighting the strengths, the potential, and the accomplishments we had observed in our work with hundreds of teens in foster care. If we could help more teens leave the system and become successful, participating citizens, then we might demonstrate to the teens in the system, to the architects of the system, and to the community that the system should institute the highest of expectations for all teens and develop programs that support those expectations.

Our position of being independently funded and operating on the fringes of the system created an unusual advantage. We had the opportunity to implement and test a high-level, future-oriented, intellectual program. If the design worked, then we would try to replicate the program.

We analyzed our previous work and carefully crafted a challenging seminar that would empower teens by helping them understand the importance and skills of self-advocacy and begin the process of taking responsibility for their own futures. We viewed self-advocacy as a critical thinking process for developing goals and plans to achieve those goals within the context of the community at large. Self-advocacy requires that an individual understands the needs and goals of others, presents a positive image of themselves, and develops solutions that will provide mutual benefits. Most everyone understood that these skills are critically important for all teens preparing for successful independence.

We developed four overarching goals for the seminar:

1. Help teens take responsibility and control of their lives
2. Advance intellectual abilities (to deal with modern economy and world)
3. Initiate preparation for a future career
4. Create relevancy and motivation for continued learning

We also broke down the self-advocacy process into components, which formed the basis for our curriculum:

> Planning and reaching your goals
>
> Fact analysis
>
> How systems and organizations qork
>
> Importance of presenting your strengths
>
> Understanding the needs of the other party
>
> Process of transitions
>
> Engaging and utilizing allies and finding mentors
>
> Depersonalizing issues and discovering the needs of others
>
> Developing solutions
>
> Self-advocacy presentations
>
> Understanding rules, laws, and rights

We were aware of no other formal programs to teach these skills; most successful people learn some form of self-advocacy in their home environment, schools, or workplace. Our legal training and professional experiences gave us a more structured view of a process that many people naturally learn from observing their parents and negotiating with them for their needs. The foster care system denied teens this natural learning experience, and without it, many are handicapped throughout their lives.

Approaching future planning through teaching self-advocacy has the advantage of being a neutral process. It neither judges the students' goals nor condones and critiques the adult world. In teaching the process, we are not asking teens to change deep-seated problems they may or may not have. For instance, our curriculum presents depersonalizing issues as an effective strategy, not as a judgment or critique on a student's attitude or supposed inability to make relationships. Students like this learning method because the process itself is depersonalized and focuses on logic rather than deconstructing entrenched psychological patterns in relationship building. Learning self-advocacy helps a student change the way he or she thinks about approaching and obtaining future goals.

Many foster care teens have developed the antithesis of self-advocacy skills. Rather than presenting their considerable range of positive attributes, the teens present problems that get attention; rather than understanding the needs and goals of others, the teens focus exclusively on their own needs; rather than developing mutually beneficial solutions, the teens personalize any resistance to helping them.

We called the seminar the Getting Beyond the System® Self-Advocacy Seminar, or GBS for short. We constructed the dynamics of the seminar based on our years of experience working with teens in foster care and observing their engagement in the learning process.

Learning Method

We needed a learning method that would be effective and engender active engagement by student and teacher. We had seen in the existing independent living programs that lecturing and imparting discrete information was an unappealing format, often rejected by students. Even students struggling to be positive and polite found this style boring, confusing, and irrelevant. We decided to use an approach that, while underutilized for teaching foster care teens, has been widely used in other education arenas for centuries: the use of stories, a case method, combined with the Socratic method.

The case method presents stories in the form of cases we have written and refined over the years. The cases are based on actual teens with whom we have worked and situations they have encountered. Each case revolves around a protagonist who has come from a challenging background, usually foster care but also from middle-class and disadvantaged backgrounds. The protagonists are in situations that require them to resolve a problem and achieve a goal. In each case, they might be treated unfairly or they may have to negotiate with a person in a position of power, find allies or mentors, or present their strengths. The cases reveal dynamics of self-advocacy, such as planning for one's goals, preparing for an informational interview, and understanding the process of transitions. The cases also focus on understanding the dynamics of the work world and the relationships between employees, colleagues, and supervisors.

YAC compiled these cases into a book, and each seminar class session consists of discussing two or three cases. Usually one case is assigned for homework with questions that must be answered in writing. Students find the protagonists realistic and their situations relevant, and so they fully engage in reading the cases. The seminar students' willingness to read the cases and critically examine facts and assumptions dispels a prevailing prejudice that students with inadequate academic backgrounds do not have the facility to do thoughtful academic work. For some, the cases appear simple, while others find them complex and filled with many nuances. But for all students, the cases are challenging and provoke active engagement in developing analytic skills and solutions. Because the cases describe life situations as the teens have experienced them, the students demonstrate less of the resistance often associated with confronting academic work.

An instructor trained in the Socratic method leads class discussions. Socrates believed that knowledge derives from the individual and that one cannot provide knowledge broken down into individual discrete elements. In modern times, almost every law school in the United States uses this method. The Socratic method is also used by a growing number of educators at different levels of primary, secondary, and college education.

Socrates recognized that teenagers empowered with information and taught to exercise their natural intellectual abilities would make good decisions in their own best interests. Socrates understood that if we believed teens should take on responsibility, then we must empower them to make their own decisions. Empowering sounds both appealing and simplistic. In practice though, empowering teens to take control of their lives is difficult to achieve.

In the Socratic learning process, the teacher's base of knowledge, although typically more extensive than the student's, will not determine what new understanding students gain. Instead, the teacher's knowledge, experience, and wisdom guides the entire group, including the teacher. The teacher steers the learning process and helps each class member develop his or her own reasoned understanding. Teachers must challenge students in their thinking and encourage them to support their conclusions, but in the final analysis, the students must make their own conclusions and accept the understandings that best suit their thinking. This learning environment supports all ideas and recognizes those ideas that the student can thoughtfully support. This method places far more responsibility than the typical high school education does on the student to fully participate as an active learner.

The philosophy behind the method is that teaching a learning process to students is more important than just imparting knowledge. Developing the ability to learn will equip a student to gain knowledge throughout his or her life. This method focuses on analyzing information and finding understanding rather than on reaching right conclusions.

Actual Application of Self-Advocacy

We wanted the learning process to include a tangible and relevant application of the self-advocacy process. We needed to demonstrate to the students that facility with self-advocacy applies in countless situations. To illustrate this point and gain their interest, we developed an application within the context of career development. In addition, it was essential to create this context outside the foster care system. Thus, we instituted an informational interview with an experienced professional in the student's chosen field of interest as the culminating assignment for the semester. This concluding project has become a cornerstone of the learning experience in both preparation and outcome.

The informational interview as a final project is a useful way of reviewing and applying all the topics studied throughout the semester. The students understand that their ability to advocate for themselves will, in many ways, determine the interview's success. Most students consider the interview highly important and are motivated to do their best at reviewing and applying their self-advocacy skills. Chapter 7 explains the full importance of the informational interview.

Promoting Personal Responsibility

In every manner the seminar had to demonstrate that students could meet high expectations. Therefore, we developed the program around the framework of a college seminar. The GBS Seminar consists of twelve weekly classes that meet for two and a half hours, usually after school, although we have taught it as a high school class for credit during school hours and believe it is also suitable for a college environment. While the seminar application does not consider past academic success, each applicant must demonstrate a motivation to do something with their lives and be willing to engage in a rigorous intellectual program. In practice, we admit any students who are interested in preparing for their future and who want to take on the seminar's challenges. We also encourage students who fear that the work and commitment of the seminar will be too rigorous to attend an orientation and even one class before abandoning the idea of enrolling in the seminar.

We learned from our experiences that we could enforce strict standards regarding attendance, lateness, participation in class, and homework completion as well as provide supportive but critical feedback. We worked on the premise that if we couldn't expect a student to attend classes during the course of one semester, how could they make it to a job every day? Or meet the demands of college? We also knew that the positive dynamics of the group and individual learning environment would diminish if we did not expect and require full attendance. When instituted, we found that students needed the structure of weekly attendance in order to remain focused on the learning objectives.

Our seminars typically attain an 85 to 90 percent attendance record, and after the initial two weeks, attrition rate is remarkably low, less than 10 percent. With a starting group of twelve students, two or three may drop by the second class, and no more than one will drop during the remainder of the semester. For a voluntary program for teens, these statistics demonstrate a high level of student commitment. The seminar facilitator tells students that they are only allowed to miss one class; if they miss two, they will be asked to drop the seminar and retake it when they are ready to make the commitment. Occasionally a student who has demonstrated active engagement in the learning process may miss a second class in the later part of the semester. The teacher is then confronted with a student who desperately wants to complete the semester and conduct his or her informational interview. Fearing the worst, the student will typically throw a range of excuses at the teacher, some very compelling. But the teacher must stop that student and remind him or her of the self-advocacy process. In essence, the teacher must step out of the teacher role to help the student apply self-advocacy principles to maintain his or her student status rather than rely on explanations of his or her victimhood. This scenario provides a powerful learning experience, and that student will not miss another class.

We also observed through our work that in becoming independent, students need and want indicators of their achievement. By testing relative achievement (progress measured individually for each student), teacher and student can then gauge success. Therefore, we instituted a number of evaluation devices including a pre-exam and final exam, feedback and grades on written homework, and feedback on the informational interview.

In the seminar, we encouraged a close focus on learning self-advocacy and preparing for informational interviews. Accordingly, we discouraged students from talking extensively about their own experiences in foster care. We were trying to help them gain a comfortable intellectual role in the group. While focus on personal issues may be therapeutic in purposefully designed therapeutic sessions, it rarely seemed conducive for educational programming in foster care. We repeatedly saw and experienced how stories of personal victimization, present and past problems, and issues brought out in a workshop or a class were sufficiently compelling to divert attention from understanding important educational goals.

In departing from the almost universal practice of discussing personal issues and problems in any foster care group setting, we risked appearing heartless and insensitive. But we had two compelling objectives that would be undermined if we followed traditional practice. First, we needed to help students learn critically important independent living skills, namely self-advocacy and preparation for taking control of their future. These objectives required total focus on the learning process. Second and equally important, we hoped to model a positive means for getting attention and support. Students needed to learn that they could get as much, if not more, attention by working toward positive goals. This approach helped to normalize the teens' sense of self as regular students, preparing for their futures. Thus, during the class the facilitator gave attention to the student who struggled with his or her homework rather than the student who had many challenges in her present foster home or group home.

We were determined to demonstrate to the students and the system that despite students' individual challenges, they could set aside time exclusively for education and preparation for independence. Within the foster care environment, this approach seemed extreme, and some child welfare workers would attack us for not caring and for underestimating the significant problems faced by teens in care. Yet, if more teens were to succeed, we had to demonstrate that most teens in the system were resilient enough to have educational and planning oases where they could temporarily disregard mental health and ordinary living problems. In fact, we believed, with support from some cognitive psychologists and learning professionals, that such an approach might actually facilitate recovery from mental health problems. Of course, we were not denying the importance of mental health intervention; we were just asking for teens to devote a small proportion of time exclusively to intellectual development.

Paul

In developing the model and exploring its usefulness, I taught the seminar for several years. Each time I taught the GBS Seminar, the first day filled me with excitement and anxiety: the excitement mounted in knowing that within just twelve weeks a group of young adults would feel their lives transformed; the anxiety stemmed from worrying whether students would overcome the significant challenges that the Seminar presented to them.

It was 3:30 p.m. on a Tuesday, thirty minutes before a new semester's Seminar would begin. Three students, two girls and a boy, had arrived, quite early. They were extremely shy and avoided eye contact with me, their teacher, and with each other. When I asked where they were coming from, they named neighborhoods that were long subway rides away. I suspected that our office was located in an unfamiliar part of the city for them. "Was it hard finding us?"

"Not really," said one. All nodded in agreement. Then one of the girls admitted, "I got a little lost. I don't really know this area."

"Do you know each other?"

They looked at each other, shrugged, and the same girl softly acknowledged that they had never met. "Well, you are going to spend a lot of time together, and I hope you will help each other," I said, trying to be upbeat and also fill the deadly silence. I am never comfortable with the initial voids in these first meetings with teens and with their reluctance to engage with strangers. I kept the conversation going on my own, sort of half musing out loud, half hoping I would get them to respond. "Are you all interested in finding out about different careers?" Slight nods in response.

I looked out the window and saw two more young girls and a guy walking toward our building. They walked with a swagger using their arms and legs to take up a great deal of space. I saw passersby giving them wary looks and extra room. If I were down on the sidewalk, I might also. In anyone's wildest imagination, these three did not look like they were about to embark on a seminar in which they would be learning self-advocacy, studying cases, debating issues, using the Socratic method, and seriously planning their futures.

The three walked up to our building, and the next moment the doorbell rang. They walked in, heads a bit down, no eye contact, and dutifully took seats. I felt greatly relieved the group was growing. These teens didn't know each other either. They ran into each other coming out of the subway station and converged as they walked toward the same destination.

I began the class about ten minutes late, which I didn't like to do, but I was hoping a couple more kids would show. By now a few other students had arrived, and we had a total of eleven. I began by telling them a little about my experience working in foster care, how I had been working in the system for many years and was still trying desperately to get out! Finally, I produced some authentic laughs and nods of agreement among the teens. They knew why I wanted out of the system.

I explained how useful the seminar would be for them and again emphasized the informational interview's importance. There was still only fleeting eye contact, there was no note taking, and there was a good deal of fidgeting and shifting about. One student was continually tying and retying a shoelace. Another was noisily digging into a large bag of potato chips.

But I knew they were listening even though they had no good reason to trust anyone or to allow their expectations to exceed their present situations. I knew they were here because they wanted to do something with their lives. I focused on their faces. These were beautiful individuals. When I did catch their eyes, they were penetrating and seemed to me to be seeking something, perhaps knowledge. Occasionally, when a smile slipped by their control, it exuded deep warmth and gentleness. I sensed their fragility. They were in the most tenuous of life situations without any stability. Yet, I also appreciated their resilience. Here they were voluntarily seeking a path to help them with their future success. In moving toward this goal, they were willing to take on unknown responsibility to do something with their lives. I was pleased that our seminar respected the duality of both the strengths and weaknesses of these students rather than focusing exclusively on one or the other.

I finally introduced myself and revealed some of the problems they would have with me. I let them know that I didn't hear too well, I didn't understand street language, I was old, and I might not understand the world as they did. I acknowledged that I didn't know them, but, from what I could guess, they had had some pretty bad luck; I acknowledged that I wouldn't have had the strength to endure what they had been through. I told them I couldn't do anything about that, but I could help them with their future. I then told them a little about my personal and professional background.

When I explained that becoming a success in the future was not only important for them as individuals but also was the key to changing the foster care system in general, the group came alive. I emphasized the importance of demonstrating that teens in the system could and did succeed. They began to talk about how much they wanted to see other kids do better and how the system did so much to keep everyone down. At this point I needed to prevent the discussion from erupting into complaints about the system.

"Okay, now let's hear who you are. When you introduce yourself, I am most interested in your telling me what you want to be doing when you are independent and what career you think you would like to have." They were attending the seminar to learn self-advocacy, but the most tangible attraction was the informational interview based on their career choice. From the first day, I would try to connect self-advocacy education to their future goals.

Darnel began. "Well, I went to the orientation and heard that girl talk about how it helped her learn about her job choice. I want to do something with computers, like design websites or fix programs or something." Darnel was assertive in his answer. We were off to a good start.

Ebony went next. She looked down and seemed sullen. "I'm going to be a singer."

"A singer, huh? What do you like to sing? My kind of music?" My vain attempt to get a smile.

She looked at me like I was nuts. "You know, R&B?"

Plenty of people would tell her it was unrealistic for her to want to be a pop star, or for another kid to dream of being a ball player. But that was not my role. We were there to help her learn self-advocacy skills and take on responsibility for her life. In her informational interview, she would learn about the music industry from a music professional and then begin analyzing her future options.

The next student introduced himself as Benny. He told the class he liked to read, and he didn't mind school. "I want to go into some field like ology."

I was confused, "Excuse me. I didn't hear. What field?"

Benny looked around at the others and with determination and a little irritation repeated, "ology."

No one else seemed confused. I guessed it was my hearing or else some slang for something I didn't understand. I tried to repeat what I thought he said—"ology?" No one corrected me or seemed to indicate that I had misspoken. I needed a translation. "Ology, what's that?"

Benny seemed deeply disappointed in my ignorance and explained, "Ology, you know! Something like sociology, psychology, anthropology, I just like ologies!"

I suppressed a smile. "Okay, explain more. What do you actually want to do?"

"I think I want to work with people, but I am also thinking about law, too."

I was impressed with Benny's ambition, wide ranging as it was. His broad approach to selecting a career field just seemed to enhance his enthusiasm. I used this opportunity to explain to him and the class that many people had wide ranges of career interests and one value of an informational interview was to find out more about their interests so they could make a more informed decision. I explained that within a couple of weeks Benny would have to choose one of his many interests so we could arrange an informational interview for him. I also encouraged him and the class not to give up on any interests until they explored them more fully.

Shermane was particularly quiet through all the class introductions. I asked her what she wanted to do. Her response surprised me. "I'm a bad girl," she shrugged and looked out the window. I was uncertain how to respond.

"Shermane, what do you think you would like to be doing when you get out of foster care?"

"Just told you. I'm a bad girl." Her words sounded more like an identification than a challenge, and I was still unsure of how to respond or what was behind this label.

"Well, there must be something you want to do?" We were talking on parallel tracks.

Shermane persisted. "Nope, I'm a bad girl, and there's nothing I can do."

The situation was nearing a standoff, and I sensed the other students carefully appraising the interaction. This was not where I wanted to go. If she drew me into the personal, I risked moving from an intellectual learning experience to a therapeutic experience dealing with past traumas or one that gave undue attention to negative behavior. I was determined to demonstrate to students that they could have significant positive learning experiences apart from the other problems in their lives. This was important for strengthening themselves as well as dealing with the community beyond foster care.

"Look, Shermane, what do you like to do? What do you do well?"

Shermane's eyes locked on mine for an instant. Then she rolled them with impatience and muttered, "Bake. I bake a pineapple upside down cake."

I sprung on this opportunity. "Great. You could be a pastry chef. That's a wonderful job." I was relieved she didn't challenge this assertion.

Nelson was the most challenging of the group. He picked up on the precedent I had just established. "You tell me what I should do. I'm the student, you're the teacher. That's your job." His tone was taunting.

The students watched to see how I would handle this. "I hope I can help you learn how to advocate for yourself and help you begin planning for your future. But it's your life, and I can't make decisions for you like selecting a career. What are you interested in doing?"

"I have no idea. This is your class; you tell me." Nelson eagerly searched among his peers for affirmation and recognition. Some of the students smiled. All appeared to be studying the dynamics of the conversation.

Nelson certainly had more stamina for this back and forth than I did. "What about a lawyer? Clearly, you would be a great lawyer. You seem to enjoy presenting challenging positions. What do you think of that as a career goal for the class?"

Nelson's smirk transformed into a full smile, as if he had won his point. "Yeah, I could be a lawyer, maybe a defense lawyer." We don't select careers for teens. However, my suggestion resonated with him. I was lucky.

I now knew that Nelson would be the challenger in the class, and more would come. I was anxious about both his strength and his ability to detract from the learning experience. But I was also impressed with his spirit and knack for going just to the line without crossing over into destructiveness for the group.

The other students introduced themselves, and we began the semester with eleven students. One dropped out the second week, and the remainder came for twelve consecutive weeks. Four students did not miss a single class. Five students missed one class. And Nelson missed two classes, which under the rules would not permit him to complete the program; however, Nelson found a way to overcome this requirement.

Four weeks later, we were back in class. The students had been working with cases that taught them to analyze difficult situations and develop strategies for the protagonists to reach their goals. Many of these situations took place in job settings. This gave them a sense of how the work environment functioned and how they could use even beginning level jobs to achieve their personal goals. Our goal was to allow the students to think proactively and rationally about their communications and negotiations and to avoid the negative, reactionary responses they had grown accustomed to using in foster care.

For this week's class, the students had read "James Asks Lishone for a Raise." This case is set in a bookstore, where James, a clerk, needs more money so he can begin taking classes at a local college. He tries to talk to his supervisor about it while she is on her coffee break, and the conversation goes nowhere, as she starts telling him about her own credit card debt.

As in all the cases, a lot of avenues for discussion and a number of learning goals exist. First, the case helps students focus on identifying strengths. The students have to figure out who James is, identify his strengths, and recommend how he can correct his inadequate approach to asking for a raise.

James has a number of strengths that are of use to the bookstore, some of which are clearly stated in the case and some of which are implied. Students develop their critical reading skills through identifying and reporting specific facts. We then have students analyze the facts they identified to discover other meanings. For example, in the James case we learn that James was in foster care. A careful reader sees that his foster care experience, while far from idyllic, also created situations that added to James's strength. In this way, students learn to think about themselves in a different, more positive light.

Additionally, the case introduces the idea that advocating for oneself requires finding ways in which one's personal goals can support the other party's needs—in this situation the book store and James's supervisor Lishone. Understanding the other side is critical for students, but it is also difficult to appreciate. The case also prompts students to think about who in an organization is responsible for making decisions. Finally, the case encourages students to consider how to make a presentation or proposal to someone in a position to help them reach a goal.

In addition to these issues directly related to self-advocacy, the context of the case presents opportunities to learn about developing a monthly expense budget, understanding the dynamics of a retail business, and learning the distinction between a formal and informal discussion. Finally, the case supports values such as the importance of higher education, reading, and volunteering to support an organization's goals.

It was 3:50, and every student was present, including Nelson, who had come late to two previous classes. Students learned quickly that the class began promptly at 4:00 p.m. I did not give late students special attention when they arrived late, and I told them after class that this would not be allowed to continue. If it did continue, then I asked them to drop the class and re-enroll for a future semester. We had to adopt this somewhat strict rule because we knew the teens needed to be held to some standards now, before they got out into the world where their lax attitudes would lose them jobs or get them into more serious trouble. We hoped Nelson was getting the idea that lateness didn't gain him any attention, and it put him at a disadvantage in terms of the discussion.

I started the class at 4:00. All the students opened their casebook to the James case and took out their written homework about the case. "Man, that James is bad. I don't mean bad good either, but pathetic." Nelson didn't wait to be called on.

"You all agree with Nelson? You think James is a real screw up?" If adhered to, the Socratic method requires that all answers come from the students.

Darnel jumped in. "Yeah, he really screwed up. Lishone, his boss, had no idea what he was talking about. I mean, she's just interested in her own life."

"So James is a total screw up. Is there anything we can do to help him?" By now, the students recognized this type of provocation from me.

Forcefully, Ebony took the challenge. "No. You're all wrong. He should never have gone to Lishone. She's just a shift manager. He should have gone to the store manager—the big boss."

In a soft voice, Benny chimed in, "You see, Lishone never knew James was serious. James should have made an appointment to talk about a raise. He also should have presented his strengths and let Lishone know how he works on night book readings. Also, he should have shown Lishone his budget."

"You're crazy. Lishone don't care about James's budget," Walter added to the discussion.

"Okay, it seems some of us think James may have screwed up. But first let's start with his strengths. What are they? Shermane?"

Shermane looked out the window, and no one was sure she would give an answer. A long time seemed to go by as we waited in silence. She began to talk as she was looking out the window. "You know, James was in foster care. He learned to deal with a lot of strange people and changes in his life. Those customers can be rude and act all crazy! So he's probably real good with them."

"That makes sense. Do the rest of you agree with Shermane?" I was working to reinforce her performance, hoping I could engage her in the class. With any luck, when she heard other students agree, this would help. But she didn't need my intervention.

Shermane continued, "You know, it says that he liked to read so he can tell customers what to read. He also wants to take classes in business and that will help the store. If he leaves, they're not going to get anyone better. He should get the raise."

"If those are his strengths, are they useful for the bookstore?" Teens from foster care typically have a limited appraisal of their personal strengths or how they can connect with an employer's needs. This type of discussion is usually enlightening to them.

"That's not the point. His strengths are good, but he hasn't a clue how to present them. And he takes things too personally. He's going to quit, and it's because he didn't present himself right." Nelson loved to pounce on the mistakes others made. I found it interesting that in his current part-time job at Toys 'R Us, he had the similar problem of overreacting and losing his cool. Nelson was clearly taking a step in the right direction by identifying the problem. Using cases defuses the defensiveness that would arise if we discussed the students' own past actions. They also allow everyone to begin with the same information.

The discussion on strengths concluded, and we moved into a discussion about James's monthly expense budget. Even though the government requires that older foster care teens learn independent living skills, many students have neither knowledge of how to develop an expense budget nor any idea of a typical range of living expenses. Our discussion pulled in all the students because it had both practical relevance and centered on the context of a character and situation with which they had become involved. It was unfortunate that we needed to break away from this discussion before we completed it. I hoped they would now see the relevance of budgeting and seek out more information about it either from their IL leaders, schools, or other sources.

"Okay, why would or should the bookstore care about James's desire to take a business class?" By this time in the semester, students were comfortable with not getting answers from the teacher. They had come to rely on their own intellectual abilities, and discussions were often robust. The students were gaining understanding of the central elements of self-advocacy, and I knew they also were gaining confidence to control their lives.

"No way. I work at a store, and all they care about is making money. They don't give a shit for us. I know." Nelson enjoyed getting attention through sharing his actual work experience with the class.

"Well, let's think this through. When you're hired for a job, even as a clerk like James, what does the store have to do?"

Walter responded. "Pay you." Walter hadn't yet achieved the level of analysis that some of the other students had reached, but he clearly read the cases. He was drawn into the discussion sometimes without prompting. He appeared pleased that the rest of us listened to him. His caseworker informed us that Walter barely attended high school and was on the verge of dropping out.

"Anything else?" There was silence. Most had never had a job experience and had rarely overheard any adult talking about job experiences. "Nelson, when Toys R Us hired you, what did they do besides pay you?"

"Well, you had to fill out some forms, like your social security." Students appeared confused. I took this opportunity, when they were particularly interested, to explain company records, the need to report income to the government, withholding taxes, and social security.

"Okay, if a company keeps changing employees, they have to keep training the new ones. Do you think this costs them anything?"

"No, because the person doing the training already works there."

"But think about this, Ebony. If you are a supervisor or even another employee and you spend your time training someone, then who does your work?"

Ebony was engaged because we were discussing her analysis. She felt pride of ownership. "But that is their job, so no one has to take over for them."

"But don't you think the supervisor has other jobs? Maybe she needs to make sure that all the cash registers are covered or that employees are helping customers or that the new book orders are up-to-date if it's a book store. Or think of it another way. What if they had to train new employees every day? Then that could become her full-time job."

"I really don't know what you're talking about. If you know the answer, why don't you just tell us?" Ebony felt intensely frustrated with the questions, and she just wanted to move on with an answer.

I tried another approach. "No, I don't know the answer. I'm really not sure, but let's think about it another way. What if all the employees stayed, and the store had no need for training?"

Ebony got excited again and came back to the Socratic process. "Oh, I get it! Then all those people who do training could do something else."

"That makes sense." The students nodded in agreement as the dialogue progressed.

"Then they could do other things." Ebony's excitement about her understanding was evident in her words and her physical manner. Her smile was expanding by the second. "It's like it's cheaper to keep an employee than to train a new one."

"Do you think it would help James if he understood this?"

Most of the students nodded in agreement.

"Yeah, James has got to tell them how valuable he is and that it will cost them more to train someone else than to give him a raise." The group seemed pleased with Ebony's summation.

"Well, what happens if the store gives James a raise and not the other clerks?"

"Just don't tell them." Nelson quickly added another solution.

"Well, in many places it's hard to hide salary rates. Think about it. James wants money to go to college. We already discussed the fact that studying business will make him more valuable to the bookstore. So how else could the bookstore support James's need and at the same time not have to increase his salary?"

"Well, they could just pay for his class, but they would never do that." Shermane made this comment with strong resentment about how the world worked; yet, she was on to something.

"Why not? By doing that, James would get what he wants. The bookstore would also get what it needs because no one else would complain about an unfair salary increase for James, and the bookstore would benefit from James's education and his loyalty and not having to hire a replacement. You know, companies sometimes pay for education expenses of employees." I added as information.

The class continued like this for the remaining two hours. We discussed two more cases. At the end of the class, I gave back the homework from last week. The students were interested in my comments, and most came up to ask me to decipher my awful handwriting or explain what I meant. No one complained about the overall grade. They appreciated the seriousness with which I took their work.

Although the class was over, no one rushed to leave. They talked with each other and even talked about some of the cases. I was exhausted but delighted because these students learned as much in two and a half hours as the most advanced students I had taught in my twenty years as a college professor.

After this class, I had another set of homework assignments to evaluate. The curriculum required students to possess a wide range of ability to complete the written homework. My first contact with students' homework had stunned me. Many of the high school students we taught were unable to write even one sentence. I remembered my initial feelings of despair and a sense of defeat before I had barely begun to teach. If it had not been for my personal encounters with the students, I would have given up.

The intelligence and creativity of the students often dramatically disconnects with their academic record. Although all the students we teach are at least sixteen years old, the education of many appears to have ceased somewhere between the fourth and sixth grades. Typically, in the first seminar sessions, some students do not turn in any homework, others give the most cursory answers, and still others give answers that demonstrate keen analytical abilities somewhat diminished by their lack of writing skills.

We instituted an approach that views written homework exclusively from a communications perspective, rather than focusing on grammar, spelling, and word usage. When students realize that what they write has power no matter how simple or rudimentary their efforts, they become motivated to communicate more effectively and then take more interest in improving their writing.

We encourage even the most resistant students to put anything to paper in answering a homework question. For instance, one case includes a question, "Why would Ms. Greer want to be a mentor for Jasda?" A simple response might be, "Because she likes Jasda." Other responses that don't appear to be well thought-out might be, "Because she has nothing better to do?" or "She wouldn't."

It's easy to understand these cursory answers as reflecting lack of interest, lack of intelligence, or even proof of assertive resistance. From my knowledge of the students, I have become reluctant to characterize these written responses. I need to begin where the student is in their written expression rather than respond in the context of my expectations. Thus, we not only accept anything a student writes as a serious expression but also provide continuing feedback that their words matter. This approach dramatically increases the student's appreciation of the intellectual. This method also teaches them that words do matter and that communication is important. We are certainly not the first to take this approach. Educators such as Paolo Freire have extensively thought about and utilized this concept. Freire found that effective education requires understanding and integrating students' language. His work helped us in developing this approach.

An example of our response to the answer "she wouldn't," might be, "I think you have something here. The question assumes Ms. Greer would want to mentor Jasda, but maybe she is just too busy or not interested. If this is true, then Jasda really has a challenge ahead of her. But when you think about it, most self-advocacy is about getting someone to do something they at first don't want to do. Because your answer is very useful, do you have any ideas about how Jasda could change Ms. Greer's mind?" This type of feedback takes time, but it has impact and pulls the student into the intellectual process. Regardless of the students' intentions, their ideas, once expressed, now have a life of their own. The student usually feels connected to his or her idea and will make the effort to further analyze the case. This approach values a student's own words and results in heightened efforts by students to engage in the written homework.

Intellectualism is a major seminar objective. Because we are outside the mandates of the educational bureaucracy, we can take approaches that create less resistance from the student. Instead of focusing on their significant educational deficits, we can focus exclusively on their ideas and analysis. All the students we meet delight in intellectual challenges. They enjoy the challenges presented in the written cases, and they take pleasure in making critical analyses. As they recognize the power and expression of ideas, they become more invested in making the expression more effective. By the end of the semester, they become much more motivated to improve their technical writing abilities.

By respecting all answers made by students, the teacher also learns to think differently. Through the process of giving intellectual merit to answers that seem poorly considered or even suggest resistance, the teacher opens himself or herself up to new ideas, and experiences the satisfaction of having to evaluate his or her own assumptions of what seems obvious. This growth on the teacher's part keeps the learning process open and energized.

By the fourth week's homework assignment, the students gave carefully considered responses and demonstrated some ability to use evidence to support a position. In that week's homework case, Nat works in a busy hardware store and needs to change his lunch hour at the last minute. In reading the case, all students were keenly aware of how poorly Nat executed this request. When I asked for better approaches, students provided thoughtful answers, such as, "Nat can compromise with his boss in getting his lunch hour changed. In return, he will do overtime," or "Nat could offer to help Alicia with her work, and, maybe in return, she could help him." "Wait until she came out of the boss's office or wait until she was finished with the customers." These were all good approaches for Nat to use in changing his lunch hour.

In the same homework, students still exhibited some unfamiliarity with vocabulary. In a question about allies, one student correctly identified the protagonist's coworker, but also included "punctuation" as an ally. The student confused the word "punctuation" with "punctuality" and expanded the meaning of allies to include general personal strengths. Yet, when I explained this misusage in the context of making a stronger argument, the student was not defensive and appeared to appreciate the correction.

"What do you do about students that have such poor academic skills?" "Our teens can't write a sentence, and reading is very difficult for them." "You can't expect a teen to attend all twelve sessions of your seminar." "It's just too much of a strain for them to sit in another class after a full day at school." We have heard these comments repeatedly since entering the foster care field. Many professionals in the system believe that teens in foster care are so poorly educated that they hold no hope for the teens to achieve in an intellectually based program.

In the beginning period of YAC, when we focused on policy work and rights violations, we engaged in informal educational programming. We met with groups of teens in foster care to educate them about the functioning of government, the foster care system, and the exercise of rights. We also conducted education sessions in which we prepared foster care teens to make presentations to graduate schools of social work, laws schools, and at conferences.

From these first encounters, I was impressed with these young people's desire and passion to learn. They soaked up information faster and more aggressively than I had experienced at the college level. I was stunned to observe the teens applying what they learned from us directly to the policy and advocacy work in which we were involved.

I observed that regardless of educational background, the students were capable of engaging in highly intellectual activities such as reading, analyzing, and applying what they learned. Why did we have such a different experience than those reported by the system in general? One conclusion seemed apparent. Students will actively engage when the learning relates to their life experiences. This engagement heightens when the student recognizes how the learning supports one of their specific goals. Carefully crafting cases around relevant experiences for the student heightened their motivation to engage in the learning process. In addition, giving them space to explore their own understanding through the Socratic Method created a strong sense of empowerment through understanding rather than through irrelevant memorization.

The seventh week everyone attended except Nelson. This was his second absence and according to the admissions agreement, I would have to dismiss him. Losing a good student this late in the semester is every teacher's nightmare. Nelson had made enormous progress in class. He had contributed to the class's understanding of self-advocacy and appeared to have developed a deeper understanding for himself. Yet, it was critical that students learn the importance of committing to a goal, showing up when expected, and extinguishing the pattern of irresponsibility promoted in foster care. Equally important, students need to learn that they will miss something of importance by not attending class. If one student doesn't follow the rule, then other students do not feel compelled to attend all classes, and it is impossible to continue a useful learning experience.

This dilemma faced me at the seventh class. Nelson had fully engaged in the seminar and was learning and finding the process useful. He was contributing to the group and advancing the collective learning experience. However, he had made a formal commitment to miss no more than one class, and somewhere he had to learn accountability for his actions. Yet, if I dismissed him from the rest of the semester, I would hurt him. Was he that resilient? But what would happen to him if I kicked him out of class? Sure, he would survive, but would it be another of a series of failed experiences?

The students noted Nelson's absence, and they would carefully scrutinize my actions. If I allowed him to come back next week without any action, I knew they would feel confused about why they should follow rules. And what would I do if Nelson didn't contact me and dropped out on his own? What if he thought he had no alternative? Weren't we teaching students that they always have alternatives?

I had to put these thoughts aside while I attended to the day's class. As with any small class, when one student was out, the dynamics changed. Without Nelson, the atmosphere had a little less energy.

After living a life in foster care, in which judges and case workers regularly broke appointments and the system paid teens stipends for not showing up at all, I had to recognize that all teens couldn't possibly change their behavior in one new experience. Recognizing this challenge, we developed a method for handling cases such as Nelson's.

After four or five days of anxiety about Nelson, he called. He sounded angry with me and told me he must talk to me after class next week. I told him we needed to discuss the issue of his second absence, and I needed to speak with him before class. Could he come in during the week? No, but he agreed to come in early before class.

"Look, I need you to tell me what I missed." he said. A typical response.

Nelson would not accept dismissal from the class. I should have felt gratified. However, if he accomplished his goal by intimidating me or playing to my sympathy, he would just continue to hone those skills until independence, when presenting oneself as a victim would have limited value. The challenge was to help him develop new self-advocacy skills that would move others to support him because of his strengths and potential to support their own professional or personal goals.

"Hold on. Nelson, you're forgetting the contract we agreed to. Remember at the beginning of the seminar we discussed how important. . . ."

"Listen to me," Nelson's rage erupted. I couldn't begin to appreciate the pressures this young man faced. "My foster mother made me take care of her kids last week. She would have thrown me out if I hadn't." Nelson quickly assessed that I didn't appear affected by his response. "Look, just tell me what I missed, and I'll . . ." Nelson's rage had gone through its range and now suddenly evaporated. "Forget it. Just forget it."

"Nelson, forget for a moment that I am the teacher. You know how much I respect you and how important your contributions have been to the class. Do you know what is upsetting me right now?" I was trying to change my role as teacher/authority figure to coach.

"Yeah. You're pissed because I missed a class, and it's against your rules." Nelson returned to a more even temper. As angry as he was with his difficult situation, I knew he would not disengage with me because the seminar and his informational interview were important to him. He was prepared to go beyond his rage for a future goal. Caught in the crosswinds of a difficult situation, a wonderful learning moment had appeared.

"You know why I am pissed? It's because you're forgetting everything you've learned about self-advocacy. As the teacher, do you think I am concerned with your foster mother? Come on Nelson, what do you think are my needs, not yours?" To give him a solid clue that he was getting back into the class I added. "You want to continue in the seminar, don't you?"

Nelson was firm and relaxed his entire face. "Yes." He was now all student.

"Okay, let's go through my needs as teacher." Nelson nodded his head. He remembered the classes about the other party's needs. "What are they?"

"You need everyone to follow the rules, you don't have time to make up a class a student misses, and you want us to do well on the informational interview." Nelson rattled these needs off as if he had prepared for this conversation.

"Why do I want you to do well on the informational interview? In fact, why do I want you to do well with your life?"

"Because you care about all of us."

Nelson either wanted to believe his last statement or believed it was the right thing to say. In fact, it was true. But it wasn't getting to the process of self-advocacy. "Nelson, you're right, I do care about you. But let's just say I'm a regular college professor with over a hundred students a year. You think I can possibly care that much about every student? Or even if I do care, what is a more important motivation for me?"

"I don't know. . . . You get paid more if I do well? I don't know."

"Now you're thinking. If my students do well, I look good, and then maybe I get a promotion or recognition. If you know this, then all you have to do is convince me you're going to do well. Get me to believe you're going to make me look good. Nelson, you're a terrific student, and I have no doubt you'll do well with your informational interview, and do well with your life."

Nelson smiled.

"Which is more important to me—the problems you have with your foster mother or the fact that you are going to do well?"

"But you're the teacher. You know who's going to do well."

"Nelson, do you want to trust me to remember everything or trust me to be a great guy? Maybe all I'm thinking about is how you challenge me in class?" We knew that opening up our thinking to students even in difficult situations provided them with important insight into human interaction and negotiations. "Or forget me and think of just some teacher who might not care as much. How do you make sure they know you are a great student?"

"I guess I tell them. Okay, look Mr. Pitcoff, I'm one of your best students. I always talk in class, I do most of my homework, I have good answers, and I'm going to do well. Nothing is going to stop me." Nelson appeared extremely satisfied.

"Now which approach do you think I or anyone would find more compelling, the problems with your foster parent or your strengths as a student?"

"Okay, okay, let me do it." Nelson went through a full presentation of why he should be allowed to continue the seminar. He based the presentation on communicating his strengths, understanding my needs as teacher, and providing solutions for the problems caused by his missing the second class. In a sense, we wish every student missed a second class to have this opportunity to be coached in their self-advocacy to get back into the seminar.

Taking the time to confront a student about his actions and then help him successfully navigate through the confrontation provides important understanding. Through this process students learn that confrontations will not always be disastrous, that they can have some power in a confrontation if they understand the process, and that the world does not believe the student will fall apart if confronted.

Later in the semester, we had the opportunity for the class to meet with a vice president at a major investment company, one of our benefactors. Part of our work was to connect the teens and our program to successful individuals and organizations in the community. Many of these individuals are moved when they hear about the teens' resilience and the efforts teens make to prepare for their independence. In addition to contributing money, these individuals commonly offer to meet with the teens and share some insights they have developed on what it takes to succeed. Some even share their personal challenges. We knew that the person we were meeting had come from a disadvantaged background and that he was eager to relate well with our students.

The students were enthusiastic about the opportunity, in spite of the fact that I could not adequately explain what function this company played in the finance world. We would learn together.

The class and I waited in marble the lobby until a suspicious but highly professional security guard fully scrutinized us. Riding the elevator up beyond the fiftieth floor, the students remained unusually quiet in the hushed atmosphere. Some important-looking people gave the students a second glance, but their own world preoccupied them.

We were ushered into a large conference room, perhaps five times the size of YAC's small office where we taught the seminar. The students immediately moved to the floor-to-ceiling windows that looked onto New York City. The view was mesmerizing. It was the first time any of the students had seen such a view of the city, from the top, rather than the limited view they get while in the foster care system.

While all the students were equally awed and wanted to connect with this world, Nelson took the initiative. "Paul, why don't we have our graduation here instead of the dumpy YAC office?"

Through the semester, I had learned that Nelson, along with many other students in the seminar, still had a spontaneous manner of making requests, but their requests were usually thoughtful. I became momentarily anxious and feared that Nelson had failed to learn self-advocacy. But I was still hopeful and rationalized that he just enjoyed aggravating me. My first impulse to his request was that he was asking too much. "It's really a great room. Guess we're lucky to have this opportunity to meet with Albert Senora," I said.

Nelson was tenacious. "Come on Paul, graduation would be so nice here. We deserve it after working so hard. Look around. No one's using the room. You can do it." Nelson had become comfortable with the Socratic model in which roles between student and teacher merge. Now he was urging me on, as if he were my coach.

When the seminar succeeds, students naturally gain high expectations. Thus, without thinking any further and accepting that Nelson's idea had merit, I responded. "Nelson, it's a great idea. Why don't you ask Mr. Senora?"

"No way! It's your job." Then, before I could respond, "Okay, I'll do it." The other students supported Nelson.

During the presentation Mr. Senora told the group about how difficult growing up in the projects had been for him. He explained that homework was like medicine, and they had to do it to have a better life. The students soaked it all up. Before their eyes stood someone authentic, who had experiences to which they could relate and who was now very successful. He explained how the bank worked and how important a college education is. He encouraged students to ask questions.

Nelson raised his hand. Would he embarrass us? "Mr. Senora, you got such a beautiful conference room, and it looks like no one uses it."

I could see Mr. Senora flinch, "Well, we use the conference room a lot, but at certain times it is not scheduled so we can clean it and prepare for another event." Was Nelson going to forget all of Mr. Senora's or his company's needs?

"Look, I know that, but this is the situation. We need a place for our graduation. Now, it looks to me as if the people who work here need to feel like they're helping teens in foster care. I mean they got to know how the world is."

"That's true. We do a lot of charity work."

"Yeah. Yeah, I know, but this way you'll meet some of the kids directly. In the elevator I could tell no one here has seen anyone like us. I mean except you. Look, if you have the graduation here, we can get some important people to come to it, and that will look good for you." The irony of a teen from foster care helping this major investment firm was apparent.

"That sounds interesting. What important people do you have in mind?"

I'm thinking the same thing. Who does Nelson have in mind? "Well, the commissioner of ACS."

Nelson not only secured a room for our graduation but got Senora's company to cater the event. The commissioner of Children's Services attended and gave a keynote speech. If one had entered the event without any knowledge, it would have looked like some special occasion for teens destined for successful careers in finance. All the students brought family members or meaningful staff people to the event. The young women received flowers from their guests, and some of the guys even wore ties.

As the students received their certificates of completion, I said something special about their performance in the seminar and their work on their future careers. In combination with the commissioner's speech about the challenges of living as a foster child, the audience was deeply impressed with the students.

YAC board member Chuck Burton rose to give a speech. He was an extremely successful attorney, and, although friendly with him, I had never heard him speak about his personal life. I assumed that he had to have come from a middle-class family to achieve the success he had and, like many in the profession, was just reserved about his background. He was extremely dedicated to our program's purpose but rarely showed much emotion.

Chuck began by expressing admiration for the students' achievements. His words were heartfelt, but in his professional manner, they lacked a connection to the teens assembled in the first two rows of seats. Then, to all of our amazement, Chuck began to recall his own childhood, growing up with a single parent and working as a teenager to help support his mother and siblings.

We listened with renewed respect for Chuck. Yet, we knew that one reason so many successful members of the community find our teens impressive is that the story of overcoming early life challenges is not restricted to teens in foster care. Hearing Chuck reveal a story that he usually kept private confirmed the importance of getting foster care teens to move beyond the system by meeting with successful community members and learning about the various struggles so many have endured.

The Getting Beyond the System® Seminar had to have a practical application and a way for students to observe what they had learned. We knew from our various experiences that contact and communications with a respected member of the community outside the foster care system was always a significant experience for teens in care and one they took seriously. Therefore, to move the seminar beyond the classroom, into a tangible experience, we designed the informational interview as the final project.

7

Informational Interviews

A Bridge from Foster Care to the Community

Understanding self-advocacy requires action. Teaching only rules and theory would inadequately prepare teens to learn how to apply self-advocacy in obtaining their individual goals. We were committed to integrating into the curriculum a way for teens to practice their skills in an authentic setting, not just through role plays in the classroom. Early on, we arranged for the teens to advocate for something they wanted in their foster care agency. Now we had raised their (and our own) vision to a farther horizon, the future, and we wanted to give them the opportunity to apply their self-advocacy skills toward getting there.

We had yet to meet a teen without some aspirations for the future. Although we had to draw those aspirations out of some, each and every foster care teen who came through our program had something in which they were interested as a possible future career. These dreams always inspired and delighted us because you could never predict what someone wanted to pursue. Given their experience in foster care, some were inevitably interested in social work, education, child care, law, investigative work, health care; usually any group featured some interested in music and sports. But then other teens surprised us. They wanted to go into robotics, archeology, book illustration, or marine biology.

We aimed to create a seminar project that not only required teens to use self-advocacy but was also relevant to each student, customized to each individual's needs. We wanted a situation that put responsibility on the student to present their strengths, do research, understand the needs of the other party, ask questions to get information, and follow through. We wanted to set up something that was genuine, carried risks, and gave students the opportunity to succeed, along with the possibility of making mistakes.

We accept all career interests as possible, even those that might seem unrealistic. How could we let kids pick any career goal? Could we expect a sixteen-year-old who reads at third-grade level to become a pediatrician? We believed that maybe some of their goals were unrealistic, but we shifted the responsibility to them to learn that on their own; in the process, they learned about other jobs and options. For several reasons we couldn't be the ones to say, "Sorry, you're not going to become a pediatrician." How did we know who was going to achieve their dreams? Predicting futures, who would succeed and who wouldn't, seemed presumptuous and beyond anyone's power.

Many teens were interested in fields about which we had little first-hand knowledge. Our belief in the goal's attainability was useless for them. Instead, we could help more by providing opportunities for the teen to learn about the nature of their intended career fields and encouraging them to make their own informed analysis. Teens were unlikely to consider the judgment of a professional from the foster care field. If we told them they couldn't make it, then they were likely to see us as just more people with low expectations for their futures. Conversely, if we told them they could make it, then they were likely to see this encouragement more as our duty or caring attitude rather than reality. However, if we adopted an approach of accepting their selected career and helping them learn more about it, then the teens would under-stand we were taking them seriously. This knowledge, in turn, made them more serious about their selections and more willing to learn from their infor-mational interviews so they could make considered and good decisions about what careers to prepare for at this moment in their lives.

Over and over we saw the teens act savvy in some ways and ignorant in others, especially about the paths to finding meaningful careers. Students hungered for information related to what they wanted to do in the world, but they were trapped in the insularity of the worlds of foster care, mediocre or bad high schools, and communities immersed in poverty. Aware that, for the most part, all the adults surrounding them were employed to care for them, they felt suspicious. Was the adult relating to them because of who the teen was or because it was their job? Did child welfare professionals give them individualized information, relevant to their particular lives, or did they homogenize, generalize, and filter down the information to the lowest common denominator? Did the world represented by the foster care system or the school in any way resemble the community they wanted to enter?

We wanted something that propelled teens beyond the system, literally away from their social workers, lawyers, teachers, and even us. Successful professionals in the system dedicate a great deal of effort to developing trust and relationships with the teens with whom they work. Often they go far beyond their job requirements to connect with the teens. They develop many good and sometimes lasting relationships. No matter how far one goes, however, these relationships still stem from the professional-client origin, rather than the collegial or personal.

At some point in the near future, the teens would not have us in their lives, nor would they have agencies and programs providing them with helping professionals. They needed to build and navigate supportive relationships with adults whom no one paid to care about them. The Getting Beyond the System® Seminar helped teens understand that they had something to offer in these relationships. Instead of getting attention and support based on their problems and victim status, the foster care students became empowered to gain attention and support based on their own merits.

For both student and teacher the informational interview served as an important final project to demonstrate mastery of self-advocacy skills learned in the seminar. We set up this informational interview with an experienced professional in the field of the student's career interest. Students recognized that by finding the career veteran in their selected field, setting up the interview, and allowing them to conduct the interview unobserved by any third party, we were providing them with an incomparable opportunity based on faith in their ability. The interview also symbolized a highly significant act of individualization, by expressing to the student respect for his or her unique personal goals and abilities.

Most professionals engage in an informational interview process at some time in their careers, either formally or informally. Seeking advice about a career or specific type of job from an experienced professional saves time in planning and making education and career moves. The individuals giving advice can do so with relative ease because they are in positions of providing support without further commitment. Even when one motivation for the interview is to arrange an appointment with someone who has the potential to actually help in getting a job, asking for an informational interview is a much easier way to set up a conversation rather than asking to meet about a specific job.

Our informational interviewers are generally successful professionals with years of experience in their field. They have ranged in age from their late twenties to their sixties. They share a passionate interest in their work and career, and most volunteer to do the interviews because they like the idea of giving advice to teenagers starting out on their career paths. Many connect to the teen through recalling memories of beginning their own journey down a career path. In remembering their own lack of knowledge and the challenge of developing a focus, they come to identify with the teen.

Even busy senior professionals find it difficult to deny our request because they have both an opportunity to talk about something they like and a tangible means of helping young people. Many enjoy the idea that they can assist in a way that goes to their strengths and provides them with the chance to give advice about something they know. This focus on their own experience and passion also keeps them focused on what they know, rather than putting them in a position of volunteering to do some mentoring type service with which they are less familiar.

Because most professionals understand the informational interview, we feel little need to give any instructions about the process. People often ask us how these professionals can conduct informational interviews without any training. In our experience, this lack of training is not a problem but is an advantage. We suspect we would not get the overwhelming participation from all the surgeons, lawyers, scientists, sports agents, computer specialists, artists, teachers, police, media producers, chefs, nurses, anthropologists, and so on, if we required them to attend trainings. In addition, training would remove a level of the authenticity from the exchange and diminish the student's trust in his or her newly acquired self-advocacy skills.

We put a lot of responsibility for the interview's success on the student. The student must know how to relate to this individual, make the participating professional believe he or she is using the time well, present a sense of future success, and actively and willingly learn from the professional. If the student fails to impress the professional with a seriousness of purpose, then he or she will not get more than the requested time of twenty minutes; in fact, the student may not even gain the participating professional's focus during those twenty minutes. Thus, the seminar becomes an important precursor for preparing properly for the informational interview.

We found little difficulty in involving professionals and community leaders this way. People in our lives outside of Youth Advocacy Center were constantly telling us they wanted to help these teens somehow, and we knew that they had much to offer. Therefore, to start the informational interview project, we turned to our friends, as well as our board members and supporters, and asked them to share their own career advice with teens. Through their connections, this personal network grew into a board of advisors in various fields committed to finding an appropriate interviewer for each and every student. When our network didn't provide someone in a particular field, we made cold calls to appropriate businesses or organizations. We feel encouraged by how many top professionals volunteer for informational interviews from these cold calls. We and the teens are heartened that so many successful and busy people in the community are willing to give some time to help young people plan their career paths.

Regardless of how we recruit the professional, our pitch remains the same. "We run an after-school program for teens who are exploring and planning for education and careers. Your experience and expertise would prove invaluable to a teen who is interested in your career as a future goal. Could you give a student twenty minutes of your time for an informational interview at your office and at your convenience?" We do not discuss the particular teen's foster care background. Discussing foster care status or experience is solely up to the student during the interview. Thus, when and if teens do

reveal their personal background or their foster care experience, the participating professional can respond in an honest manner, appropriate to the discussion context.

We are excited to break through the insularity of the system and broker
these relationships for teens. We enjoy using our personal and professional
connections and don't mind putting our reputations on the line. We know
that most of these teens would not get the meetings without our initial help,
just like most young people need the help of parents, family members, and
alumni associations to get their first contacts in the work world.

Paul

By the semester's ninth week, students no longer viewed the informational interview as abstract. They recognized that this project would have a
dramatic impact on advancing their ability to achieve specific career goals.
They understood the interview's importance in terms of getting valuable
information, testing their self-advocacy and presentation skills, and beginning to develop a professional network. Therefore, they recognized the value
of learning self-advocacy and working hard to achieve these goals.

Ebony, the aspiring R&B star, was meeting with someone who supervised
production at a major recording studio. Like all our informational interviewers, he was a busy professional absorbed in his own career.

"Okay, let's go through this again. You have the address and day and time
of your appointment. How should you prepare to get there?" I enjoyed
observing the students' enthusiasm and concentration as they made final
preparations for their informational interview.

"I wrote it down in my book and also on another piece of paper I have in
my wallet." In the first four weeks of the seminar, Ebony never wrote anything
down, even if I directly suggested she do so.

"Fine. You wrote it down, but how are you going to get there?" I could
take nothing for granted. Foster care agencies probably shy away from
sending teens out on their own like this due to the risk that kids will fail to
show up or get lost along the way. But if they can't start to take trips like
this, how are they going to make it when they are out of foster care and on
their own?

"The appointment is way downtown. I'll take the train." Ebony's confidence had markedly increased each week of the semester. In the early sessions of the seminar, I had difficulty getting her to answer any question without tremendous prodding.

Benny worked diligently to prepare for his interview at the Museum of Natural History, and he expected everyone else to hold to his standards. "What train? You ever been downtown? How do you know you won't get lost?"

"I'll take the A and then ask someone where to get off." Ebony was speaking with growing confidence.

"You won't have time that day. Or you may be late. You should find out now how to get there. I called the museum and asked the information desk what train to take and where I should get off." Benny sharing his experience created much more impact than I would have had in telling Ebony how to prepare.

"Why do you think Benny wants to plan the trip before the day of the interview?" The class was already engaged in dialogue, and my input was minimal. Students were now familiar with and accepted the Socratic process as the means for understanding. The class had come together, and the students were providing mutual support for each other, creating a safe and supportive atmosphere.

"Yeah, Ebony, you don't want to get lost. You also know you're going to be nervous, and maybe there won't even be anyone to ask that day. If you don't get there on time, he may not wait for you." Nelson still had to get into every conversation.

"It's 4:15 on Thursday," Ebony said. "I'll get there at 4:10. And if the train gets stuck and I'm late he'll wait there, because it's at his office." For Ebony and others in the class, getting to understand the importance of even arriving five minutes early for an appointment required a big step beyond the time culture of foster care. While cutting it close, she at least understood the concept of getting to the appointment early to ensure she was on time.

"Why is it important to get to your appointment early? Before you answer that, do you think Ebony's interviewer will wait if she is late? Shermane, what do you think?"

"Well, Ebony says he's there anyway. But I think he won't respect her if she's late. I think he'll think Ebony doesn't care much about the interview." Darnel cut off Shermane.

"Yeah, he may still meet with Ebony to be polite, but he won't like being disrespected. Ebony, you got to remember that this guy is doing you a favor. He don't have to do it so you ought to show respect. I'm getting there a half hour before my appointment because I want to start right."

"That's a good point. When you arrive communicates something. Remember all our discussions. What do you want to communicate to your informational interviewer, Ebony?" At this part of the semester, I only had to occasionally focus the discussion.

"That I'm responsible and that they can have faith in me. That's why I got to be on time."

"That's right, but what else? What will make them most interested in helping you?"

Benny answered as if he had waited all afternoon to jump on this question. "I know. I know. You want them to believe you're going to succeed, that if they help you, you're going to reach your goals. Then they can be proud they helped you. You got to show them your strengths and show them that nothing is going to stop you from getting where you want to go."

Benny said it better than I could have and in terms to which the students could relate. His answer needed no refinement. I refrained from jumping up and hugging him for his comprehensive and excellent answer and instead accepted it as part of the course of discussion. "Those are some good points that I think we need to keep in mind. But how do we accomplish those goals? Is it just showing up on time?"

"No. No. Showing up on time is easy, and it's just one step that you have to do." I would not compel Ebony to change her estimated arrival time from five minutes before the interview, but I began to feel that, judging from her answer, Ebony was concluding that on her own. "No, you got to talk about your strengths. You got to tell them because they don't know anything about us."

"I think you're right. What strengths will you talk about?" I was enjoying the discussion.

"Well, I'll tell him that music is the thing I care most about. And I'll tell him I love to sing and that I'm going to get my high school diploma."

"That's great, I think he'll be impressed because what does that demonstrate?"

Darnel joined in. "Well, it shows that Ebony sticks it out and won't settle for a GED."

"Anything else?"

Ebony looked a little dejected. "That's not enough? I guess I could talk about my basketball, but why would he be interested in that?"

I looked around the room. "What else? I think it's something you all should consider discussing because you all have it. What's special about all of you?"

The class turned silent for the first time this session. I allowed the silence and thinking to play out for a little while. "Look, you're all just starting out. Do you think the informational interviewer expects Ebony to be an accomplished singer, or Shermane to be an experienced chef, or Darnel to be fully knowledgeable about computers?" The students shook their heads, and some mumbled no. "Okay, then what else is the person interested in? Look at it this way—strengths often relate to past achievements and your developed skills, but can strengths relate to your future too?"

Benny again jumped in with enthusiasm. "I know . . . it's like we talked about. Our future goals are strengths. A strength is that we want to do something with our lives."

"I think Benny is right. It's called ambition. The informational interviewer is very interested in whether you have ambition. Do you have what it takes to succeed? And having future goals and a passion to reach those goals, no matter what it takes, is ambition, and you will always impress an informational interviewer with it."

As the discussion continued, the students gained understanding of the purpose and dynamics of an informational interview versus job interview. As the next step, they prepared written agendas for their interviews. The agendas would help them come up with and remember questions they had and points they wanted to make about themselves.

The informational interviews rely solely on the two participants, the self-advocacy student and the participating expert. Styles and outcomes range widely depending upon effectiveness of the student and the personality and experiences of both parties. At the same time, many informational interviews play out similarly because most students do focus their agenda on getting useful career information, and the normal dynamics of an informational interview are typically supportive.

We use the following case, which is an example of an informational interview, to help students identify the dynamics involved in an informational interview.

> Derek wants to work in the video field. He is seventeen years old, and although he thinks video will be a lifelong career, he knows very little about the profession. Derek is completing high school next June. He has done well in a history class and an art class and not so well in many other subjects.
>
> Derek lived with his family in the Caribbean until his mother brought him to the city when he was six years old. Sadly, she became ill and was unable to take care of him, and by the time he turned ten, he was living in a foster home. That foster mother treated him very kindly, but she couldn't continue foster parenting, so his caseworker moved him when he was twelve. Since then, he has been in two more foster homes and a group home.
>
> Derek has heard that many teenagers have a tough time getting started after they graduate from high school. Often they cannot find work or a suitable place to live. Many graduates from high school don't seem to ever get a job they really want. Derek has decided that he desires a better life. He wants to have a family someday, and he wants to work at something he will enjoy, as well as make a decent living. Derek thinks he would like to pursue a career in video. He heard that he should try to find out about what he needs to do to get into the video profession so he can prepare for after he completes college.
>
> Derek has decided to do some informational interviews. These are interviews with experienced professionals in a career field in which you are interested. The purpose of these interviews is to find out more about the line of work and to learn how people prepare to get jobs and begin a career in the field.

It is Tuesday at 7:30 a.m. Derek is meeting with Sharon Simms, producer of institutional training videos. She designs these videos for companies that need to train their employees in some type of new activity.

[We want students to recognize that their interviews are extremely important, and therefore they may have to reach out to meet the participating professional's needs, such as meeting very early in the morning.]

Derek: "Thank you for meeting with me. I understand that you started in this business as a production assistant intern and now you are producing your own shows. Your experience of starting at the bottom and then getting your own shows would be very helpful for me. I want to work in video."

[We want students to understand how important it is to initially focus on the participating professional and explain why and how their help will be particularly useful.]

Sharon: "Have you thought about what area you would be interested in?"
Derek: "I think I would like camera work, but I want to find out more about the entire field. Like, what's the best way to learn about the field, and how do I get hired?"
Sharon: "Why do you want to work in video?"
Derek: "Because it looks like fun. You're not working at a desk, and everybody watches what you produce."

[We prepare students for a number of specific questions about their goals and why they selected these goals. This preparation also forces them to begin analyzing their own goals.]

Sharon: "Tell me a little about yourself."
Derek: "I will graduate high school this June. I did very well in my art class and in a few history classes. I enjoy reading and spend a good deal of time reading adventure novels and watching all types of programs on television.

"I think I'm very quick at learning how to do physical and technical things if I watch someone else do them. I've lived in many different places because of my family situation—you see, I've been in foster care. That experience hasn't been easy, but I learned how to adapt to many different situations and how to deal with a lot of very different people."

[Our students learn the importance of communicating their strengths, something that is difficult for most of us, but especially for them since the system has taught them to focus on their troubles and victim status.]

> Sharon: "In a way, maybe your experiences will help you in the end. The media field is very stressful, and you have to deal with lots of different people. Learning from watching is very important."

[Another skill is analyzing the participating professional's response. Prior to the seminar, many students personalize all reactions. When adults ask hard questions, don't smile, and move a conversation along quickly, teens consider them mean and unsupportive. Students need to learn to look for different kinds of clues and to interpret interactions differently. Hard questions may, in reality, show interest in the student, appreciation for his or her potential to handle such questions, and careful attention to the conversation. Here, Sharon is demonstrating interest by repeating back her understanding of Derek's strengths.]

> Derek: "Is producing videos fun?"
>
> Sharon: "It can be fun, but it's also a lot of hard work. The biggest mistake people make coming into the field is that they think it's glamorous. When you start, you spend most of the time carrying heavy equipment, getting people sandwiches, getting yelled at by producers, crew, and clients."
>
> Derek: "I can do that. I'm used to yelling."
>
> Sharon: "Then, when you make it, you spend long hours fixing problems and dealing with difficult people. You may find the clients, the talent, and the crew all very difficult to deal with at times. Everyone is under a lot of pressure. But yes, producing videos also can be fun when the show comes out okay and everyone has worked hard to get it to succeed."
>
> Derek: "That must be great."
>
> Sharon: "You want to be a cameraperson. So do a lot of other people. The field has a lot of competition. You should also think of many jobs that people don't always think about. Lighting, gaffing, sound, production managing, directing, assistant producing, location scouting, researching, props designing, picture editing, sound editing, and on and on."

[Students often have one specific career goal, usually the most visible or recognized, and are frequently unaware of a range of related jobs and careers that they would also find interesting. Most students consider this sort of information very useful.]

> Derek: "How do I learn about what all these jobs are?"
>
> Sharon: "If you really want to work in this field you can. There are several ways to go about it. You're just at the right age to begin interning. Try to get an internship with a production company. The bigger companies usually like you to be in college before they give you an internship, but some smaller companies will take high school students."

[We stress understanding the importance of internships. They are an avenue to learning about a career and making connections for a job. The foster care system too often overlooks or does not encourage internships in a student's particular career interest. One rationale is that the students need to begin earning money, and long-term career goals are too unrealistic for this population. Yet, while in foster care, a student's financial needs are more secure than when they leave foster care. In addition, if a student becomes passionate about a career path, he or she can go to college and successfully work toward a long-term goal. An internship can contribute to this passion and provide a useful guide for achieving a career goal. The alternative is preparing for low-level jobs without career horizons, and in most urban setting, these types of jobs will only place the student on a path to poverty or subsistence living.]

> Derek: "How do I get an internship?"
>
> Sharon: "It's hard. Everyone wants them. You need to keep calling and going to as many production companies as possible. Offer your services. Tell them what you are good at. Tell them you're definitely going into the video field, and you want experience and are willing to do any work to get it. Get to know as many people in the business as you can and keep pursuing them, nicely of course, for an internship. You'll get one."
>
> Derek: "I hope so."
>
> Sharon: "And then when you get it, treat it as a real job. Show up on time. Do the best you can. Volunteer to do more. And get yourself known by everyone on the production. If they ask you to get lunch for everyone, don't screw up the order. If they ask you to deliver a video to an editing studio, get it there as fast as possible. Show them you are super at whatever you do. The first years in the business, you can never think anything is beneath you."

Derek: "Is that what you did?"

Sharon: "I sure did."

Derek: "What about school? Should I go to one of those video trade
schools?"

Sharon: "Maybe. But I recommend college. Look, you should talk to
other people too, not just me. Get their advice. It will be different. And then you'll have to decide what advice suits you. But
I'm a big believer in college. You won't get far without a college
education. It's always good to learn something about what you
are videotaping and a college education really helps. Take
classes in all subjects, not just communications."

[We believe in encouraging every teen to explore a college education. The
teens in the system could potentially benefit from a college education, and it
is of fundamental importance for preparing them to live a full life with different and changing career opportunities. The established community recognizes this fact, and almost all participating professionals strongly advocate a
college education without any prompting from us. Advice from a respected
stranger has a great impact, and many students attribute a renewed interest
in college to their informational interviewers.]

Derek: "This has been very helpful. Are there any books I should
read?"

Sharon: "Absolutely. Read lots of novels. Videos are stories, and you
need to get as much experience with different ways to tell
stories. Watch films. Not just new ones but old ones. Any film.
Watch them again and again to see if you understand how they
are made. Read some books about film and video. I'll give you a
list."

Derek: "Can you give me any suggestions of who I might go to for an
internship?"

Sharon: "Try Meg Halpern at HYT, which is a small producer of travel
videos. Also try Harold Jackson at National Express. It has its
own video unit and might be interested."

Derek: "Can I say that you suggested I call?"

Sharon: "Certainly."

Derek: "Thank you so much. Can I call you in a few months and let
you know how I am doing?"

[One of the differences between teens growing up in foster care from those
in middle-class families is the lack of connections and unfamiliarity with

networking. Teens from foster care could benefit a great deal from developing a network of support within the community. The informational interviews are a first step in this direction.]

> Sharon: "I would like that. Sorry, I have to go now, but my shoot begins at 8:00 a.m."
>
> Derek: "I know this is a lot to ask, but could I watch today or at some other time?"
>
> Sharon: "You're here. Why don't you watch this morning? I won't be able to talk with you. I'll be too busy, but you are welcome to stay."
>
> Derek: "Thanks, I really appreciate it!"
>
> Sharon: "Would you mind first getting me a cup of coffee and a muffin? I haven't had anything yet this morning. Here's some money, there is a place on the corner of Twenty-seventh and Seventh."
>
> Derek: "Sure. I'll be right back."

Students enjoy this case and find it has many dimensions of analysis in terms of self-advocacy, and it promotes wide-ranging discussions about career development.

The seminar is now in the eleventh week, and many students have gone on their informational interviews.

"Ebony, tell us about your interview."

"He was so great. I mean, I learned so much! That place is huge, you never seen a lobby like that with so many elevators, and I had to go up to the thirty-fourth floor! And I didn't even realize that this one company has all these labels with like, a hundred different artists. And I saw the studios, and he gave me some CDs. . . ." Ebony couldn't get the words out fast enough, and her smile said even more. It came from deep satisfaction with having a new vision for her life. She sat visibly taller and straighter. The experience clearly exceeded her wildest imagination.

Over the years, the reports from both students and professionals are that the dynamics of the interviews work and usually exceed both parties' expectations. Students are exhilarated. They report getting useful, specific information about the career field, including recommendations for particular educational and experiential paths. They report that the interviewer gives them particular information, related specifically to their individual goals, strengths, and personality.

Students believe that this personal approach is extremely important, especially compared to group information sessions which often neglect a student's specific questions and needs.

In addition to giving them valuable information, this individualized attention greatly increases the student's sense of their potential to succeed. The experience provides feedback from a respected professional, and allows the student to visualize himself or herself as a future professional or even future colleague of the informational interview. This identification potentially creates a reservoir of energy and motivation to seriously pursue advanced education and prioritize their lives to focus on achieving their goals.

"What was he like?" I asked

"His name is Gil Rodgers. He's really nice . . ."

Students report that the informational interviewers do not talk down to them and treat them like "a real person." This attitude delightfully surprises the students, and they often attribute it to the niceness of the interviewers, in spite of our efforts to help them depersonalize the situation. While participating professionals may be nice, we need to remind students that an interview succeeds based on a relationship that requires both parties. The engagement of the interviewer is more a response to the students' abilities to communicate and present their strengths, than it is to the interviewer's inherent character.

I asked her to elaborate, to go beyond nice. Did he give her useful information? Did he think she could make it in the recording business? Did she get across her strengths?

"It's really funny because I was surprised how much we could relate to each other. He's a producer but started out as a musician, a drummer. He still plays drums, but his job is as a producer. He told me he started out just like me. He wanted to be a drummer and nothing else."

Students are pleased with the concrete information they receive from the interview and the fact that they understand it. They thrill at explaining to the seminar class the dynamics of the recording business, the role of a sonogram technologist, how a graphic artist has to interpret the meaning of a book, how a computer expert has to understand their clients' needs, the importance of certain internships, what an anthropologist does at a museum, and so on.

"But he told me you have to have a back up plan. It's not so easy getting jobs as a musician or singer so you need a back up, like another job in the business. Then he said who knows . . . you may even get a break as a musician if you work in the business." This statement was coming from a girl who seven weeks ago was insisting that just having the goal of becoming a singer was sufficient.

I asked if she thought the interviewer's advice was a good idea. "Yeah, he said I got to go to college. He explained that I had to go to college and be sure to take some business courses because it's a business; it's not just about music. He also said I got to try to get internships when I go to college."

Ebony continued, "Want to hear something else? He told me he really screwed up his first year of college and almost flunked out, but then he got serious and worked hard."

When our students look out at the world, they often believe that successful people are born into success. Especially for a teenager in foster care, this perfect rise to success seems daunting. A shaky start consumes many foster care teens. They know they have endured considerable challenges in their life that have left significant scars and trauma. Students often waver between feeling that their backgrounds make it unlikely they will ever succeed and occasionally believing that their tremendous resilience will allow them to rise above their past. Thus, when informational interview experts reveal their own screw-ups and failures, especially when they were young, our students pay particular attention. We never have suggested to the professional to engage in such revelation, but consistently they do so.

Learning how successful professionals almost failed out of their first year of college, got fired from their first job for calling in sick from a party, or had to support their brother who was sick, or any of the range of struggles most people encounter, diminishes students' own insecurities about their high school record or some trouble they experienced. Life as a teenager means experimenting and failing. This is a universal experience. When professionals share their own experiments, failures, challenges, and responsibilities, the students can then see themselves as possibly succeeding in a career.

"What do you think he thought of you?" I asked.

"He liked me! I think he did. He said I had ambition just to do this interview and that impressed him. He also said he thought I was strong and could deal with pressure. He talked about me, not someone else, and he really took his time to make sure I understood. He said I should keep in touch with him."

Then, looking at everyone in the class, Ebony repeated solemnly, "It's so important to have back-up plans." She said this as if she were the one who thought of it. The tables had turned, and Ebony was now informing her peers of the importance of a back-up plan if you wanted to do something as competitive as professional singing. Any sign of belligerence or resistance to this idea had vanished.

"I mean, I still want to be a singer, but I didn't realize I could work in the business and that was a way to maybe get a chance to sing. But even if I don't sing professionally, I can have a good job and be connected to music."

We cannot underestimate the importance of teens visualizing themselves as future professionals. For many students, the informational interview is the first time they physically enter a work or college setting outside the foster care and public high school systems. Impressive strangers greet them and treat them as potentially belonging to a new group, a group of professionals. The professional shows them around, gives them tours, and brings them to an office, all in the context of this future identity. They pass and often meet or see people that look like them and recognize that they can fit into a professional setting too. Their sole identity within the community is no longer as a foster child, but as a future colleague.

"Sounds interesting," I said, "What will you do next?"

"Yesterday I went to meet with a guidance counselor at my high school. I never even knew who that was. But this totally changed my mind about college. I mean, he's right, I have to have a back-up plan." She repeated those words again, almost to herself, with some obvious satisfaction.

Repeatedly, we see how these interviews have transformed the students. Many in the system would tell Ebony that counting on a career as a singer was foolish. This approach would only have made her angry, more resistant, or even more withdrawn. In her mind, anyone associated with the system was part of the group always telling her what not to do, or how limited her life would be. She would even find my credibility low if I had told her that becoming a musician was unrealistic or that she had to have a back-up plan. What did I know about her life? And what did I know about her chances in the music business? Connecting her with a professional in the music business and letting her go to the informational interview on her own placed her in an environment she could trust where she could gain more unbiased and informed information. Ebony was now pursuing a path based on her own understanding.

The other students listened attentively to Ebony. They smiled, made comments of encouragement, and appeared genuinely pleased with Ebony's achievements. None of the other students knew Ebony before this class, but the class time and especially the shared challenge and anxiety of conducting their informational interviews had drawn them all close. They understood the magnitude of Ebony's preparation to succeed in her interview. Students benefit from our seminars by coming together around an important shared experience. Many teens have not formed close relationships in the context of group experiences. The bonding experience of going through a challenge related to improving one's life appears to bring many students closer to each other and to help them to develop continuing relationships.

When I turned to Shermane, an uncharacteristic broad smile appeared on her face. Shermane finally stopped saying she was a bad girl. I had learned that her vibes of aloofness and separateness from the group had nothing to do with her engagement in the class, and she more than equally contributed.

I asked her how her twenty minutes with the pastry chef went. She too could hardly contain her words.

"What are you talking about twenty minutes, Paul? He spent an hour and a half with me!"

I no longer felt surprised that the requested twenty-minute interview usually lasted longer, sometimes to an hour or two. Because YAC never asks for the extra time or continuing relationships when setting up the interview, such an achievement is solely individual and in the students' hands.

"You should see this restaurant! It is like so fancy! I mean, the desserts are twelve dollars! He talked to me for almost an hour and then took me on a tour of the kitchen. He introduced me to everyone who was working there. So many people, and each one does a special job. The stoves are huge! He told me the best thing is to try to get to a four-star restaurant or deluxe hotel. And you're not gonna believe it, but his favorite dessert is the same as mine, an upside-down cake! He even wrote down some names of cooking schools for me and told me they might give me some scholarship money. He said I could call him for help if I need it. He was just so nice."

This was not the same young woman who had started the class. She was now excited about a future rather than identifying herself with the past. She expressed self-confidence and shared a positive experience willingly with her peers and me.

Her interview had occurred a week and a half before this class. I asked if she had sent a thank you note. We don't require the students to do this but rather explain the importance and give them some ideas of how to customize them. Knowing Shermane's weak academic skills I had some concern she might find the task too difficult. I was willing to help her after class.

"Well, I did . . . but it came back in the mail." I figured she got the address wrong and asked if she checked it.

"Of course I did." Shermane, like some of the other students, tended to respond to me as if I were slow.

"Then how come it came back?" I assumed that Shermane had screwed up something, but I would remain supportive. "Maybe the post office made a mistake?"

"No, they didn't—he no longer works there. I went to the restaurant and found the new restaurant he works at. I sent the letter there," Shermane said, as if she normally handled countless situations in this way. But I knew this was a big deal for her. I was particularly impressed that she took the initiative to find out where the chef was now working. She knew the importance of this contact for her. She exhibited the capacity to figure out the rest without anyone telling her specifics. Shermane's thoughtfulness and actions proved wrong the system's belief that someone must teach teens every single step of a process because they wouldn't figure it out for themselves.

In a week, we would reach the semester's end. Nine of the students had completed their informational interviews. Each member of the group appeared much more confident and mature. They exuded a sense of accomplishment as they talked excitedly about the experiences they had going to offices, studios, restaurants, and laboratories for their informational interviews. They talked about new adult characters in their lives that had nothing to do with their foster care situation.

I felt thrilled to see how far they had come. No one expected to see such involvement in preparing and planning for their future careers. One student had never actively participated in a class through more than three years of high school; another young woman had never read aloud in any class; a third girl had lived in foster care for seven years and lived in nine different placements; an agency had considered another a significant problem and continually denied her visits with her biological mother; a caseworker told yet another student that college was an inappropriate plan for her. The system at one time or another had considered all of these young people to have had an attitude, yet there they sat, discussing careers and the components of self-advocacy as any college student preparing for a successful future.

One very simple but critical goal we have accomplished in securing and preparing students for informational interviews is to expose them to an environment different from foster care. More important, this context directly relates to their future planning for successful independence after they leave foster care. This idea goes back to some of the earliest work we did at YAC, for example, when Carlos and other teens led graduate school classes. When we place teens in a situation in which they bear responsibility and prepare them to take a leadership role, they accept it and begin to thrive. And the expectations around them change, and others begin to see them differently. People no longer identify them as the group home kids destined for the streets, the shelters, and the prisons.

Certainly our teens impressed and moved their informational interviewers. One television producer wrote us:

> The most surprising thing about my informational interview was that when the meeting ended, I was the one who left deeply impressed and felt empowered. I was producing a new series and

invited her to meet me in one of the editing bays. It was near the end of production, at the harried, crisis stage, and I had already rescheduled, but I was determined to keep the appointment because I knew it was important and was flattered to have been asked. I took the meeting seriously and was prepared.

Allison [the teen] was equally prepared with questions about how to achieve her goal to become an on-air reporter. But it wasn't her polite manners, good listening skills, or informed questions that impressed me. It was her drive, confidence, and sense of self that was so present in the face of such personal adversity and challenging circumstances that are endemic to being raised in foster care. Her determination still sends tingles down my spine.

Upon completing the meeting, the interviewers enthusiastically report a range of elements that excite them and motivate many to volunteer to do additional interviews. Most are sincerely impressed with the student they meet. The interview turns into a connection with the student. Students impress the interviewer with their commitment, positive attributes, resiliency, and desire to contribute to the community at large. When the interviewer turns the twenty minutes requested time into more than an hour, they are as surprised as the teen. Most volunteers handle demanding professional and personal schedules and would rarely allocate such time for anything not directly related to their work or personal life. They report that they enjoy the conversations with the student and find that the student's questions often get them to reanalyze their own understanding of their work and the paths necessary to achieve their goals. They enjoy the candidness of the students and their openness to learn.

Informational interviewers give a wide range of information because the students appear vitally interested and focused on the discussion topics. Interviewers often mention complicated concepts, describe unfamiliar experiences, and use words and expressions unfamiliar to the student. Yet, the student's understanding of self-advocacy, their motivation, and the relation of the discussion to their personal goals creates willingness and often the ability for them to persevere with the conversations. Students then learn from and integrate this new information into their own lives.

Almost everyone who learns about our use of informational interviews for teens in foster care agrees that the interviews have proven to be a great idea. Many parents of teens outside the foster care system express a desire to see their own teenagers experience an informational interview. Its value is easy to appreciate.

After many semesters, the informational interview project continues to be immensely successful for helping teens take control of their future and develop their self-advocacy skills. It helps teens get beyond the foster care system in a demonstrable, tangible way. It helps them physically move out of the foster care arenas into the spaces and places where they aspire to be. We designed it around their individual strengths and needs, and thus it speaks to their unique desires and dreams. Successful individuals commonly use this process to move ahead in education and careers, and teens from foster care should have access to it and benefit from it. It respects and, in fact, requires the engagement of the intellect in planning and execution.

The informational interview attacks the segregation of foster care teens from the rest of us. It creates a bridge, a space for people to meet across class, race, and family issues. It gets people outside of the system interested in helping these teens and, for some of them, interested in changing the system. We see it as an exciting way to break down the system's insularity and raise the expectations for what we, as a society, should provide for these teens.

Our next question was, would the system accept a different approach to preparing teens for independence and consider incorporating the Getting Beyond the System® seminar and the informational interview?

8

System Resistance to Empowering Teens

We had been running the Getting Beyond the System® Self-Advocacy Seminar classes for teens at our office for two years. We enrolled a few students from a number of different agencies in New York City to form a class. Usually the students were encouraged to attend our seminar by independent living specialists who were committed to seeing teens prepare for their transition out of foster care. These classes helped us learn how to run the seminar and demonstrated the effectiveness of the curriculum and informational interview program.

We had seen in our program that empowering teens through self-advocacy was an independent living skill. Engaging intellectually, understanding the needs of the other party, setting goals, assessing and communicating personal strengths, negotiating, and practicing communication skills are essential in many arenas one encounters in independent life. These skills transfer to job hunting, to finding someone to help you apply to college, to getting help with a health issue, to successfully pursuing a career, to becoming and remaining a productive participating citizen.

Naturally, we believed that foster care agencies, which struggled to prepare their youth for independent living, would jump at the opportunity to adopt the GBS program and include it in their efforts to empower all their teens. We developed a method to train foster care agency staff to run the GBS program on their own. We even included in the training a facilitator's guide that we had tested and proven effective. By transferring our model to the agency, many more teens would have the opportunity to better prepare for independence. Of equal importance, GBS was not terribly resource dependent. At a time when many program managers and funders looked to leverage resources, GBS was providing an invaluable new resource, the informational interviewer, almost without cost.

We decided to approach some foster care agencies and organizations involved with foster teens to discuss the possibility of incorporating our self-advocacy training into their independent living programs. To facilitate the seminar's adoption, we offered to run the program independently for the organization or train them to run the program. In addition to reaching more teens, we also believed that if the agency ran the seminar, it might affect their practice methods for empowering teens. Integrating GBS into an organization's programming would encourage staff to focus more on planning for the teens' futures, recognizing each of their individual strengths, and identifying the teens with a future goal rather than a past problem or trauma.

The enthusiasm of GBS graduates and many professionals aware of our program did not prepare us for the resistance we would face from foster care agencies. They expressed resistance in different ways. Some professionals worried that we would take their best students away from their existing program, others felt the seminar challenged their teens too much, others didn't want teens traveling to a different neighborhood, and still others could not understand the necessity for attending all classes.

In our journey to help more teens learn self-advocacy and take control of their futures we had more lessons to learn. Although we had developed an effective seminar that was transferable, we needed to understand the nature of the foster care system's resistance to such programs and find ways to break through this resistance to serve the teens in care. This new journey began.

Paul

Sex was the last thing on my mind as I arrived at Grand Central Station to meet Norman and Faith. But knowing we were going to a foster care agency to talk with teens, I should have known better. Sometimes I thought that the people who worked with teens in foster care obsessed about sex more than the teenagers did.

Faith and Norman, two recent graduates of our twelve-week self-advocacy seminar arranged to meet me at Grand Central Station. In two hours we were presenting to teenagers at an agency outside the city. Through the presentation we intended to orient teenagers who would be taking our seminar. This was the first time an agency had shown interest in offering our seminar at their facility, and we were determined to make the arrangement work. As our first step, we would explain the seminar to the teens whom the agency had selected to attend in hopes that it would interest them.

Faith and Norman knew we had a train to catch. They also knew my expectations and that I would not wait past 11:10. But Faith and Norman had long experience in a culture of low expectations, and I was a bit anxious because I had not called to remind them, nor would I wait for them.

As I scanned this great space, my eye momentarily caught the contrast between business people rushing with purpose and a lone young man leaning against a distant wall. His posture was one of all toughness and attitude against the grace of the marble wall. As people hurried by to important appointments, this man projected an invisible barrier. The commuters instinctively responded and allowed him just a bit of extra space as they dashed to offices or trains.

I approached the information booth, reassuring myself that I was early. As I calmed myself, a familiar voice from behind simply said, "Hi." I turned and saw Norman. "I've been here two hours," he said, as he pointed to the space that was previously occupied by the young man I had just noticed. Norman was clearly excited about Grand Central Station and today's presentation. The young man who had looked so off-putting was as enthusiastic as a little boy, describing what he had seen during the last hours. He talked about the stars on the ceiling, the people, the glitzy stores, the huge buildings outside. At eighteen, although a lifelong resident of New York City, he said he had never seen Grand Central or even been in midtown. Just absorbing this atmosphere filled him with enthusiasm. Norman appeared to take measure of this world and whether he could fit in.

Norman and Faith practiced their presentation on the train ride. They decided to explain how learning self-advocacy skills helped them in their own lives. While they practiced, they sat with less nervous energy, their expressions serious as they struggled to find the right words. They sensed the importance of their responsibility. As graduates of our seminar program, they had prepared for the day's presentation by taking an additional two-session training course and worked on developing their presentation agendas on their own time.

Erica, the agency's independent living director, met us at the train station with bad news. She informed us that Floyd Philips, the agency school principal, had left us a message just an hour before, while we were on the train, telling us that we shouldn't come. Apparently he had never arranged for the teens, the seminar candidates, to be available for our presentation.

Faith and Norman had experienced some of the greatest disappointments in life. One might think that separation from their families and the multiple changes in their foster care placements might have made them immune to smaller everyday disappointments. Yet, I felt pained seeing the sadness wash across their faces. How many disappointments did it take to dampen a young person's hopes? In this environment of broken commitments, teenagers in foster care were somehow expected to learn how to meet responsibilities and become independent.

Over the past few months, we had planned the presentation we were supposed to have made that day. Herb Hodos, the executive director of the agency, wanted to offer our program to teens in his agency. We first met Hodos three years earlier, at conferences and at various committee meetings. He immediately captured our interest. Not only did he and his agency have a good reputation for innovative programming, but he was well versed in the systemic problems of the foster care system. Hodos appeared determined to reverse the failure rate of teens emancipated from the system and was committed to returning children to their families. Hodos was an energetic and tireless crusader for families and kids. Increasing the number of beds or the stay for children at his agency for the sake of building his budget never seemed like issues on his agenda. Betsy and I felt reassured that he was a caring leader in a high position who could actually implement meaningful reforms in the foster care system.

Executive directors of foster care agencies have many pressures and extensive responsibilities. The lives of the children in their care are literally at stake. Too often bad things happen, and many times someone should have and could have prevented them. Screening and monitoring foster placements, hiring, training, and supervising staff, taking care of children, working with biological parents, and preparing each child's case for legal review and monitoring by the local government administration are often conflicting demands that need to be managed. These factors combine with a constant sense of impending crises.

Although the agency's public face is one of a charity for children, it also has many parallels to a big business. Some agency budgets total more than fifty million dollars a year. New York's dozens of social services agencies compete to get foster care children to enable them to renew their contracts with the city government and maintain and increase their annual funding. This focus on revenue filters down to the staff. Children who leave foster care or switch agencies diminish an agency's revenue stream, and the consequences can significantly impact salaries, services, staffing, and facilities. This pressure to maintain funding and therefore children is occasionally explicit and often implicit in contributing to the decisions around reuniting children with their biological parents.

Young children often have a chance of reuniting with their biological family or getting adopted; therefore, the agency is continually vulnerable to diminished revenue flow. Teenagers, however, represent a more consistent revenue source for foster care agencies because of their length of stay. Typically, after the courts assign them independent living as the discharge plan, the agency is less pressured to reunite teens with their biological families or find adoptive families. Thus, if the system places a teen in the independent living category, he or she can legally and practically remain in foster care for two to five years, depending upon the state's maximum discharge age.

Because most revenue comes from government contracts, the agency devotes an inordinate amount of time fulfilling mandates, regulations, and paperwork. Without compliance and reports, the government may not pay the foster care agency, and the agency may lose its contract. For most, losing a major foster care contract would be a devastating blow that could drive them out of business. Along with addressing mandates, the executive director needs to communicate the agency's merits to the political leaders connected with foster care, as well as to private donors.

Clearly, executive directors and senior administrators work under so many conflicting pressures that one would have difficulty understanding how they could possibly attend to any new, creative solutions to the problems faced by children in their care. At the same time, they need to continually demonstrate that they are doing more and providing improved services for these children. One way they can do this is to adopt new programs like ours and let their funders and the government become aware of the innovative attempts they are making to serve their teenagers. However, many so-called innovative programs appeared questionable as to whether they changed practices or impacted outcomes for teens discharged from foster care.

Although we knew that the agencies had priorities other than the teens' futures, we searched for the exception, an agency willing to dedicate resources to help teens prepare for a successful future. At the same time, we were aware that some agencies interested in our program were just looking for ways to improve their public image but had no capacity to fully adopt the seminar and change their approach to preparing teens for independence. When Hodos agreed to a joint project, we believed that he and his agency were sincerely committed to exploring better ways to prepare teenagers for their transition to independence; we hoped that, with his backing, the agency had the capacity to host the GBS Seminar.

A series of meetings took place. The meetings quickly ripened into a bureaucratic atmosphere. Everyone was very particular about start dates, logistical arrangements for the teens, the exact nature of our curriculum, individual responsibilities, and exactly which teenagers would enroll. After we made each decision, the associate director noted it in his pad. The deliberation and precision should have comforted me. At the same time, we increasingly realized that few people from the agency understood our program. Everyone's ideas of the seminar's purpose conformed to their own notions of what teenagers needed.

Hodos's agency had an existing collaboration with a large national travel company. The travel company had set up a job-training program for the teens at the foster care agency, in which it trained teens to use specific data entry programs for travel arrangements. The agency hoped that their teens would get jobs, and the company was looking for a source of low-end employees. Initially, the program appealed to me. It appeared useful for teens in foster care looking for job experience. Yet, as I learned about the details, many problems became apparent.

At our meetings, Ron Wendel, the travel company executive, spoke frankly about his frustration with what he called the low caliber of the teens showing up for his training, and the foster care agency was aggravated by how few teens they could interest in the program. Wendel was appalled by the teens' lack of work ethics. He described how they were irresponsible and challenged the rules too often. Wendel shared his concern that our program might be inappropriate; instead of learning to advocate for themselves these teens needed to learn to take orders and not live in a world of entitlements.

The strange thing about my reaction to Wendel was that I agreed with some of his observations. Most teens in foster care are not responsive to the culture and mores of a non-welfare system. Our disagreement was with the cause of these problems. He saw the problem as innate with what he called "these types of kids." We saw their inability to adapt to work situations as a continuation of the behavior and skills the teens had learned in the foster care system. The system too often supported a poor work ethic by communicating diminished or negative expectations for the teens and not providing any significant opportunities to handle personal responsibility.

The more I heard Wendel talk, the more I began to suspect that the travel company was not really offering the teens anything of great importance. Yes, they wanted to train teens to do data entry. However, no part of their plan called for career advice or even educating the teens on the types of significant job opportunities that existed in the travel business. Their expectation went only so far as hoping teens could perform data entry for the rest of their lives or until another program or system made their work obsolete. This diminished expectation certainly got communicated to the teen. Just getting a job for the rest of one's life does not particularly appeal to teenagers.

We explained to Wendel and the others that we had based self-advocacy and the seminar on understanding the needs of the other party and finding ways to support those needs in achieving one's own goals. If the travel company could demonstrate how these teens could find a meaningful career beyond data entry, the teens might respond more enthusiastically in their training. The agency staff remained noticeably quiet through this exchange. Everybody felt the tension. The agency did not want to offend either Wendel or us. I was saddened to witness the lack of support for their teenagers communicated to the travel executive, who was clearly new to understanding the foster care situation.

Oddly, these meetings never included Floyd Philips, the principal of the agency's high school program where the seminar would be offered, or Erica, the independent living director who coordinated such programs and had supported us in the past. However, those in attendance assured us that they had set up everything for us to begin running the seminar at the school. We confirmed and reconfirmed the date and time of an orientation session.

Now it was that date, half an hour before the seminar orientation, and I was standing on the train platform, looking at Norman and Faith. I knew we could not turn around and go home. Their faces no longer showed sadness. It had been replaced by an icy look that betrayed no emotion, a look they had acquired from years of learning how to armor oneself from disappointment. I was pained and frightened to see this in the faces that were so animated just ten minutes before. I told Erica that because we had prepared and had made the trip, we wanted to go to the school. "Perhaps the principal could find a way to arrange to find the students selected for our presentation," I suggested.

When we arrived at the agency's school Erica left us standing in the hall while she went to check in with the principal. The school displayed no student work or projects in its hallways. The only decorations and color interrupting the gloom of the institution were glossy travel posters advertising the travel company and exotic destinations. Soon Erica returned and apologized for the fact that the principal refused to personally welcome us.

She led us to a room in the basement, with tables along the walls and a few computers set up. Four staff people were having coffee on one side of the room, and I assumed that, if the presentation was to happen, we would be sharing this space and competing with other ongoing activities for the teens'

attention. This setup was typical at foster care agencies. Staff rarely designated a room solely to an activity for teens. Random people came in and out
of any type of presentation and class. Staff freely pulled teenagers out from a
class if they wanted to talk with them. All these distractions made it hard, if
not impossible, for leaders or students to focus.

We sat for forty-five minutes past the designated time for the presentation. Erica left the room and every ten minutes or so popped her head in to
tell us that the principal was rounding up some teens for our presentation.
She apologetically forewarned us that he could not find the original
teenagers selected for the seminar, but at least we would have some kids to
present to.

Eventually, two childcare staff arrived with six teens. Erica introduced
the staff, Mr. Firmly and Ms. Pleasant. I found this introduction useful
because I had difficulty telling who the mature staff were and who the kids
were. This wasn't as much because of their similar baggy jeans, big shirts,
and do-rags, or because of the small age gap, as much as it was because of
the attitudes. Firmly and Pleasant and a number of students were arguing
bitterly. Norman, Faith, and I were invisible to them.

Jerome, a thin, muscular boy with light brown eyes was in a rage. He
turned on Firmly, "You have no right to stop me from seeing my mother . . .
you ain't nothing, and I can take you on."

"We'll see about that." Firmly did not allow a second to pass after this
challenge. "I'll take care of you right after this meeting."

Jerome was not put off. "You and who else?"

The other teen participants were intently watching. When Jerome fell off
the argument, others jumped in with their own issues with Firmly and Pleasant. "I ain't going anywhere till I get new clothes," hissed Tamika, a pretty girl
who clearly had made an effort to look attractive. "I've been wearing the same
pair of jeans for four months," she burst out screaming, as her fury mounted.
The charge in the atmosphere had been ignited.

The three of us had no role here. The seminar and our presentation were
completely irrelevant. As the sounds of human torment intensified and the
feelings of long suffering flared, we could only connect with these teenagers
through our sympathy for them.

Erica tapped Mr. Firmly on the shoulder and whispered something to him. He abruptly switched gears and informed the group of teenagers that they should be respectful to their guests. "Now y'all pay attention. NOW." He yelled for compliance. He sat back, folded his arms, and nodded to us to begin.

A somewhat older looking participant, Curtis, who I thought was sleeping through this prelude, picked his head up off his chest. "Look. I just want to get out of here. Why do we have to be here anyway? I know everything I need to know about sex." Because the scene was surreal, Curtis's comment about sex did not strike me as particularly bizarre or significant. But Curtis unwittingly came to our rescue. The teens hushed briefly and focused attention on us.

Politely, I addressed Mr. Firmly and Ms. Pleasant and told them we were here to present the self-advocacy orientation for the teens, and perhaps they would like to come back after we finished to resolve the problems they were discussing with the teens. I added that if that was not possible, perhaps we should just tell Mr. Philips, the principal, that we couldn't do this today because of these other problems. Using the threat of the principal was terribly demeaning, but I had become acculturated to the foster care bureaucracy.

Indeed, the threat caught their attention and prodded Firmly and Pleasant in a different direction, though their tone did not change. They yelled at the teenagers, "Be respectful. . . . You have a lot to learn from these good people." How could we not dislike Firmly and Pleasant? They patronized us, threatened the teens with bodily assaults, created anguish with their bureaucratic use of the rules, obviously hated being here, hadn't a clue of what we were doing, and, worst of all, had the lowest expectations for the teens. How could these individuals be in charge of the lives of even one teenager?

At the same time we sympathized with Firmly and Pleasant. They were probably paid minimum wage and were not sufficiently trained or respected by the management. They had the hardest jobs at the agency, dealing with the teens on a day-by-day, hour-by-hour, minute-by-minute basis. The agency and the teens expected them to resolve all kinds of problems on the spot.

They were given the critical responsibility of caring for teens traumatized first by separation from their families and then by the foster care system.

On reflection, at another time and in a more rational space, I realized that Firmly and Pleasant were not lone actors in this neglectful and abusive treatment of teenagers. They were the product of a society that, on one hand, promoted "family values," and, on the other, failed to help to keep families together, one that removed children from parents and did nothing substantial to reunite them and repair the wounds. A society that warehoused teenagers who were separated from their families and offered no worthy program to prepare them for independence and personal responsibility. Entrenched private bureaucracies focused on the revenue derived from every day a teenager was kept in foster care. In the end, Firmly and Pleasant suffered from the same lack of empowerment as the teens.

I jumped into the momentary quiet and began the presentation by introducing our organization and asking Norman and Faith to introduce themselves. The teen participants briefly glanced at me but became intensely interested when our teen graduates explained that they too were in foster care. Faith began by trying to explain self-advocacy. Faith was the type of teen that many had said couldn't make it. She had a heavy lisp and a disorganized manner when she spoke. She was sweet but at times seemed a little out of it. Yet, here she told a story about how she advocated for herself to have her foster care agency pay for a trip to visit a college in which she was interested.

Faith asked if anyone had a problem that they could solve using self-advocacy. Everyone was silent. Annoyingly, Firmly and Pleasant had been talking with each other in a distracting low whisper. The sudden silence among the teens startled them, and they returned their attention to the group. "Answer the young lady's question," Pleasant barked at the teens. Curtis in a boisterous voice complained, "What's this got to do with sex? I know all I need to know. I told you that already . . . I'm leaving," and he started to get up.

"Wait, wait," I tried. "Why do you think our presentation is about sex?"

"Philips, the principal, told me to come here, and I would learn more about sex! Y'all know I'm an expert in this area, but he said I should come anyway."

The rest of the group snickered. "Were the rest of you told the same thing?" My sense of reality was shaky. They shrugged and nodded, and the truth came out that, indeed, Principal Philips had told them that our presentation was about sex, not self-advocacy. Apparently Philips believed this was the only way to get teenagers to attend a presentation about planning their life goals and learning self-advocacy.

We had observed a pervasive belief among adults working in foster care that only sex, food, and quick money motivated teenagers. The bait and switch of using sex to lure teens to our seminar was a manifestation of low or nonexistent expectations for these teens to take on responsibility to prepare for independence.

Norman had a heightened ability to understand the subtext of human interactions. He combined this skill with an uncanny sense of timing and willingness to get involved. At first I didn't appreciate this skill when Norman, in the seminar, had aggressively challenged me. The longer I knew Norman, the more I realized that he could use his ability to challenge in a positive way, not only to benefit himself but also to support others. Norman knew what was happening and took the initiative to try to neutralize a charged situation and move away from sex back to self-advocacy.

"Here . . . self-advocacy is really good. You take this class for twelve weeks, and you learn how to do a lot of things. Take me . . . I work at a big store. The customers are always abusing me. I get angry and curse them. I took this class, and now the customers don't get to me. I realize I have more important thinks to think about. They have nothing to do with my life. I'm working on my goals. I'm going to be a sound engineer. That's what the seminar is about."

Listening to him describe what self-advocacy had done for him and hearing his conviction that it had helped, produced tears in my eyes. I knew from talking to Norman that the store had come close to firing him a number of times for mouthing off at customers who wanted him to drop what he was doing for one customer to serve them or magically produce something out of stock from the back. Now he was giving a message that his fellow foster care peers could apply to their lives. His capacity to endure and to change was inspiring.

Curtis was now sitting forward, elbows on knees. All the teens were pay-ing attention. "Hey, I'm looking for a job now . . . help me?"

Norman straightened, as Curtis asked him for guidance. "Sure, it's like, you take this program, and you'll learn what kind of work you really want. And how to plan to get it because you might have to do something you don't like to do to get to do something you want to do. I'm telling you . . . this is for you."

A lively conversation developed and the teenage participants seemed vitally involved. Yet, they were constantly interrupted and distracted by people who were coming in and out of the room and working on computers to the side of the relatively small room. Firmly and Pleasant were discussing unrelated things. In the middle of our presentation the principal interrupted us saying that he just wanted to "pop in to say hello." All these ancillary activ-ities reinforced the fact that the participants' expression of ideas, as well as their time and dignity, had little importance to the adults around them. The situation was another example of role modeling behavior that a serious school or workplace would have found unacceptable.

We concluded the presentation by handing out applications for the sem-inar and letting everyone know that they'd be expected to attend every class, do homework, be on time, complete a major final project, and take and pass a final exam. I repeated this and explained that, unlike experiences they might have had in the past, we would hold to these rules. The teens didn't seem deterred as they started filling out the applications.

Going back into the city on the train Faith and Norman expressed their frustration. "Bad for them. . . . It's real bad!" observed Norman. "I thought Firmly and Pleasant were never going to let us speak, did you see how nerv-ous they got when Faith and I were introduced?" Having been in foster care for more than six years Norman could read all clues from the adults who worked in the system.

We were frustrated but wanted to move on and help the teens who had shown up, even though they were not the actual teens selected for the pro-gram. Because Hodos had indicated a keen interest in our self-advocacy pro-gram, we decided that to ensure success, we would let him know our problems and recommendations for solutions.

I wrote to him that the presentation got off to a rocky start but that we wanted to move ahead. I suggested how to proceed and expressed willingness to discuss our approach. Three days later I received a phone call. Whoever was on the line began yelling, "I called two hours before your scheduled appointment. How come you didn't pick up? Didn't you get the message? Don't you even check your messages?" This one way conversation with Philips, the principal, achieved no concrete results.

The next week I was on the phone with Hodos and his associates several times. They said they wanted the seminar to continue but were sorry that they couldn't seem to get their own principal on board. Therefore, regretfully, they could not guarantee that students would successfully enroll for the twelve-week seminar.

I began to suspect that part, if not all, of our seminar's appeal was window dressing. The agency could use the self-advocacy seminar to impress their Board, ACS, the community, and their funders by showing that they were involved in innovative work. Yet, aside from Erica, no one at the agency had expressed any elevated expectations for the teens in their care. The agency never criticized our goals or methods, but apparently providing a context that supported high expectations for the teens was too foreign to them.

From this experience, we learned that foster care agencies had many motivations for trying new programming. We had assumed that the audience for the seminar was primarily the teens and the executive team. We failed to understand the significant pressures on agencies from funders, donors, and the government to guarantee continuation of their operations. These constituencies seemed more prone to view teens in care as victims that need protection and benevolence rather than young adults capable of successfully participating in the adult community. The combination of low expectations for the teens and other priorities defeated efforts to substantially change any of the approaches to preparing teens for independence. We had failed to understand that the lack of high expectations, or really any expectations at all for the teens, indicated that the agency would not commit to any serious attempt.

This experience haunted us. It tempered our hopefulness about changing the system through working in partnership with agencies. We analyzed the situation and decided that failure was a part of any enterprise, and we must keep going because the teens needed something better and success would come. Next time we would find an agency dedicated to higher expectations for its teens.

Within six months after our failure at this agency, we set up a meeting to present our program to Pete Koren, a well-known executive director of one of the most prestigious foster care agencies in New York. This foster care agency had a national reputation for doing great work with families and children throughout the city. His personal reputation and work indicated a commitment to high expectations for all children. Some of the senior staff who oversaw programs directly related to foster care teens also attended the meeting. I explained the GBS Seminar and the value of the informational interview and getting students to take on more responsibility for preparing for their futures. When I finished, two senior staff members patiently explained how their independent living program already reached the same objectives as ours. Those objections did not interest Koren. He asked us many questions and was fascinated as to how we placed more responsibility on the students to plan their futures.

Koren was interested in piloting the seminar. We agreed that the best and most cost efficient way to adopt the GBS Seminar was to teach their staff how to run it. This method would take between a year and eighteen months of training and technical assistance, and then the seminar would become completely theirs to run. Koren turned to his staff and said, "You know, we must be honest. We don't give anything this worthwhile to our teenagers right now. While they are with us, we owe it to them to offer this program." The director of foster care, Sue Pearson, was obviously uncomfortable with this criticism and with having an outside program thrust on her.

By the end of this first meeting, I understood that we needed to do a lot of work to get the support of principle staff, including the supervisor of social workers, the independent living coordinator, the education coordinator, and several other professionals all assigned to the teen unit. I had no idea how much work that would be.

A series of meetings began two weeks later.

Most of the agency foster care staff worked out of a nondescript office building in Manhattan, and there we held the first of the many of our planning meetings. I arrived at 9:20 for our 9:30 meeting to begin the planning for how to initiate the seminar. A couple of staff members were also early, and I made an effort to connect. One was Cora Flume, a young woman in her mid-twenties. She wore her dark hair pulled back tight in a short ponytail, and she had a sour expression on her otherwise pretty face. She was the acting director for independent living, a temporary position. I wondered why the agency hadn't made her permanent director of independent living and if she was bitter about being passed over. The other early arrival was Helen Jackson, the coordinator for education for the agency. She was in her fifties and had a fixed, calm look on her face, a smooth reassuring way of speaking. She radiated kindness.

In our informal conversation, Cora and Helen readily expressed anxiety about so many changes at the agency, budget cuts, and vacant staff positions that needed to be filled. They told me that Sue Pearson, director of foster care, had just arrived at the agency herself. They said the agency had difficulty recruiting new staff that would remain more than a couple of years. The agency was staffed either by individuals who had been around for more than a decade or were just starting fresh out of school, who gave little reason to believe they would remain long at the agency. I was not surprised since teens in foster care placed the turnover of agency staff high on their complaints list. Teens resented telling their stories repeatedly to new workers and going through the process of loss after making attachments to workers who moved on or out of the system. The instability of staff assignments and continuing changes in placements added immensely to the anxiety created for teens in foster care and their feelings of impermanence.

At 9:45 Sue Pearson arrived with Marie Smalls, another staff person, and two assistants. The meeting could now begin. Sue noted that she did not have much time left for the meeting because she had another appointment shortly. I quickly outlined the seminar program and suggested some scheduling targets. The staff politely nodded as I proceeded. Then Cora Flume, the acting director of independent living, responded sharply, "Well, this sounds good, but we already have way too much to do. I just don't see how we have time for another program, especially if it's once a week for a whole three months." Cora added that she had such a hard time getting the teens to existing programs.

In explaining her resistance, Cora expressed her fear that if we focused on the eight teens who regularly attended her IL programs, she would lose them. I appreciated her concern and explained that the seminar usually created a heightened interest in attending other agency programs that supported IL. She was not convinced.

Helen Jackson continued the resistance and explained that all the teens in care suffer from severe educational deficits. A seminar like ours would demand too much from the teens and would produce another failure in their lives. I explained that we had run the seminar for several years and had enrolled a wide range of foster care teens, including those from more restrictive settings such as residential treatment centers. During those years the majority successfully completed the seminar, attended 90 percent of the classes, and completed written homework for 80 percent of the sessions. Some students did not achieve every objective of the seminar, but all achieved some levels of success.

Marie Smalls, who had some undefined administrative role and had reported that she had been at the agency for eighteen years, reminded Sue that they were having a very hard time finding new foster homes for teens. Her tone became serious as she said that the agency could not overburden foster parents who already had teens with additional programs for their teens. For the assembled staff, the threat of losing foster parents was a conclusive argument for putting the seminar aside.

The group was now unanimous in rejecting the seminar. Helen Jackson tried to create closure by reiterating the idea that the seminar's objectives were not a priority. She reminded everyone that, until the agency filled all the vacant positions, they had no time for any additional work, especially given the upcoming state audits.

The cordial staff members from twenty minutes before had transformed into resistant defenders of the status quo. Perhaps some of the aggressive resistance was directed not at me but at Sue, their new director. In any case this group was uninterested in considering alternative and perhaps better ways to prepare their teens for independence. In general, I would expect resistance to a new program; however, their duplicity of sitting with the executive director two weeks ago and making no public objections was stunning.

Sue made no effort to intervene. Perhaps she was torn between satisfying her staff and moving ahead with the executive director's directive to implement the self-advocacy seminar. In an effort to help her gain internal support, I offered our availability to meet with teens, foster parents, and the entire foster care staff to explain the seminar's purpose. Sue thought that was a good idea and invited me to the full staff meeting the next Tuesday morning.

On Tuesday, I was back at the agency building. This time the meeting was in a large conference room filled with about forty social workers, case workers, supervisors, and legal professionals who worked in the foster care unit. Standing at the front of the room, Sue explained to the staff that the first item of business was a presentation by a consultant who was reviewing the way the agency kept files, in accordance with government regulations. I tried to follow the consultant's earnest presentation, but I found myself getting lost in the acronyms and numbers that he used to identify various forms, procedures, and bureaucratic entities. How could anyone view a teen as an individual in the context of this bureaucratic system?

Sue introduced me. I talked about the great potential of the teens at their agency to succeed and how our self-advocacy seminar would complement their work to make this happen. While four or five staff members seemed interested, in general, the group appeared preoccupied. Those who were interested raised their hands to ask insightful questions. The remaining staff members appeared to focus on the new forms they were given. At the end of the meeting, some of the interested staff members approached me and offered to contact specific teens who would benefit from the seminar. They let me know how important this self-advocacy seminar would be to their teens. No one from the planning group, including Sue, the director of foster care, attempted to speak with me. Yet, I left the general staff meeting hoping that the few individuals to whom I spoke would support the program.

I respected the agency's need to recruit, counsel, and retrain foster parents. Thus I suggested that I meet with the foster parents to explain the seminar's value for their teens, as well as for helping them with new tools for their parenting responsibilities. Sue agreed that this presentation would be useful and arranged for me to attend a meeting of the foster parents advisory board. She assured me that these were the best foster parents, the leaders of their community. I looked forward to getting to know these parents who had opened their homes to teens. I respected their willingness to take in foster care teens and deal with the system bureaucracy.

Four foster parents gathered for this meeting. Marie joined us. She explained to the group that we would be offering a new program for their teens. Immediately, the floodgates opened.

"The problem we have," said a pleasant looking, if somewhat disheveled, woman, who introduced herself as Gloria Jones, "is that we don't know who these kids are. You see, the agency drops them off with no information! Sometimes in the middle of the night! I got to wake up and meet this child, with no idea who she is . . . if she's a good girl or trouble who's going to steal everything I got. What can you do about that?"

I knew this happened in the system, that agencies placed kids at any hour, with no preparation for them or for the homes that were taking them. It sounded horrendous for all concerned. I could not picture myself opening my front door in the middle of the night to welcome a strange child or teenager, with no idea of their identity.

She didn't wait for a response from me. "Not like you get extra for that either. I have a hard enough time getting the checks they owe me. . . . Processing is so slow these days, and I don't have money to lay out for these kids. They always eating and wanting new sneakers. I tell them, got to wait for the agency check to come." She turned to the social worker, "I am still waiting for that $356 from last month. In case you don't know, a teenager eats a lot of food."

Marie gave an apologetic acknowledgment and looked a bit flustered. "Now you know we are working on that with the main office, Gloria. We will be cutting your check, and if I have time today, I'll check on it again."

I interrupted, "Let's talk about the teens. . . ."

Another foster mother named Rita spoke. "These poor babies need someone who understands them. I have had oh, maybe twenty-seven foster kids over the years, and these are babies that need some loving. But it ain't easy with some of them because they won't trust you; they've been so abused." She shook her head in sorrow.

"You don't want these girls out getting pregnant under your roof," said Gloria with an air of authority. "I tell them, you are coming to church with me. Then I got to tell them, you cannot wear that outfit out of my house, with your belly showing, that is not appropriate."

"Yeah, and that's when they call the Children's Rights on you!" Rita cut in. "Tell 'em you going against their rights! These kids, they think they can always get over on you, get what they want from the system. They don't know how good they got it. My own kids didn't get everything these kids get."

Either the foster parents just welcomed the opportunity to vent, or they were presenting this barrage of issues and problems because they hoped I could solve them. I listened and realized that to get them to support sending kids to our program, I had to demonstrate that our seminar would help the foster parents in some way. When I finally broke in, I attempted to explain that, in our experience in foster care, empowering teens to take on more responsibility often diminished the acting-out behavior because teens became more focused on their long-term objectives. I described how the seminar would focus their teens on positive future goals that the foster parents could support and would provide their teens with a method for taking more responsibility in their lives.

I felt like maybe I was speaking another language when one of them responded, "Responsibility! When I was a girl, back in my country, they gave us a cow to take care of. That's how we learned responsibility. That's what these kids need, a cow."

"What they need is a good whupping. That's what my daddy always gave us, put us right over his knee and got the belt. And there were eight of us kids so it kept him busy."

"Agency don't allow that though. They don't back you up on this stuff. But that doesn't stop me from taking out the big wooden spoon. All the kids in my house know about the big wooden spoon if they are not behaving themselves."

In desperation, I tried to start wrapping up the presentation by reiterating that the self-advocacy seminar would give foster parents something positive they could share with their teens. But I was losing steam. How could we overlook that the foster parents themselves were un-empowered, largely uneducated, poor, and with limited opportunities in their own lives? The agency complained that they had a difficult time recruiting foster parents, especially for teens, but what did it give them? How did it treat them? In general, the expectations for the foster parents did not seem much greater than for the teens.

Often people ask me if foster parents "do it for the money." Although it can cost the government $40,000 or more a year for each teen in foster care, that money doesn't end up in the pockets of the foster parents, who receive a mere twenty dollars a day to care for a teen.

In the meetings with the foster parents, the full foster care staff, and the group assigned to the seminar project, the agency leadership made little to no effort to promote the seminar. Agency staff were not hostile, but they communicated a sense that the seminar would go away if they just went through the motions. They appeared completely unconcerned with empowering teens in preparation for independent living, and I realized that we were wasting our time and the time of the agency staff. My frustration became overwhelming. I called Koren, the head of the agency. I told him as plainly as I could, without any recriminations, that his staff opposed the seminar too much and that it would be best if we called it off. Koren listened and asked me to please hold off on making any decision. He graciously invited me to lunch, a somewhat unexpected gesture.

The next week, we met over lunch. He was forthright about the challenges of implementing a new program in foster care. He explained how many of his staff were overwhelmed by the mandates of the system. He offered his view that the kind of individual who ended up staying at a foster care agency was often one attracted to following rules and mandates. Social work outside the foster care system, with less mandates, required more flexibility and responsibility, and some people just didn't want that. He urged me to be patient with the staff's lack of risk taking and unfamiliarity with creative ventures. He reiterated that YAC's self-advocacy seminar was important for their teens. Koren offered to get re-involved and ensure that the program would move forward. "Our teens need it," he kept saying. Koren was supportive, collegial, and encouraging. I could easily see how he had become a respected leader in the child welfare field.

Koren's word was good. He set up another meeting for the distinct purpose of restating his intention that the director of foster care and her staff implement the seminar. Personally involving himself in this particular pilot program was highly unusual for an executive director engaged in administering an agency with hundreds of programs spread throughout the city. I was not proud that we needed his specific involvement to get the program going, but we too were committed to finding ways to help teens in foster care.

Uncharacteristically, all the staff members with whom I had been meeting arrived on time at his office and appeared attentive throughout the meeting. The executive director told the assembled group, including Sue, Cora, Helen, and Marie, "I want this program. You know, and I know, we don't have anything that comes close to giving our foster teens such a good start on preparing for their independence. They deserve this program, and I want it." He paused, and no one responded. "This is your chance to tell me what you need to make it work. I'll do what you ask, and then you must make it work." He made eye contact with each staff member assembled around the table.

Helen went first. She explained this seminar was an added responsibility. She argued that staff involved with the seminar needed to get a bonus. I couldn't believe the speed of Koran's response, "Fine. Done. Anything else?" Money was no longer an issue.

Marie explained to the executive director that they still needed to fill vacancies in the foster care unit. He assured her that Sue had the lines allocated and all that was needed was for them to bring suitable candidates. Cora Flume seemed more sullen than usual, and I figured she really was angry about not getting the job of permanent IL director. She raised her hand and declared somewhat petulantly, "I need some books, like dictionaries and interesting reading material, for my resource room."

Koren appeared startled. "This has nothing to do with this project. You should have all the books you need in the IL resource center, and it's your responsibility to make us aware of your needs. Nothing will stop us from having what is needed." Staff continued for another five minutes, until no one could think of more requests. "This is your opportunity. Do you need anything else? Say so now," he warned. "I want this seminar. Now I am going to leave, and I want you to sit here and figure out how it is going to happen."

If the articulated reasons for the resistance to our seminar were the actual causes for the resistance, then Koren made every attempt to address them and provide for any of the staff's needs. I was hopeful that setting up the seminar would move along now. I thanked him, and after he walked out, Sue, Cora, Helen, Marie, and I agreed to hold yet another meeting to plan how to recruit students for the seminar through an orientation workshop.

The seminar team met within ten days of the meeting with the executive director. Cora began the meeting, explaining to Sue that they must devote a good deal of time to picking balloon colors. I couldn't determine if she was joking. She looked at me in a way that showed the seriousness of the issue and continued, "We find that having balloons, especially the right color, makes the teens feel more comfortable and makes them think the event will be fun."

"How do you normally recruit teens to come to these types of meetings?" I inquired. I had been planning to share some of our past successes in recruitment, along with the backgrounds of the Youth Advocates who would present at the recruitment workshop.

Cora and the group ignored me. She was leading the meeting. "We need to have sandwiches. Teens will not come to anything unless there is food."

I had mixed emotions as the conversation continued. On the one hand, I sensed that the recruitment/orientation session was going to happen. On the other hand, no one seemed prepared to discuss substance. The group was planning a party rather than an educational program.

Cora continued authoritatively, "The only way we can get students to come is to do it at the end of the month meeting, when they get their stipends." All nodded in agreement.

"But what about the ones who normally don't attend IL programs?" I asked, knowing that many don't attend.

"They'll show up for at least fifteen minutes, just to get their checks," Helen reassured me.

"Our policy is to give stipends even to students who don't always make the programs. They may have other issues going on. It wouldn't be right not to give them their stipends; it would be discrimination," Cora challenged. This didn't make any sense to me, but I heard the edge in her voice. I was silent.

Marie spoke gently to me, as though explaining this to a very slow person. "You'll have to offer stipends for your program if you want anyone to show up. It wouldn't be right to ask them to come without that."

Trying not to sound confrontational, I explained YAC's philosophy that teens needed to learn the value of education. They should understand that education was not usually something one got paid to do. Paying students to take training or educational programs gave the impression that only the teacher or organization benefits from offering the program. Most people in the world paid for advanced education or training, or else they won scholarships or borrowed money for tuition. Paying students to take classes was not the common approach outside the foster care system, I noted, and as I said it, I realized I was directly challenging their system. They acknowledged my thoughts with silence.

Understanding that I would make no progress with the stipend issue, I backed off. I acknowledged respect for their tradition and suggested a compromise, "We will reach both of our objectives if we pay stipends only to students who complete the entire seminar. The stipend could consist of a savings bond or promise to pay a college expense. This would support the future focus of the seminar."

They found this compromise unacceptable. They shook their heads in unison. "No, our policy is to pay students for each class they attend rather than wait till the end of the semester. They won't wait that long. Also, some students have crises in their lives, or other meetings come up." Sue nodded as Cora stated the obvious and continued, "Our policy will remain. Payments to students enrolled. We can't penalize them for not attending the full seminar."

By the end of this meeting, they had agreed to the date, color of balloons, and menu. These matters left no time to discuss the agenda. The next time we met would be at the recruitment and orientation workshop.

As we all got up to leave, Sue asked whether I would mind stepping into her office. "I have something that needs to be said." She sounded ominous and certainly demonstrated to her staff that she was calling me into the woodshed.

I followed her in, and she closed the door behind us. Her office was unremarkable, with one wall covered by a city map with push pins marking all the neighborhoods in which this agency had offices or foster homes. How impossible it was to be an individual in this system. We both remained standing. I had the feeling we were not about to discuss how to move forward. "Look, things are clearly not going well. There is a lot of friction between you and the staff. The best we can do is to keep processing this before we move on. I suggest another meeting to discuss the problems they have with you."

What is remarkable about the foster care system, from family court throughout the agencies and the government administrations, is that staff have the power to ignore initiatives they don't like through covert resistance. Rarely are the real reasons for the resistance discussed, negotiated, or mediated. If staff, including the director of foster care, would not honestly negotiate with their director about what they believed to be useful or nonuseful programming, how could we expect that teens would learn positive ways to empower themselves and negotiate their lives within the community at large?

This agency may have had well-founded resistance to our seminar. It overworked its staff and needed more people. However, the manner in which they defeated the seminar was disingenuous and could not lead to better programming for the teens in their care. They displayed disrespect for not only our work but also their own time and efforts. Clearly, they had the power to defeat the seminar, but neither the power nor inclination to offer better approaches.

One could criticize the staff. Why would they work so hard to deprive their teens of a program that many believed could be useful? Perhaps they had worked too long in a system that provided little pay and little respect while placing awesome responsibilities on them. Perhaps, while "empowerment" was a nice new catch phrase that professionals high up in the administration were using, at their level the demands of just finding suitable foster homes, keeping the kids safe, and dealing with all the problems that erupted overwhelmed them. Perhaps the system had so disempowered them that they could not be open to helping teens achieve more than they had. These were all speculations for the moment, but we had heard each of them numerous times by foster care staff we met who were open to talking about their situations.

These thoughts flashed through my mind. Perhaps the system promoted too much processing and not enough education? I took a deep breath and said, "I'm sorry, Sue, but we really don't have time for these processing meetings at this point. Why don't we all focus our energies on the recruitment workshop and see how that works out?"

Sue looked a bit chagrined but went along with it. "I know you have the support of our executive director, but I just don't think this is going to work. They just don't seem to like you." Sue was a professional social worker with years of experience and proven abilities. She was a leader in her profession. She had agreed, in front of the executive director, to do what it takes to offer the self-advocacy seminar. Could leadership in this situation mean the ability to stall the project long enough for Koren to forget about it?

I tried to empathize with the staff and understand the pressures they felt from taking responsibility for the teens in their care, working with foster parents, complying with the maze of government regulations, and contending with continual turn over. Those who had been there for years, like Helen and Marie, had seen countless revisions in programming, supervisory shifts, and general staff adjustments. None of these changes had any significant impact on the major burdens they carried. In their minds, we most likely represented just another new fancy of the executive director. From long experience, they felt confident that he could and would become distracted, and then we would disappear. Cora would either join their ranks of the career foster care worker, or she would burn out from the unrealistic responsibilities of teaching fifty teens independent living skills and quit.

With Koren's encouragement and support from students in our own model seminars, we were determined to move forward. I selected Chantel and Antoine, recent seminar graduates, to present at the recruitment workshop. They both believed the seminar helped them greatly and that other teens should participate. They devoted a good deal of time preparing written agendas and practicing what they were going to say. Again we were pleased that this was one of the outcomes of our program, that teens were willing to present themselves in new situations and stretch themselves.

We arrived fifteen minutes before the scheduled time for the recruitment workshop. The staff had ringed the large conference room with chairs along a wall, food and drinks on a table to the side, and half a dozen red and yellow balloons attached to the table of food. A lot of discussion for six balloons! Three agency teens had already arrived. They tried to look disinterested. Betsy and I greeted them, and then Chantel and Antoine started chatting with them about neighborhoods, schools, and so on.

At 5:20 p.m., twenty minutes after the appointed time, perhaps a dozen teens had joined the meeting. We asked when everyone would arrive. They told us that "this is probably it."

"No, it's stipend day, more will be here," offered one of the teens.

"Yeah, but they'll come at 7:00, just before it's over so they can get their check without having to listen."

"No, I know someone who gets their check from their social worker even if they don't show at all."

A few more straggled in. We asked if anyone had seen Ms. Flume (Cora) and Ms. Jackson (Helen) and got shrugs.

At 5:30, half an hour after the scheduled start time, we decided to begin the recruitment presentation even though none of the appointed agency staff had arrived. I had seen Cora when we first came in, but she had now disappeared. Everyone got quiet, and we explained a little about why we were here and introduced Chantel and Antoine. In a soft voice, Chantel began explaining why the seminar had been instrumental in helping her to decide to go to college and pursue her career goal of becoming an early childhood educator.

The door to the room opened, and I heard a loud jovial conversation. Cora Flume and Helen Jackson moved a few steps into the room and stood loudly talking and laughing. They acted as if the meeting had not started. This interruption distracted Chantel. She stopped and looked toward these two adult authority figures to get a clue of how to proceed. She then looked to me for a signal. Cora and Helen appeared oblivious to what was going on in the room. I motioned to Chantel to keep going. The conversation between the staff members grew louder. Again Chantel stopped and seemed uncertain about whether to continue. The teens in the audience began to shift their attention to Helen and Cora.

Betsy became exasperated with this interruption and walked over to Cora and Helen, to ask them if they could carry on their conversation in the hall or somewhere else, so we could continue. She gestured toward Chantel and explained that she was having difficulty concentrating while other people were speaking in the room. In an instant, two cheery colleagues transformed to combatants. They glared at Betsy and told her that the meeting couldn't have started yet since they had been dealing with a crisis. Then they announced to the whole group that the meeting could now begin.

Cora took charge. "Caleb, take off your hat and pay attention." Caleb smirked and turned his hat to another position. "Caleb, we won't begin this presentation until you take off your hat." Focusing on the most resistant student usually reinforces the idea that those who act out and present the most problems get the most attention. This confrontation was taking center stage for the group of assembled teens.

"It's okay if he wants to wear his hat," I said, trying to diffuse the situation. Antoine chimed in that he liked the hat.

"Now everyone, pay attention and sit straight. You're not getting any sandwiches until you listen up to what these people have to say. This is going to be a good program. We want all of you to pay attention." Cora had shifted the context from motivation through informing to using authority to establish the mood. She was effectively moving the seminar's appeal into the static of typical agency hyperbole. Her recommendation, "good program" was of dubious value since it diminished the opportunity for students to make independent judgments. Coming from agency authority figures, teens considered dubious anything with the word *good* before it.

I took back the focus and explained again that our presenters would talk about the seminar, followed by questions from the group. I asked the students to think about whether they would like to learn self-advocacy and begin working on their future. If anyone was interested, after our presentation we would have applications for them to fill out.

After this shaky start, the presentation went well. The teens listened intently and asked relevant questions. Most teens enjoyed talking about their future career ambitions and were visibly engaged when we took their career choices seriously by listening carefully, asking specific questions, and reinforcing the soundness of their choices. The assembled teens respected YAC's teen presenters and after the formal meeting, approached them as if they were celebrities.

After the event ended, Cora and Helen interrupted Betsy and me while we were answering questions from one of the teen applicants. "Can we see you out in the hall? We have a real issue here and need to talk with you now." Safely in the hall, they began yelling.

"No one has ever been so rude to me in my entire life!"

"You can't talk to us that way in front of children!"

"You have disrespected us in front of our clients!"

They pounded Betsy and me with a volley of invectives. It seemed relentless; their team approach was well executed.

"I'm sorry," I protested, "but we had already begun the meeting, and our presenter was having a very difficult time being heard."

Cora was defiant. "That's no excuse. The meeting doesn't start until we start it. You had no right . . ."

"But we had all agreed to 5:00 p.m. We began at nearly 5:30. We assumed something had come up for you, and we needed to start to get through the program."

The intensity was rising. "You people have no understanding of the crises we have to handle. Things come up. You're rude to begin without us."

I was trying to be calm, but they had shaken my self-control. I told them what I really thought. "Be honest, you really don't want to talk about the program or see your teens in it. We can't engage in this shouting match. I think the best thing for you to do is inform your executive director that we are too rude, discourteous, or whatever to work with and that you insist we not offer the seminar. Stand up for what you believe."

With that said and embarrassed that things had so disintegrated, I started to walk away. I claim that nothing shocks me in foster care. That isn't true. As I stepped away, my arm was yanked backward as Helen pulled me back. I was so stunned, I began to pull my arm free, and in a moment, was engaged in a physical struggle with her for my arm. I heard myself demanding my arm back. I was burning with outrage and bewildered with how I got to this point. I felt like one of the teens. I finally retrieved my arm, Helen apologized for the physical contact, and we all parted without further words.

The recruitment workshop had some success mixed in with the failures. Eleven teens completed thoughtful applications to attend the seminar. These students wrote out answers to questions about their motivation to reach future goals, and most of them had some sort of general career goal. Chantel and Antoine told us that many teens came up to tell them that the seminar seemed like an exciting opportunity for them. Although I could consider the eventual recovery of my arm a success, the confrontation and its level of escalation was a failure. I had completely failed to gain the support of the staff in charge of the program.

A year passed, and the agency hired a new independent living director before we successfully ran one pilot seminar for the agency. No one from the agency agreed to be trained, and thus I taught the seminar. The teens who participated in the seminar worked hard, had useful informational interviews, and felt they had gained more focus in their lives. One soon went off to college. Some of their foster parents gave positive feedback, noting that they saw differences in the way their teens took on responsibility. We had a good attendance and retention rate.

Unfortunately, the seminar's success could not move the entrenched resistance of staff, and they made no effort to continue the program. Koren, the executive director, gave up all contact with us, even after we sent reports and offered to meet again. One of the assigned project directors explained that the agency's priority was to find foster care families. Without foster families the agency would lose the number of teens assigned to them and lose revenue. Offering a new program to help teens prepare for the future was simply not a priority to which they could give attention.

Frustration is an understatement for anyone who works in foster care. Our direct experience working with a dozen or so foster care agencies helped us understand the nature of the resistance to providing quality programs to foster care teens and to empowering them with education and opportunities. Within the foster care system, government mandates determine most of staff's daily activities, and they have little opportunity to utilize their professional skills in creative and effective manners. When they do have time, little training is available to help them acquire new methods for educating and preparing teens for independent living. The teens with whom they work are under inordinate stress owing to their placement in foster care. The primary imperative of the system is safety, and thus staff are often thrust into the role of controlling the actions and behavior of the teens. When teens see the primary role of their workers as controllers, a natural tinder box of conflict is created. Finally, the system and the individual leadership are too fearful of taking the necessary risks for supporting teen empowerment. Under these pressures, we more than understand why the system breeds the type of resistance we described.

In reflecting on our experiences with foster care agencies, we could have easily villainized the workers and foster parents who appeared insensitive to the teens' needs. Yet, the majority of professionals care deeply, and they struggle daily with ways to help their teens. The system is filled with thousands of talented professionals who want to help teens in substantial ways and who, in a supportive context, are willing to take on new initiatives and new approaches to preparing teens for successful independence. This great resource often goes underutilized. GBS or any other useful program needs the involvement of these professionals both as facilitators and as supporters of empowering teens to take control of their future.

We learned that we had to find ways not only to involve these professionals but also to help them in their own struggles to make the system more conducive for effective and relevant independent living programs. Therefore, Youth Advocacy Center began offering two-day training sessions to social services professionals who want to bring the GBS model and approach to their youth, in New York City, in other cities, and at specific agencies. Each training has encouraged us about the growing interest in and demand for the methods we developed for the seminar. We are gratified to train and collaborate with professionals from around the country working with teens who are looking for new tools and program designs. It saves them time to devote to their direct work with teens and provides a means for finding different and better ways to utilize GBS approaches to teaching self-advocacy. These trainings give us the opportunity to continue to learn about other effective approaches to helping foster care teens gain control of their lives.

In our trainings and collaborations around the country, we use our experiences developing GBS to talk about what it means to empower teens to take on responsibility for their lives. We also explain specific methods we have found effective—the Socratic method and narrative approach and introducing participants to the value of informational interviews.

A primary goal in developing the GBS Seminar and our approach to empowering teens was to develop a method that would maximize the talents and experience of the seminar teacher or facilitator—in effect, empowering the facilitator as well. The effectiveness of GBS relies on the curriculum and the facilitator's creativity, experience, and individuality. The curriculum is designed to make the process interesting, exciting, and fresh for the facilitators, no matter how many semesters they have taught. Whether they are child welfare professionals or individuals from outside the system, all GBS facilitators appreciate the fact that the GBS approach allows and requires them to utilize their own unique talent and creativity. The GBS curriculum is only a tool for talented facilitators. Teens in foster care need the dynamics associated with interpersonal connections that develop when facilitator and student feel free to make intellectual explorations. Thus, GBS and all programs for teens in care must recruit and rely on effective facilitators to bring life to the learning experience.

The idea of youth empowerment has currency in child welfare and social services right now, but it means a lot of different things to different people. This became clear to us at training in Detroit where we worked with a group of individuals with a range of professional and personal backgrounds. Each group member participated because of a strong commitment to exploring different paths for helping teens gain empowerment. Most had faced the bureaucratic challenges of working in the foster care system but remained hopeful about change. They freely challenged almost every proposition we presented. Their openly critical and challenging nature and diverse perspectives helped us develop better understandings of the challenges and approaches to empowering teens to take control of their futures.

This group in Detroit was used to listening to teens. In the process of determining whether to replicate the GBS Self-Advocacy Seminar, they sent a group of teen leaders to meet with graduates from our seminar in New York. They used their recommendation as a determining factor in deciding to pilot our program. Yet, this same group struggled with how far we could go with empowering teens.

They asked what we would do in our seminar if a teen selected the supposedly wrong career. Are we really saying we should support that decision and set up an informational interview? The conversation went something like this:

"Yes, we would. And help the student get as much information as possible. We have to trust that in the end, it is his or her decision, and the student will make the right decision."

"But isn't this risky? And unrealistic? So many of my kids want to be NBA stars or rap singers or criminal investigators—you know all the stuff they see on TV."

"Well, let's think about it. What are your alternatives?"

"We tell them they are wasting their time and don't have a chance, and then we get them interested in something else."

"Sounds good—but will they listen?"

In response to this, the professionals shrug or, with a smile shake their heads, especially if they have their own teenage children.

"We really don't have another alternative than to give them information and let them make informed rather than uninformed decisions. Every teen we have sent to a NBA star has come back telling us they need a back-up plan or that they are going to pursue a different career. They respect information that is unbiased and is accurate, and they do listen and can make good decisions."

By offering our tools to these partners, and through them, to teens across the country, we are on the path to achieving a better future for teens in foster care. Although our experiences in the system taught us about the resistance to new thinking, we are still hopeful because many professionals are now becoming our partners through learning from our trainings and curriculum and sharing their own experiences with us. We need new thinking and partnerships to create lasting changes that will prepare teens leaving foster care for the future.

Conclusion

Consensus is growing that the foster care system needs to be rethought for teens.

Our journey with youth in foster care led us to conclude that foster care for teens should have different goals, strategies, and structures than foster care for younger children. Adolescents in foster care have needs and priorities different from small children. In addition to safety and efforts at family reunification, teens in care must be prepared for adulthood. This vital objective requires a different kind of system than child welfare currently offers.

Many professionals recognize the need to rethink the objectives of foster care for teens in light of the need to prepare them for independence. Providing for teens in foster care is a process that the system must examine continuously and renew. This process requires continuing accountability. We have learned that a good approach or an effective solution today will most certainly need to be reviewed, modified, and even abandoned as the needs of teens and society change. Therefore we not only need a different current approach to foster care for teens, but a system that is more adaptable to economic and social changes in society.

The philosophy and program we have developed through our work at Youth Advocacy Center has roots in the American ideal. Every child, regardless of his or her background, must receive the necessary preparation to achieve their maximum potential and become a successful participating citizen. By that we mean that these future adults are citizens not just by having a job and paying taxes, but also by contributing to the community, achieving some sense of personal satisfaction, and fulfilling their potential as well as meeting their responsibilities to their families. We must make it possible for every teen in foster care to have substantiated hope that no matter how rough their beginnings, how dysfunctional or disrupted their family life, how poor their neighborhood, and how inadequate their early education was, they can improve their lives. We need to give them a vision of a hopeful future and provide them with some essential skills and understandings to become successful adults.

We must establish a new system of preparing these teens for participating citizenship, and the foundation of it must stem from higher expectations for what teens in foster care can achieve. We ought to instill in every teen an expectation that he or she can make it—which should mean more than merely struggling on a subsistence level. For the past two decades an underlying assumption in the foster care system has been low expectations: if a teen gets a fast food job, then this is viewed as a grand success and perhaps final attainment of a lifelong career. This view is not only unsatisfactory but also insulting to young people in care. If we set higher expectations, then many teens will rise to meet them; the bar will be raised for all.

Although there may be many ways to establish and convey higher expectations, we propose that a greater focus on education for teens in foster care is a logical and important start. We could begin by acknowledging that foster care teens indeed have suffered traumas in the past, and that perhaps making their families whole or finding them all new permanent families simply cannot be the exclusive objective of foster care. At the same time, we could acknowledge that, despite their past ordeals, foster care teens have intellectual abilities, strengths, and desires to succeed, and they deserve to be educated to the highest degree possible. Imagine if preparing these teens for education and careers was the system's main priority, rather than treating them as dysfunctional and traumatized victims who require continuing intervention for their incapacities. This new emphasis would create a different attitude among caretakers and policy makers about teens' performance in school and after-school programs.

Therefore, one possible goal is to expect that some large percentage of teens, if not all teens, should graduate college or complete advanced vocational training, and the system should expect that all are given opportunities to prepare for meaningful careers. The natural intellectual talent is present; it is up to us to find ways to make college education and advanced training a reality. Our experiences demonstrate that many teens in the system could and should prepare to attend four-year colleges. For students not interested in a four-year college education, other opportunities in trades may require advanced training or apprenticeships. For others, community colleges have become a proven method to gain further education and a chance to continue at a four-year college.

This goal is not idealistic but definable and measurable, and a necessity for teens to reach future self-sufficiency and success. Within this goal is the imperative to focus on and develop support for existing and new programs that will prepare more foster care teens for higher education. This valuable goal does not narrowly define the method because students can be prepared for and motivated to attend and graduate from college or seek advanced training in many ways.

We recognize that teens in foster care have encountered and will continue to encounter many significant challenges. Some of these challenges are unique to the experience of being removed from one's biological family. But despite the nature and uniqueness of these challenges, we have no reason to believe that teens can't overcome many obstacles. Foster care teens are deprived of certain experiences one has while living in an intact family, such as high expectations—a reminder that you can be what you want to be; a positive vision of the future; a sense of hope that you will achieve something; a continuing lesson in learning how to negotiate and self-advocate to reach personal goals; authentic stories of how others 'made it' to overcome problems and obstacles. Our Getting Beyond the System® model demonstrates that one can offset these deprivations enough to help young people increase their chances of having fulfilling, independent lives.

In moving teens toward independent adulthood, we must give more responsibility to teens themselves. No good reasons exist to prevent teens from taking on more responsibility while in their adolescence to prepare for their future independence. Rather than doing things to or for teens, the system must develop programming that requires their genuine initiative and active participation. Only by transferring responsibility to teens can we help them develop plans that meet their individual needs.

Running foster care for teens as a welfare system will never succeed.

To do justice to young people and to the community, the foster care system must get beyond the welfare mentality of minimal expectations and top-down prescriptions for orderly behavior. Limiting our vision of success for foster care teens tragically disregards their potential. For teens to succeed, they must have the ability to understand and negotiate nonwelfare situations. Foster care for teens must be taken out of the welfare context and put into a context that prepares them for independent adulthood. The government must abandon the present foster care system for teens that rewards behavior management and control in exchange for policies that promote education goals, personal responsibility, and control of one's future.

The Getting Beyond the System® program demonstrates to the system that teens in foster care can rise to the challenge of a high-level intellectual program and take on more responsibility for their future. GBS is not a poverty program that only has potential for teens from disadvantaged backgrounds. Most families that learn about GBS, no matter their economic or social class, understand its merits and attractiveness. Parents from all backgrounds have said they wished they could find a GBS program for their own teens. Designing GBS as a high-level program is purposeful in that it demonstrates the parallel between the capabilities of foster care teens with those of any other teen, a comparison that gives us every reason to elevate our expectations for teens in foster care.

We recognize that countless talented individuals in the system are committed to helping individual teens succeed and do everything in their power to support them. However, the present system sadly corrodes their commitment and talent, and eventually prevents them from achieving success. Long-standing structures in the form of government mandates and bureaucratic inertia simply prevent the development of effective approaches to reverse the high level of failure for teens seeking independence.

The foster care system is controlled and fueled by an overwhelming array of government mandates. The system rewards compliance with these mandates rather than success in preparing teens for independence. Change must come at all levels of the system, but the most significant change must first derive from society's understanding of foster care's purpose. The challenge is to recreate a system that will support the future dreams and hopes of every teen in foster care. We, through our government as custodian, must establish preparing adolescents for participation as successful and independent citizens as the primary goal of foster care for teens. This goal must become part of the formal permanency planning for independent living and must displace behavior management and control as a central focus.

Bureaucracies such as the foster care system require innovation from outside their systems.

To change the foster care system for teens, businesses, independent programmers, foundations, community members, and others can and should play an important role in developing innovative ideas and implementing them. We need a more progressive approach to public/private partnerships because overcoming system challenges requires fresh insight.

In maintaining its bureaucracy, too often the foster care system has segregated teens from the general community. This setup is unfortunate for both the teens and the larger community. Teens can only gain new ideas and insights about the functioning of the adult world if they are provided with authentic experiences outside and beyond foster care. An untapped reservoir of resources in the general community is able and willing to assist teens making the transition to independence. Changing the foster care system for teens must include drawing on this resource. If teens in care are to succeed in the adult world they need to have more experiences interacting with successful adults outside the foster care system, similar to the experiences they have with informational interviewers in the GBS program.

If the foster care system were to take full advantage of community resources, then it would build bridges to directly include community experts in the process of changing the system. The general public has a significant role to play in improving opportunities for teens from foster care. We have demonstrated that many people can be relied upon to give individualized advice, offer professional contacts, and, in some cases, provide internships and jobs. The informational interviewers have become active in increasing community respect for teens in foster care. These informational interviewers are leaders and decision makers, who represent a wide range of commercial activities. Their meetings with foster care teens allow them to give career opportunities to graduates of foster care. This is a first step. Our experience demonstrates that professionals outside the field of mental heath have a desire to become involved in finding better ways to help teens in foster care. Educators, business executives, lawyers, sports professionals, robotics engineers, and others have devoted time and resources to trying to understand the problems and offer solutions.

We must find ways to build on this first step toward breaking the insularity of the foster care system by bringing these resources into the system. Teens need and will benefit from increased contacts with the community outside of foster care. The system must develop more programs that prepare students for informational interviews so as to include the countless successful citizens who want to help teens in foster care. We know that for every single teen in foster care, a number of highly successful professionals would gladly provide informational interviews. This resource has unlimited value for helping teens properly plan for their futures.

In addition, citizens must not wait for the system to call upon them. They need to involve themselves in the workings of foster care. Many have valuable experiences and skills to share that directly relate to helping teens prepare for a career and further education. These people should be more assertive in their offers to help and not be intimidated by the closed nature of foster care and the unfamiliar rules, regulations, and government mandates. Citizens can learn about specific independent living preparation, evaluate current practices, and offer their own wealth of experiences and wisdom to the process of foster care change. Community members need to act as resources and as accountable agents to ensure that the system raises its expectations and provides high-level programming and that the foster care agencies become open to including existing community resources.

The media have a strong responsibility to continue to act as the public's observer and reporter of child abuse and physical neglect, but they must also tell the story of the equally harmful neglect related to the inadequate preparation of teens for independence. In addition, the media have a role in celebrating the talents, achievements, and resilience of teens in foster care. Presenting more stories of teens who have successfully achieved their goals in the adult world will encourage teens currently in foster care and raise expectations of both teens and adults. Further, the media must assess their own accountability for contributing to the stigma of foster care and the prejudice held by some that teens in care are either troubled children or problem kids.

Child welfare policy making—at conferences, in academia, in government, or in child welfare institutions—must begin to include professionals from a wider range of disciplines as equal participants. While the entire world outside of foster care changes, foster care remains an insulated system based on a design from another time and for other needs. Our teens want and deserve to be included in our new world, and it will not happen unless we invite those successful in working in the "outside" world to participate in designing independent living preparation for teens in care.

The system must be more open to utilizing a wider range of community resources that cut across disciplines. This approach encourages individuals to think beyond their professional disciplines to bring innovation to their work and to be less defensive in questioning existing practices. The interdisciplinary approach to finding ways to help teens in foster care reminds us that we must continually reevaluate our thinking and practices and use methods that can adapt to the transitions in life.

Empowerment for foster care youth is integral to change.

In recent years, there has been a growing interest in youth empowerment. Many youth empowerment programs have organized around creating youth leadership boards, designing youth speakers' bureaus, helping youth learn their rights, and instituting other mechanisms for youth to be heard in the system. Empowerment programs arrange for teens to voice their concerns to adults responsible for their care, including, in some cases, legislators and other government policy makers. These programs can be effective and have important goals, such as pressing for reforms in the foster care system or for policy changes at individual agencies. These empowerment programs can also elevate teens' sense of their importance.

However, as we saw in our own work teaching teens their rights and involving them in policy advocacy, empowerment programs must be careful not to ignore the importance of empowering youth to become adults. In every empowerment effort, successful independence must remain the prime objective for every teen in foster care. If we view empowerment in the broadest sense, it can and should be the building block for preparing teens for adulthood.

To change the system to promote success for foster care teens, policies and practices at foster care agencies must integrate empowerment, which cannot be separate from the main agency business, if it is to truly lead to success for teens. Instead of trying to control teens' behavior, we need to provide them with necessary information to make decisions and give them the skills to be fully empowered adults in all arenas of their lives.

First, teens must be allowed to make decisions. To make decisions, they need information, they need to know how to get information, and they need the skills to weigh and process that information. Throughout our work with young people, we have observed students gaining new tools and new understanding to become effective self-advocates. With this new knowledge, teens did not need someone else telling them what to do. Instead, they learned for themselves and thus became more motivated and more attached to their personal goals. Specifically, in the GBS seminars, we have seen that if provided with information about a career and paths to attaining that career, youth will make decisions that are in their best interests.

Inevitably, teens will sometimes make poor decisions—what we might see as mistakes. Empowerment means not just allowing these, but creating opportunities for mistakes and for recovery, and allowing teens to learn from the process. This departs from current practice that attempts to protect teens and does not provide them with sufficient opportunities to fail. In our work, the GBS seminar maintains high expectations and encourages students to seek more information, but allows us to remain nonjudgmental of the individual decisions and applications of self-advocacy by each student. The risk of failing to meet the significant requirements of the class is always present, along with the risk of messing up an informational interview. In either case, we do not prevent students from failure. Through this experience students, as well as professionals, see that they have as much to learn from failure as from success in the GBS process. Setbacks, mistakes, and failures are steps of the path to empowerment rather than indicators of a lack of capacity. Without these experiences, youth can never achieve the level of empowerment they will need to become successfully participating citizens.

Second, to empower teens for adulthood, we must give them opportunities to test and assert themselves beyond the system. Nothing is inherently wrong with teens learning to advocate for themselves about foster care issues within the system, and meeting with government officials about foster care issues can certainly be interesting. Yet, young people need to test their adult skills outside the system and see themselves as having something to offer the larger community. The informational interview is one example in which students advance their individual goals in ways totally unrelated to the foster care system.

Third, to integrate empowerment into foster care for teens, everyone who comes into contact with teens, not just the independent living specialist, but every group home worker, foster parent, and therapist, should be aware of their responsibility to empower teens, the importance of high expectations for teens, and the need for teens to go beyond the system to succeed. There are certainly many ways to accomplish this, but one technique we have found useful in developing intellectual empowerment is the Socratic method. Using the Socratic method for learning in foster care is not just a trendy new approach, nor is it politically charged. This method has survived more than two thousand years and permeates our society in many direct and indirect ways. The Socratic approach has always been appealing to teenagers because it allows respect for the teen's thinking. If we can support the use of such methods for the many adults who interact with teens in the system, then we will be taking steps toward empowering teens and preparing them for independence.

Empowerment methods in the long run make everyone's job easier. If a teen takes on more responsibility, the staff has to handle fewer issues. If a teen learns to understand situations, then there is less need to have continuing sessions devoted to memorizing or repeating individual independent living facts. Less behavior management issues will occur if teens are focused on both concrete planning for their futures and envisioning opportunities rather than hopelessness. Thus, we need to help foster care professionals view empowering methods as a way to make their work easier and more useful for teens.

While empowerment may have gained recent attention in foster care, our nation is founded on the principle of empowerment. Most of us believe in empowerment, even if we haven't clearly articulated its meaning. When we know of the repeated failures of teens trying to leave foster care for independent lives, and, at the same time, the incredible potential and strengths of these young people, we can better understand the urgency of empowering them to become participating citizens in our community.

Large bureaucratic systems such as foster care are effective at resisting significant change and are hostile to encouraging client empowerment. These systems, such as foster care, are poorly suited to serve individual needs and elevate individual expectations. All of us who work inside foster care and those citizens outside the system are left to recognize the challenges, pursue intelligent review, elevate expectations, and require accountability. We must continue indefinitely to bring new visions and perspectives to a closed system that requires more transparency. Empowering teens to take on more responsibility and utilize existing and willing community resources is an approach no more costly than the present system. If pursued to a successful end, empowerment will be less costly than our present system of diminished expectations.

We hope that this book has provided the reader with an inside view of the potential of teens in foster care and some impediments these teens face in preparing to successfully integrate into the community. By sharing our experience in developing a self-advocacy educational program, we have presented hopeful evidence that we can bring about change to benefit teens in care. Although we have experimented with many approaches and worked in countless different settings with a large number of teens, our primary goal remains. If we raise our expectations and provide support to achieve those expectations, many more teens will succeed. We are encouraged by the resilience, the talents, and the insights of the young people we have met and the growing consensus that we can all play a role in creating a better future for teens in foster care.

Notes

Introduction

1 Roseana Bess and Cynthia Andrews Scarcella. *Child Welfare Spending During a Time of Fiscal Stress.* [online] The Urban Institute, 2004. http://www.urban.org/url.cfm?ID=411124 (Accessed 23 June 2005).

2 *Why are Post-Adoption Services Needed in* NYS? [online] New York: New York State Citizens' Coalition, Inc., 2000. http://www.nysccc.org/Post%20Adoption%20Services/whyarepasneeded.htm (accessed 23 June 2005).

Chapter 1 • **First Impressions of the Foster Care System**

1 *Program Goal and Accomplishments.* [Online] New York: NYS Citizens' Coalition for Children, Inc., 2004. http://www.nysccc.org/Purpose.html (accessed 23 June 2005).

Chapter 2 • **Education for Foster Care Teens**

1 A 1994 study states that the "average high school completion rate among [youth entering adulthood from foster care] was 58 percent. National estimates of the percentage of youth in foster care who leave care with a high school diploma range from 37 percent to 60 percent, depending on the size of the population studied and other research constraints." *National Youth Permanence Convening.* [Online] Stuart Foundation, 2003. http://www.jimcaseyyouth.org/docs/stuart.doc (accessed 23 June 2005).

2 Nationally only half of all black, Hispanic, and Native American teens in the United States will graduate from high school, according to education and civil rights advocates, while the graduation rate for white students is 75 percent. New York State has among the lowest graduation rates for minority students in the country, with only 35 percent of black and 32 percent of Hispanic teens reaching commencement. G. Orfield, D. Losen, J. Wald, and C. Swanson, *Losing Our Future: How Minority Youth are Being Left Behind by the Graduation Rate Crisis.* [Online] Massachusetts: The Civil Rights Project at Harvard University. Contributors: Advocates for Children of New York, The Civil Society Institute, 2004. http://www.advocatesforchildren.org/pubs/losingOurFutureMainReport.pdf (accessed 23 June 2005).

3 *Campaign for Fiscal Equity v. New York.* 100 NY2d 893, 935 (2003).

4   "Can They Make It On Their Own? Aging Out of Foster Care—A Report on New York City's Independent Living Program" |Online| Citizens' Committee for Children of New York, Inc., 2000. http://www.cccnewyork.org/publications/OnTheirOwn.pdf (accessed 23 June 2005).

5   *Campaign for Fiscal Equity v. New York.* 100 NY2d 893, 934 (2003).

6   *Foster Care Education Policy Reform Initiative* |online| New York: Advocates For Children of New York, Inc. http://www.advocatesforchildren.org/pubs/FCrep7-11.htm (accessed 23 June 2005).

7   Marni Finkelstein, Mark Wamsley, and Doreen Miranda. *What Keeps Children in Foster Care From Succeeding in School?: Views of Early Adolescents and the Adults in Their Lives.* Vera Institute of Justice (July 2002), 1, 16.

8   Advocates for Children, *Foster Care Education Policy Reform Initiative.*

9   Ibid.

10   Ibid.

11   Wamsley and MirandaFinkelstein, *What Keeps Children in Foster Care From Succeeding in School?,* 16.

12   Jessica Martin. *Foster Youth Desire College, Study Shows, But Face Roadblocks to Learning.* |online| Washington University in St. Louis, website, 2 Oct. 2003. http://mednews.wustl.edu/tips/page/normal/452.html (accessed 23 June 2005).

Chapter 5   •   **Preparing for Independent Living**

1   By the late 1990s the government recognized what teens in care and their advocates had long known: existing foster care independent living programs for teens don't work very well. The Government Accounting Office reported to Congress that the few available studies show a substantial portion of former foster care youth don't complete high school, depend on welfare, become homeless, and generally have trouble becoming self-sufficient; state and local program administrators acknowledge that independent living services fall short in key areas; there are few evaluations that link program objectives to outcomes. As a result, the Foster Care Independence Act of 1999 doubled available funds and increased flexibility in spending. In its investigations surrounding the enactment of the FCIA, Congress made several findings. Among them were that adolescents leaving foster care have significant difficulty making a successful transition to adulthood and exhibit high rates of poverty, homelessness, nonmarital childbearing, delinquent or criminal behavior, and victimization as the target of crime and physical assaults. Congress urged state and local governments, with financial support from the federal government, to "offer an extensive program of education, training, employment, and financial support for young adults leaving foster care," beginning during high school and continuing until they "establish independence" or reach age twenty-one. *Foster Youth: HHS Action Could Improve Coordination of Services and Monitoring of States' Independent Living Programs.* |online| United States Government Accountability Office, Nov. 2004. http://www.nrcys.ou.edu/nrcyd/publications/pubspdfs/gaoyouthreport.pdf (accessed 23 June 2005).

2   "Can They Make It On Their Own?" Citizens' Committee for Children of New York, Inc.

Index

About the Authors

Betsy Krebs and Paul Pitcoff cofounded Youth Advocacy Center in New York City to teach teenagers to be advocates for themselves and take control of their lives. Using their backgrounds in law and higher education, together they created a nationally acclaimed model of using the Socratic case method to teach teens self-advocacy and prepare them for informational interviews in the community. They have co-authored numerous articles, columns, and publications about topics ranging from adolescents aging out of the foster care system to self-advocacy and teen mothers in foster care. Their book, *On Your Own as a Young Adult*, is used across the country to teach teens self-advocacy. Their approach to teaching self-advocacy and helping teens take on more responsibilities for their futures at Youth Advocacy Center, has been recognized as highly effective and innovative locally and nationally by social services professionals, foundations, governments, private sector leadership—as well as by teens themselves.

For her work at Youth Advocacy Center, Betsy Krebs was awarded a fellowship from George Soros's Open Society Institute and was elected as a fellow to the Ashoka: Innovators for the Public, a global organization that identifies and invests in leading social entrepreneurs. Betsy received her J.D. from Harvard Law School and worked as an attorney representing foster care children for four years before cofounding Youth Advocacy Center.

Paul Pitcoff, cofounder and director of Education at Youth Advocacy Center, was a filmmaker, founding chair of the department of communications at Adelphi University, and tenured professor for twenty years, and is now Professor Emeritus. He has won the Outstanding Educator Award as well as numerous international film festival awards for directing, producing and camerawork. Paul received his J.D. from Cardozo School of Law and MFA in film from New York University.